FEMALE SEXUAL AWARENESS

Achieving Sexual Fulfillment

Also from Carroll & Graf

Sexual Awareness by Barry and Emily McCarthy
Male Sexual Awareness by Barry McCarthy

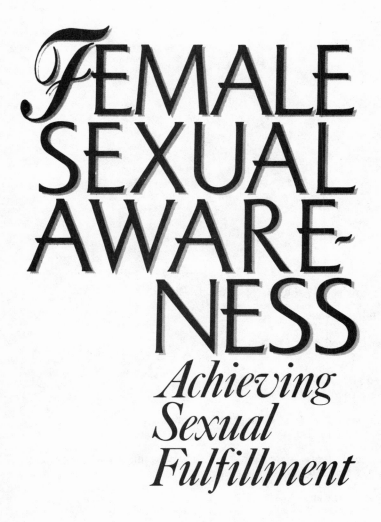

FEMALE SEXUAL AWARE- NESS

Achieving Sexual Fulfillment

Barry AND Emily McCarthy

Carroll & Graf Publishers, Inc.
New York

First Carroll & Graf edition 1989

Carroll & Graf Publishers, Inc
260 Fifth Avenue
New York, NY 10001

Library of Congress Cataloging-in-Publication Data

McCarthy, B. (Barry)
    Female sexual awareness : achieving sexual fulfillment / Barry and
Emily McCarthy.
        p.   cm.
    ISBN (invalid) 0-88184-479-4 : $9.95
    1. Women—Sexual behavior.   2. Sex.   I. McCarthy, Emily J.
II. Title.
HQ29.M454   1989
306.7′088042—dc19   89-610
                                                              CIP

Manufactured in the United States of America

Contents

I. FACTS—
INCREASING YOUR AWARENESS

1
FEMALE SEXUALITY: MYTHS AND REALITIES

When did you first think of yourself as a sexual woman? In our culture it is supposed to be when you first have sexual intercourse. In truth, you are a sexual woman from the day you're born to the day you die.

In previous generations, a woman cared for her husband and children but had little personality of her own nor was she supposed to be aware of her sexuality. Sex was the man's domain. Care-giving was the woman's. For the woman, sex produced children, not pleasure. It was acceptable for women to care about romance and affection, but not to value sexual expression and orgasm. Men and women alike feared that if a woman became too interested in sex she would run wild and destroy the marriage and the family. Female sexuality was so strong it had to be kept under control or its destructive potential would break loose and wreak havoc.

Although the media trumpets the "sexual revolution" occurring in the 1960s, the fact is that the major change in female sexual expression occurred around 1910 and the changes that followed are part of an evolutionary pattern. The second empirical reality of the "sexual revolution" is that it consists largely of changes in female attitudes and behavior, rather than male. The 1990s will give women more cultural permission to think, feel, and express their sexuality than any other time in history. Yet the sexual fears, misinformation, and demands on the woman are as burdensome as at any other time. Is the woman to become like the male and focus on sexual performance goals to prove her sexuality? Or is she to be the loving caretaker in the family room and combine that with being the sexual athlete in

3

the bedroom? Is she to be superwoman—a great care-giver, a perfect mother, a take-charge career person, while staying up until midnight having multiple orgasms?

Until the advent of AIDS, the subject of female orgasms was the hottest topic in the field of human sexuality. Orgasm was put on a pedestal, as if it was totally apart from the process of intimacy and sexual pleasure. The "big O" was the defining characteristic of female sexuality. This obsession with unrealistic sexual performance has proven deleterious for female sexuality generally and for orgasmic response specifically. The appropriate association is between "sex and pleasure" not "sex and performance." A woman's sexuality is an integral part of her as a person—involving her thoughts, feelings, and values, as well as her body, genitals, sexual arousal, and intercourse. Orgasm is neither a measure of satisfaction nor of femininity. Orgasm is a positive, integral component of female sexuality, a part of the sexual experience, not a performance goal apart from sexual pleasure.

There are a number of myths and misunderstandings about female sexuality. How much do you really know and to what extent are you misinformed? To find out, we suggest you take the short true-false test that follows. Don't worry about your score—the results will not be posted. The test will help you find out what you know about female sexuality.

1. There are two types of orgasms, clitoral and vaginal.
2. Female masturbation inhibits sexual response with a partner.
3. Breastfeeding is an effective means of contraception.
4. Women in the United States have one of the highest rates of sexual dysfunction in the world.
5. Men and women have many more differences than similarities.
6. Most women ejaculate during orgasm, just like men do.
7. Fewer than 1 out of 100 female children are sexually abused.
8. Prepared childbirth is beneficial for neither the mother nor the baby.
9. Fathers do more sex education with their children than do mothers.
10. Fewer than 10 percent of women complain of inhibited sexual desire.

11. Separation and divorce is usually initiated by the male.
12. Most women have their first orgasmic experience during intercourse.
13. The rate of unplanned, unwanted pregnancies has dramatically decreased in the past ten years.
14. Fewer than 15 percent of women will ever contract a sexually transmitted disease.
15. As long as they regularly have orgasms, women have no complaints about their marital relationships.
16. Divorced women enjoy their sexual lives more than do married women.
17. Women who have extramarital affairs begin them after ten years of marriage.
18. Women who identify with a religious belief evaluate their sexual lives as poorer than nonreligious women.
19. Women who fantasize about forced sex or group sex are psychologically disturbed.
20. Rape usually involves a stranger who wields a knife or gun.
21. Having a sexual thought or fantasy involving sex with another woman is a sign of latent lesbianism.
22. Lesbian women are not able to have children nor are they interested in parenting children.
23. Birth control is conscientiously and competently used by over 80 percent of unmarried women and 90 percent of married women.
24. Female sterilization is cheaper and safer than male sterilization.
25. As long as there is a loving, affectionate relationship sexual satisfaction is not important for women.

Count the number of "trues" you answered. What this tells you is the number of sexual myths you believe—this was a sex myth test. For comparison, the number of myths believed by the general public is approximately eight, and college students in a human sexuality course believe an average of five. These myths along with correct information and more facilitative sexual attitudes will be explored in subsequent chapters.

The premise of this book is that the more understanding you have about sexuality in general, and female sexuality in particular, the better it is for your sexual and psychological well-being.

A woman who is aware of and comfortable with her sexuality will act responsibly and make sexual choices that are in her best interest. Knowledge is power, and that is especially true in the area of female sexuality. For far too long women have been encouraged to take an ignorant, inhibited stance and told to leave sexual matters to male experts (especially gynecologists and ministers) and/or to their husbands.

The last three decades have introduced a new and refreshing approach to women and their sexuality. The combination of the feminist movement, dramatic changes in birth control, abortion, and sterilization practices, better education and career opportunities for women, and increased information about female sexual responsivity and dysfunction have heralded a new era. Thus far the era has not lived up to its claims for greater personal and sexual fulfillment, but we will not regain lost inhibitions or return to belief in discredited myths. The challenge to women in the 1990s is to integrate knowledge and positive attitudes so that sexuality can enhance their lives and intimate relationships.

THE ROLE OF SEX IN LIFE

Just how important should sex be in a woman's life? Too much of a man's self-esteem is tied up in his penis; why should the woman fall into the trap of defining her personhood by her vulva? Or is love and intimacy the really important thing, and sexuality only a minor footnote? Our belief is that sex is a good element in life and not a bad thing, that a woman's sexuality is a positive, integral part of her personality, and that sexual expression involves more than her vulva, intercourse, and orgasm. Sexuality includes attitudes, behavior, and emotions that can and should enhance a woman's life and intimate relationship. Sexuality plays an important role in a woman's body image, self-esteem, self-respect, and relations with other people.

When sexuality goes well in a relationship it accounts for perhaps 15–20 percent of the sense of well-being, but when sex is problematic it can be the negative, controlling factor and take over 50–60 percent or even 80 percent of a person's psychological energy. Sexuality is best viewed as a positive, integral part of a woman's life and personality, but not the most important element. People who make major life choices such as who to marry, where to live, whether to leave a marriage or stay, based primarily on sexual factors are setting themselves up to make a poor decision. Sexual factors should not serve as the rationale for vocational, marital, or life-style decisions. It is too easy to make an emotional, impulsive, and self-defeating decision on the basis of sexuality. Such decisions must be carefully thought out, taking into account a range of factors including the psychological, interpersonal, financial, and practical. Sexual feelings, attractions, and responses are one dimension, but not the major one.

Traditionally, women have been encouraged to focus their whole lives on loving a man and taking care of children. We are in favor of both marriage and parenting, but not in the way they have been traditionally practiced. In the traditional equation if the woman feels sexually attracted to the man and sexually responsive with him that means she is in love with him, should marry him and plan her life around him. This is the myth of "romantic love" that has victimized hundreds of thousands of women. Sex is a wonderful aspect of life, and sexuality is an integral part of being a woman, but it does not deserve the power it has traditionally wielded in women's lives and decisions. Sex and sexuality work best when they're rich components to life but not controlling forces. Make decisions that are in your best interest, not for sex or for the sexual or psychological needs of another person.

WHAT IS THE RELATIONSHIP BETWEEN SEX AND LOVE?

In the traditional view, sex, love, and marriage all went together for women (but not for men). Love and marriage gave women cultural permission to be sexual. The scientific reality is that sex and love are separate phenomena. It is possible to be very sexually attracted to and responsive with people you don't know or even like. It is also possible to be very loving and emotionally intimate with someone and still experience sexual dysfunction. No matter what your mother or minister told you, love and sex are separate. This does not mean they are incompatible. On the contrary, we believe that the most satisfying sexuality integrates sexual expression with trust, closeness, and intimate emotional expression. The most satisfying relationship is one in which the woman and man have both sexuality and emotional-intimacy skills and express them in a respectful, trustful, and caring marriage. We are in favor of the traditional values of marriage and try to practice them in our own life.

Seeing sex, love, and marriage as three separate phenomena is in keeping with the scientific facts, but even more important allows the woman a clearer, more aware, more responsible basis for understanding herself and for sexuality to work well in her life. It is the myth of romantic love that has had such a devastating effect on women. We prefer the term "emotional intimacy" to "romantic love," because the term "love" has been so misused and abused in our culture. We encourage both women and men to develop the attitudes and skills needed to sustain an intimate relationship. Women must not delude themselves or let society delude them into believing that love and sexuality are the same thing. What's true is that sexual expression can enhance the intimate bond.

ARE WOMEN AND MEN TOTALLY DIFFERENT CREATURES?

The scientific data are very clear. Intellectually, emotionally, and behaviorally there are many more similarities than differences between women and men. This is also true in terms of sexuality. Women and men are both capable of sexual desire, arousal, orgasm, and emotional satisfaction. Women and men go through the same cycle of sexual response governed by the same vascular and neurological processes. In the typical sleep cycle, the woman has sexually oriented dreams and vaginally lubricates just as the man has sexually oriented dreams and erections. There are as many nerve endings in the clitoral area as there are in the penis. The idea that women and men are vastly different and/or incompatible is a myth.

What are the sexual differences? There are two major differences, one in conceptive functioning and one in sexual functioning. It is a woman who has a menstrual cycle, conceives a baby, and lactates (can breastfeed). In terms of sexual functioning, the woman typically needs more time and more direct genital stimulation to become aroused. Both females and males experience orgasm, but female orgasmic response is more variable and complex than male orgasm. Remember, the issue in orgasm is not better or worse, but different. Typically, the male will have one orgasm per sexual experience and it will occur during intercourse. The woman might have no orgasm, a single orgasm, or multiple orgasms, which can occur during the foreplay/ pleasuring period, during intercourse, or in the afterplay time. Women need not try to shape their sexual response to be like men (have a single orgasm during intercourse), but be aware of and enjoy their unique sexual response pattern. Remember, sex is for pleasure not performance. The sexual differences between men and women are complementary not adversarial. If understood, communicated, and integrated into their sexual style, differences in orgasmic response can enhance sexual pleasure.

DEALING WITH NEGATIVE SEXUAL EVENTS

One of the realities of sexuality is that it never reaches the idealistic standards set for it (whether those be traditional or liberated). Negative, confusing, guilt-inducing, or traumatic experiences do occur. By age twenty-five, 95 percent of women report at least one negative sexual incident (this is also true for men). We have to confront the reality that negative sexual events happen to almost all women. These range from unwanted pregnancy to incest and include child sexual abuse, rape, guilt over masturbation or fantasies, being exhibited to, peeped on or rubbed against, contracting a sexually transmitted disease, being rejected, humiliated, or harassed, having a sexual dysfunction, etc. You need not feel controlled by the experience or see yourself as a sexual victim, but should view yourself as a sexual survivor. It is rightly said that "Living well is the best revenge." You should neither deny these negative sexual incidents nor give them power over your sexual self-esteem. You can learn from the negative incidents, acknowledge that you did cope and survive, and develop a positive sexual self-esteem.

SEXUAL DYSFUNCTION AND DIFFICULT SEXUAL ISSUES

In reading the popular women's magazines, it is easy to become sexually intimidated. You worry, Am I normal? Each woman has her own sexual style based on her family background, experiences, values, prior relationships, etc. For many, if not most women, this may include difficult problems such as a sexual dysfunction or dissatisfaction, dealing with an extramarital affair (your own or your partner's), dissatisfaction with your body image, marital conflict, and/or infertility. Rather than feeling indadequate or stigmatized by the sexual problem, you can gain greater understanding and learn to deal with it in a positive way. One of the major tenets of sex therapy is that the best way to conceptualize and treat a sexual problem is to see it as a "couple problem." This goes a long way toward breaking the cycle of guilt, blame, and stigma. Conceptualizing a sexual problem as a couple problem helps the woman and her partner work cooperatively to develop a sexual style that is satisfying for both people. Women without regular partners can learn accurate information about sexual functioning, develop healthy sexual attitudes, improve sexual skills, and feel more comfortable with their sexuality.

A particularly difficult issue is a sense of guilt or shame over past sexual experiences (whether an unwanted pregnancy, sexual humiliation, or being rejected) that continues to plague a woman and inhibit sexual functioning. Guilt is the most self-defeating of human emotions. Feeling guilty leaves you vulnerable to repeating the negative patterns, lowering your self-esteem, and continuing in a self-destructive cycle. Guilt inhibits you from communicating about the sexual problem and taking steps to solve it. You cannot change the past, but you can devote psychological time and energy to improving present and future sexual expression.

ARE MARRIAGE AND CHILDREN THE JUSTIFICATION FOR SEXUALITY?

Our answer to this is a resounding No! We are in favor of both marriage and children, but neither is necessary for sexual expression. Sexuality needs no justification. You can feel good about yourself as a sexual woman whether or not you are married, and whether or not you have children. Marriage is the most popular way to relate intimately, but it is not the only way. One of the purposes of sex is conception, but it is not the only function or the most important one. Equally important functions of sex are as a shared pleasure, as a way to build and reinforce emotional intimacy, and as a tension reducer. (Yes, this is as true for women as for men).

You can feel good about yourself as a sexual woman whether eighteen, thirty-eight, fifty-eight, or seventy-eight, regardless of your childbearing status. Women of the latter two ages have completed their childbearing years, but certainly not their sexual years. The average number of children a woman gives birth to is two. Does that negate the other nonconceptive intercourse experiences? Absolutely not! Sex can be particularly exciting when you are trying to become pregnant, but conception is not necessary for sexual pleasure and sexual intercourse.

THE NEGATIVE LEGACY OF PREMARITAL SEX

The double standard of female-male sexual behavior is overlearned during the premarital period. It is hard to pinpoint which lessons are most harmful for adult female sexuality because there are so many. The median age for women to marry in the United States is twenty-three. Yet most of the sexual emphasis is on premarital issues, rather than enjoying adult sexuality. Traditional premarital sexual education focuses on the women's responsibility to say no to the man, to prevent pregnancy, to protect her reputation, to talk a man into marrying her, and to save her parents from the disgrace of having a sexually active daughter. All these are antithetical to a healthy approach to adult female sexuality.

Premarital sexuality is better conceptualized as a training ground for later adult sexuality (usually in a marital relationship). The first step a woman should take is to develop a good feeling about her body (including breasts and vulva). The second is to feel good about herself as a woman, especially her ability to choose and to be assertive. She can choose a partner who she feels comfortable with, trusts, and is attracted to. As an adolescent, she can enjoy the experience of kissing and touching (necking and petting). Sexual expression ought to enhance the relationship rather than cause pressure, discomfort, or trauma. She needs to learn to act responsibly to prevent unwanted pregnancy or sexually transmitted diseases. Most important, she can utilize her premarital experiences to learn more about herself as a person and about intimacy in relationships. The premarital experiences can serve to establish a pattern of lifelong sexual learning. Premarital sexuality has traditionally been a source of great stress and pressure for women. It need not be so. It can serve as an education about themselves, their sexuality, and their relationships. Ultimately, these experiences can enhance their adult lives.

IS SEX INTERCOURSE?

Perhaps the single most negative premarital sexual lesson is the equation of sex and intercourse. Women are told by men that holding, touching, kissing, caresssing, fondling, manual stimulation, etc., are not "real sex." These touching activities are tolerated, but once intercourse is introduced, they are abandoned or relegated to the category of "foreplay." Touching is not valuable for itself, only as a means to get the woman ready for the only sexual expression that matters: "intercourse." The male view that real sex consists of the penis, the vagina, intercourse, and the few seconds of orgasm controls the woman's sexual expression.

Do not cheat yourself and buy the myth that real sex equals intercourse. Touching, kissing, caressing, holding, and nongenital sensuality is good in and of itself. It has value whether you're clothed or unclothed, whether it occurs outside or inside the bedroom. Throughout this book we will be speaking of the "pleasuring" process instead of "foreplay." Foreplay connotes a preparatory activity that is wasted and silly (or immature and juvenile) if not followed by "real intercourse." Our belief is that pleasuring is a major glue that bonds the couple and is of great value in itself. Often pleasuring will lead to intercourse, but it need not. Sensuality (which entails a range of primarily nongenital touching activities) is the basis of sexual expression and a way of experiencing pleasure and intimacy.

THE NONDEMAND CONCEPT

A major subject throughout this book is nondemand pleasuring. This means experiencing and enjoying a range of sensual and sexual activities without feeling a demand or pressure toward intercourse, orgasm, or any other sexual activity. Neither the culture nor a male has a right to demand that a woman do anything against her will. Sexuality is a voluntary, cooperative experience in giving and receiving pleasure. The concept of nondemand pleasuring is frequently violated in our culture not just in the extreme acts of sexual abuse and rape, but in many interactions between men and women, even married couples. One extreme example is marital rape where the man says, "Since you are my wife I can use and abuse you as I like." More common is the husband's feeling that if his wife is enjoying the touching experiences and he's sexually aroused that it's her duty to proceed to intercourse. The corollary is if the woman does not want intercourse she should avoid touching him. This attitude cheats both people of the pleasure of affectionate, nondemand touching and results in less intercourse, not more. It reinforces the self-defeating view that intercourse is the only "real sex."

Nondemand touching is a vital ingredient in an ongoing intimate relationship. It is not the woman's role to convince the man and win him over to this viewpoint (although that would be in his best interest and be better for the couple). She does not need his permission to engage in and enjoy nondemand touching.

THE WOMAN AS AN AWARE, RESPONSIBLE SEXUAL PERSON

The more knowledgeable of sexuality the woman is, the better for her and the person she is involved with. The woman can feel responsible for herself sexually and realize she can make sexual choices that enhance her life. This is not a "Cinderella" or "fairy tale" view of female sexuality. Women have to deal with the difficult areas of contraception, sexually transmitted diseases, sexual dysfunction, sexual trauma, fear of AIDS, sexual harassment, etc. Awareness and responsibility do not guarantee sexual satisfaction nor do they protect you from having to deal with difficult issues. But being aware and responsible will give you a broader perspective and better resources to plan and choose how sexuality can play a constructive and fulfilling role in your life.

WHAT THIS BOOK IS ABOUT

There are two main focuses of this book. A prime goal is to present the most accurate, reliable information on female sexuality presently available. Second is to help the female reader integrate her sexuality with her personality and express sexuality in a way that will bring her greater fulfillment and satisfaction. Sex is much more than your genitals, intercourse, and orgasm. Sexuality refers to the whole range of attitudes, behavior, and emotions concerning you as a woman. This book is addressed primarily to women, but men are encouraged to read it as well. Indeed, since sexuality is the most intimate form of human communication, it can be extremely beneficial to a couple's relationship for both partners to have an understanding and appreciation of female sexuality.

This book will be comprehensive in covering a variety of issues of interest and importance to women. You could read the chapters consecutively as a survey of female sexuality, but you will be better served to use the chapters as a reference source for the specific questions and issues most relevant to you. The book is divided into three sections: chapters on facts to increase your knowledge, chapters on ways to enhance your sexuality, and chapters on dealing with problems that interfere with sexual satisfaction. Where there are questions of attitudes and values, we have committed ourselves to a particular position based on personal and professional experiences. However, you need to take into account your own background and values in deciding how relevant these guidelines are to your life. In our opinion, the range of normal sexual behavior includes any private activity between consenting individuals that provides a sense of sharing and pleasure, is not coercive, does not involve children, and is not physically or psychologically destructive. The choice is yours and depends on what you and your partner find pleasurable and satisfying.

A PERSONAL NOTE

Emily and Barry McCarthy wrote this book together, each bringing complementary skills and attitudes to the project. This is their third joint book, and the one they are proudest of. It is the culmination of twenty-two years of sharing their lives as a married couple. They have learned from and positively influenced each other.

Emily's preparation for writing this book comes both from her academic degree in speech communication as well as her forty-three years of being a sexual person. She grew up in a small town outside Peoria, Illinois, in a working-class family where males and females were treated very differently, with women viewed as second-class citizens. The double standard was strong, with Emily's brothers encouraged to be sexual early and to marry early. Emily's mother encouraged her to go to college and break out of the male-dominated life she'd grown up in. Even in college, the options women could pursue were limited to nursing, teaching, and social work. Emily enjoyed the independence of college and charting her own way in the world, but sexuality played a relatively minor role in her life.

She was highly motivated to lead her life differently from her parents, especially in developing a marital bond that was more respectful and equitable. She had seen Barry on campus, but their first date wasn't until months later on Emily's twenty-first birthday. Emily looks back fondly on a romantic, exciting dating time that included midnight swims and going for long rides on a motorcycle through the beautiful rural countryside of southern Illinois. However, it was not a "romantic love-is-blind" match—they talked and negotiated a view of life and marriage that would require major changes for both. Emily was assertive in saying she would not tolerate physical violence in the marriage, they would live away from Illinois and their families' influence, and that she wanted an equal say in decisions about work, home, children, and life-style.

It was an interesting marital ceremony in that everyone assumed Emily was pregnant (a very common reason to marry) and people were surprised when nine months passed and there was no baby. Mark was born two years after the marriage, Kara was adopted two years later, and Paul was born two years after that. As the marriage progressed, Emily has been more aware and assertive about the sexual issues, but she was less so early in the relationship. Looking back on early sex, she remembers it as frequent, sometimes exciting, but usually low quality. Emily and Barry are a good example of a couple who needed over six months to develop a sexual style that was functional and satisfying for both.

As the relationship has progressed, there have been a number of issues and transitions to deal with, and no doubt this process will continue. Maritally and sexually you cannot rest on your laurels. If sexuality is to remain a positive part of life and a marriage, it requires continual time and attention. Making time to be a sexual couple is very different when children are babies as opposed to when they are adolescents. Emily really enjoyed delivering her two biological children through prepared childbirth and the breastfeeding process. However she was pleased that Barry had a vasectomy and they no longer had to deal with contraception. She plans to welcome the "empty nest," which will allow her more individual time and freedom to pursue her interests and do more traveling as part of a couple. Emily has found that balancing the roles of an individual, wife, mother, and sexual person has been a challenge, at times draining, but worthwhile.

Barry's preparation for writing this book comes from his academic background of a Ph.D. in psychology, his clinical work in sex and marital therapy, teaching human sexual behavior to college students, and conducting sex therapy and sexual trauma workshops for professionals. His professional experience and beliefs are in marked contrast to Barry's own sexual development as a child and adolescent. His experiences were typical of the majority of males in our culture. As a boy in Chicago, he received no real sex education from family, church, or school. His parental model of marriage and sexuality was a poor one. His father was involved in work and was a quiet man who kept his emotional distance from everyone including his wife and children. Barry's mother was a full-time homemaker with low self-esteem who tried to live her life through her children. Their marriage fit the man's needs better because he was taken care of, but was frustrating and depressing to the woman. Barry finds it hard to imagine they were a sexual couple.

As an adolescent and young adult, Barry had some dating and

sexual experiences that he greatly exaggerated to male friends in an effort to appear "macho." In his early sexual encounters he took no responsibility for contraception, seeing that as the woman's role. By the time Emily came into his life at twenty-three, Barry was disillusioned by the disappointment and hurt experienced in dating relationships. Barry enjoyed the emotional openness as well as the romantic intensity he felt with Emily, and he was the one who pushed through opposition from both families to an early marriage.

Barry carried with him into the marriage many of the erroneous and destructive assumptions about sex and sex roles he had learned earlier. This led to problems and conflicts, especially during the first year of marriage, that had to be confronted and resolved if this was to be an emotionally and sexually satisfying marriage. He was shocked when Emily confronted him with the reality that their sex was high-quantity low-quality, and that he needed to be more communicative, slower, more tender, more experimental, and more emotionally intimate. Barry has had a number of surprises in the marriage—the satisfaction of having a spouse who is his best friend, the joy of seeing his children born and adopting his daughter, the complexity of the father role (both joys and stresses), deciding to have a vasectomy, and frankly, surprise at being involved as a teacher, writer, and clinician in the area of human sexuality. Perhaps the biggest surprise is realizing that the quality of sex is better after twenty-two years of marriage.

FOCUS ON FEMALE SEXUALITY

Our assumption is that the more comfortable, aware, and accepting of sexuality a woman is the better she can choose to express herself in a manner that promotes her self-esteem and intimacy in a relationship. We will be dealing with various topics relating to the female life cycle, with methods of enhancing self-esteem, with decisions and responsibilities that are a necessary part of sexuality, and dealing with problems that inhibit the full expression of female sexuality. Throughout, we will draw on case studies of clients Barry has treated (their identities have been disguised), as well as our own personal experiences, to provide relevant illustrations for the concepts being discussed.

This is primarily a book of ideas and information, not a do-it-yourself sex therapy book or a treatise on sexual techniques to teach you to have better orgasms. If, by presenting a positive and integrated view of female sexuality, our book can help you examine your attitudes, feelings, and experiences, we will be satisfied. We hope this book will be helpful to you and the people you care about.

2
BODY-EXPLORATION AND MASTURBATION

From Greek artists to modern-day advertisers there has been a deep and abiding interest in the female body and intrigue with female genitalia. The woman's breasts are up front and visible, although artists and advertisers go through cycles of preferring certain sizes, shapes, and muscle tone. More intriguing and secret is the vulva, which is in the folds of the labia. The fountainhead of sexual pleasure, the clitoris, is small and hidden in contrast to the glans of the man's penis. The vagina, an amazingly flexible organ, is another source of great mystery.

Unlike artists who delight in secrets and mysteries, you can become more aware of and accepting of your body, especially your genitalia. The most efficient and effective way to learn about your body is through self-exploration and masturbation. This has only been recognized by sex therapists in the past fifteen years and is still not accepted by the general public. It is ironic that masturbation, which had been blamed for everything from facial blemishes to blindness, has turned out to be the treatment of choice for women who have never had an orgasm. Ten-session groups led by a female therapist that focus on teaching women to explore and stimulate their bodies report over 90 percent success in helping participants reach orgasm through masturbation.

A SELF-EXPLORATION
Just think how much more helpful information about the female body and sexual responsiveness would be to an adolescent or young adult woman. Could you imagine your mother or doctor

19

or health teacher encouraging you to explore your body, be aware of your genitals, and learn about your sexual responsiveness? Why is our culture so afraid of female genitalia and sexuality? Why is there a fear of women learning about and controlling their own orgasms? By age sixteen, over 90 percent of males have learned to be orgasmic through masturbation, but fewer than 30 percent of women have. By age twenty-five over 95 percent of men have reached orgasm through masturbation, but fewer than 60 percent of women. It is not until adulthood and after marriage that 75 percent of females have masturbated to orgasm. Is it the fear that women will become "hung-up" on masturbation? The reality is that women who are orgasmic through masturbation are more likely to be responsive and orgasmic with partner sex. There is no evidence that masturbation has harmful effects on female sexuality or couple sexual expression.

Why don't we encourage our female children to engage in body exploration? At less than a year old, the baby girl has found her genitals in the process of discovering and enjoying her body. Is this discovery greeted with delight by her parents? It is usually greeted with concern. Most mothers are sophisticated enough not to slap their daughter's hand. However, they do guide it away from her genitals. Why not let her "play with herself?" Most people find it hard to answer that question. It's the irrational feeling that "good little girls" don't touch their genitals. It reflects the fear that if the baby girl, or the prepubescent girl, or the adolescent girl is too aware of her genitals and sexual pleasure that some ill-defined damaging thing will happen. It is perfectly normal and natural for female (as well as male) children to explore their genitals and to continue touching them because it generates pleasurable feelings.

As the baby grows into a toddler and the toddler enters preschool and then elementary school, her fascination with her body and genitals continues. The big difference is that it becomes private and secretive. A two-year-old can run around the house naked, a five-year-old cannot. The self-exploration occurs in the bedroom or in the bathroom while taking a shower or bath. As a child develops and grows, you encourage her to explore her world and increase her awareness. That same message can and should extend to her body and genitals. By the

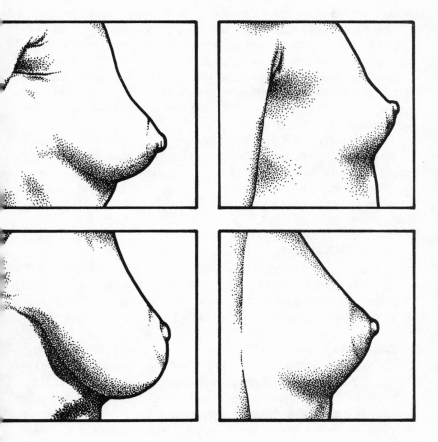

Typical variations in the appearance of the female breast.

time a girl begins menstruation (the normal range is between ten and fourteen) she can have a good sense of her body.

Being comfortable with one's body is particularly important. Our culture sets unrealistic standards for youth and beauty so the woman's body image is constantly challenged. She feels pressure to be thinner, to have bigger or smaller breasts, to change her nose or hair, to continually strive to be perfect, and she always fall short. Young women (and, in fact, women of all ages) base too much of their self-esteem on physical appearance. This obsession with the perfect body is a major cause of eating disorders in young women. The remedy is not to strive for the perfect body, but to develop a body image you are comfortable with.

Menstruation need not be a scary event. It is best viewed as the beginning of becoming a sexual woman and opening a new door to personal growth. Menstruation heralds growth in breast development and pubic hair, as well as an increase in sexual feelings and responsivity.

MASTURBATION

The ten- to fourteen-year age range is the time that males typically begin masturbating to orgasm. This is not the usual pattern for females, but the age is certainly opportune for women as well. A significant minority of women do begin masturbation in their early teen years. The traditional cultural fear is if these young women experience orgasm, it will serve as an uncontrollable urge to have sex with every available boy. This is a falsehood, although believed by many, especially parents. What is true is that young women who are comfortable with their bodies and have learned to be orgasmic via masturbation are more likely to be responsive and enjoy partner sex. It does not mean they will begin partner sex earlier or have more partners.

Adolescence and young adulthood is the time when women begin experimenting with partner sex, including intercourse. There is an increase in masturbation activity, although not dramatic. It's as if the young woman says to herself, I need to learn about men, not myself. Are those two needs incompatible? Not at all. Young males pursue sex with girls (which they brag about), but the majority of orgasms for young men come through masturbation, not partner sex (they don't admit it, but it's true). Throughout their lives both women and men (whether twenty, forty, or sixty) find it easier and more reliable to be orgasmic during masturbation than during partner sex. This is not because they prefer masturbation; contrary to people's fears women do not get "hooked" on masturbation. Women find it easier to be orgasmic with masturbation, but they find greater emotional and sexual satisfaction during partner sex.

The greatest increase in women masturbating occurs after marriage. That might seem surprising, but it shouldn't. The movie image of the newly married couple is romantic, idealistic, and untrue. The act of getting married does not guarantee good sex. For many women, the quality of early marital sex is disappointing.

The cultural expectation that sexual expression will be more satisfying with the mantle of marriage proves untrue for many women. With increased sexual activity, but not increased orgasmic response (perhaps none), many women turn to masturbation to provide an orgasmic release. As the woman's body responds with masturbation, it is likely she will become responsive with her partner. She will learn a crucial lesson—masturbation and partner sex are complementary, not either-or opposites. This accounts for the second major reason for an increase in masturbation with marriage— a heightened awareness of sexuality fosters an increased interest in a variety of sexual outlets, including masturbation. Masturbation enhances sexuality and can serve this role throughout the marriage.

By age thirty-five, about 75 percent of women will have experimented with masturbation, and more than half continue to masturbate, at least on occasion, throughout their lives. Viewed from this perspective, we find that self-exploration and masturbation is a normal, healthy sexual experience that can and does exist throughout the woman's life. It serves a positive function in and of itself, as well as contributing to the development of couple sexuality.

Iris

As twenty-eight-year-old Iris was standing at a reception for high-achieving IBM technical staff, she mused to herself that she was a woman of the 1990s. Professionally she was ambitious and competent. She had a two-career marriage where both she and her husband were actively involved in parenting their two-year-old daughter. Iris was comfortable with her sexuality, both in terms of sex with her husband and with masturbation.

Iris traveled at least every other week. Although she missed her husband and daughter, she appreciated the time alone. Unlike colleagues who hung around bars or went to restaurants for rich, expense-account food, Iris used her nights on the road to relax, exercise, catch up on professional reading, write letters to friends and relatives, and to masturbate. Iris would prepare a bubble bath about nine at night and let herself luxuriate for fifteen minutes with classical music in the background. She would slowly towel herself dry and without putting clothes on lie on the bed. She changed the music to light rock, which she found erotic, and lowered the lights. Iris's pattern of masturbation was to mix breast stimulation with clitoral stimulation. She surprised herself by how rapidly she could become aroused and reach orgasm, usually in less than five minutes. When Iris read about women who slowly and gently caressed themselves and took half an hour to reach orgasm she felt more than a little envy, but she accepted her more intense, focused pattern of masturbation. She laughed at claims that women dissipated their sexuality with masturbation. When she returned from a trip, she was more desirous of being sexual with her husband.

Iris had begun masturbation at age seventeen. She was dating a fellow high-school senior and the relationship included heavy petting (genital stimulation) for both. She did not feel ready to make the commitment to having intercourse. Frankly, she did not want to go to a gynecologist for birth control and did not trust her boyfriend to use condoms. Iris was pleased with their sexual relationship and noticed that he was satisfied and relaxed when he achieved orgasm with her manual stimulation. She'd read about and heard orgasms discussed on "The Phil Donahue Show," and she was interested in experiencing orgasm for herself. When she returned home from one of their dates she engaged in genital self-stimulation. Iris experienced a mix of feelings including excitement, guilt, anxiety, and a desire to continue experimenting. After two weeks, Iris had her first orgasm after engaging in self-stimulation for forty minutes. Once she'd discovered she could be orgasmic, subsequent experiences with self-stimulation were more comfortable and easier. Within two months, Iris discovered the masturbatory pattern of combining breast and clitoral stimulation that she continues to use today. The majority of women use sexual fantasies or read sexually explicit material while engaging in masturbation. Iris has tried this and does use images occasionally, especially if she's been to an erotic movie, but usually she focuses on the erotic sensations.

Throughout early adulthood, Iris used masturbation as sexual expression. She would often masturbate three or four times per week. She seldom talked about it with female friends or boyfriends, but if asked she would say that she did masturbate and that it was normal and healthy. After marriage, she talked to her husband and learned that he, too, engaged in masturbation. Masturbation was viewed by Iris and her husband as something to do privately. She guessed that when he took extra long showers he was using that time to masturbate. Neither worried that masturbation would detract from marital sex or be used to avoid couple sexual contact. Masturbation was an alternative mode of sexual expression, not a substitute for or a challenge to couple sexuality.

VIBRATORS

Perhaps the major technological inroad in female sexuality is the increased use of vibrators, both in self-stimulation and to a lesser extent during partner sex. Vibrators are a relatively inexpensive (most cost under thirty dollars) means to enhance pleasure and lead to orgasmic response. A generation ago vibrators were viewed as "kinky" equipment and many were shaped like a penis (a dildo). This was based on the myth that what a woman wanted and needed for self-stimulation was a large, firm penis substitute. Another type of vibrator was a vigorous massager that you strapped to your hand. It is amazing how myths and misconceptions build on themselves.

The process of manual stimulation and vibrator stimulation is similar. The focus of stimulation for most women is the labia and clitoral area, not the inside of the vagina. The preferred vibrator stimulation is not overwhelming speed and shaking intensity, but a steady rhythm focused around the clitoral area. The most popular vibrators are battery-operated, hand-held models that have two speeds. Some have a choice of three to five rubber attachments that provide a variety of stimulations. Vibrators can be purchased at women's erotica stores or via mail order. They are more likely to be purchased at a large department store and labeled as a back, face, or whole body massager. Vibrators are no longer thought of as "dirty" or "perverted." They are instead viewed by many as a sexual toy or aid—as an enhancer of sexual pleasure.

Some women use a vibrator to have their first orgasmic experience—"special help from a friend." For most women, the vibrator serves as a transition to enhance manual self-stimulation. Although some articles warn about the dangers of becoming "hooked" on vibrator stimulation, this occurs with relatively few women. Women find it easier and faster to be orgasmic with vibrator stimulation because of the focused, steady rhythm of the vibrator. However, it is not the vibrator that is doing this "to" or "for" the woman. She is in control of the stimulation. She lets go, gives herself permission to enjoy the erotic sensations, and allows them to proceed to orgasm.

This attitude can extend to use of vibrator stimulation during partner sex. Some couples utilize vibrator stimulation as an extension of the pleasuring process. This can involve the man as well as the woman. Vibrator stimulation is used as a genital arousal technique to increase receptivity for subsequent manual, oral, or intercourse stimulation. Another variation is to have the partner or the woman herself proceed to orgasm with vibrator stimulation. Some couples will use the vibrator as a multiple stimulation technique along with intercourse. Other women prefer vibrator stimulation during afterplay if they have not been orgasmic with intercourse. The vibrator is a very adaptable aid to increase sexual pleasure.

GAINING COMFORT WITH BODY-EXPLORATION AND SELF-STIMULATION

Many therapy clients find that reading about their bodies and masturbation is liberating and serves to change their attitudes. However, when they engage in self-stimulation they confront feelings of discomfort, inhibition, and embarrassment that negate the experience. A sexual experience that is meant to be comfortable and pleasurable turns into an ordeal. How can a woman who has not enjoyed masturbation succeed in doing so?

There are two key elements—first is to become comfortable with body exploration and the second is to focus on pleasurable sensations in a nondemand, non-goal-oriented manner. If you choose to engage in genital self-exploration exercises, the focus needs to be on discovery, not orgasm. There are detailed exercises in our book *Sexual Awareness,* in Heiman and Lopiccolo's book, *Becoming Orgasmic*, and in Barbach's book *For Yourself.* We recommend these resources if you desire to follow through on a detailed, semistructured program of exercises. Another option is to join a women's sexuality group that provides peer support to help you confront the guilt and inhibitions and encourages sexual expression. These groups usually meet for ten sessions. Those interested in participating should contact a female sex therapist in their area.

Let us present the following guidelines and suggestions. The first step in building comfort is to be open to exploring and discovering what kinds of touch on which parts of your body result in good feelings and sensations. Allow the touching to be slow, exploratory, and nondemanding. The focus is not on arousal but on comfort, sensuality, and pleasure. Instead of looking at your body with a critical eye, worrying about wrinkles and fat, see it in a more accepting manner as a pleasure-giving part of you. Many women find this easier in the context of first taking a hot bubble bath while playing their favorite music and sipping a glass of wine. Other women prefer a shower where they feel clean and refreshed. Some women do body exploration in front of a three-sided mirror so they can look at themselves from a variety of angles, whereas other women would rather lie in bed with the lights dimmed or perhaps a candle burning.

To look at and explore your genitalia, you can use a hand mirror. We've included a drawing to help you identify the different parts of your vulva. Your genitalia will not look exactly like this drawing—a vulva is like a face, every woman has her own features. Begin by looking at and touching the bony area covered with hair, which is called the mons. Touch and examine your pubic hair—be aware of its texture and color.

Move your fingers around the labia majora (outer lips) of your vulva. These folds encompass and protect the labia minora (inner lips). As you look at and touch your labia, be aware of a warm and sensuous feeling. The inner lips come together at the clitoral shaft. The clitoral shaft connects to the clitoral hood, which covers the clitoris itself. The hood protects the clitoris, which is a very sensitive small organ filled with pleasurable nerve endings. The clitoris is the most important source of sexual pleasure. It is amazing that an organ so small and so difficult to identify is the source of sexual arousal.

As you continue with genital exploration, spread your inner lips and locate the urethra (from which you urinate), a small opening above your vagina. Look at your vagina, and especially the vaginal opening. The vagina is amazingly adaptable; it opens up and lets the penis in and then adapts to the size and movement of the penis during thrusting. It expands to allow a baby to pass through in the childbirth process. The outer one-third of the vagina contains the most nerve endings. Greater awareness of vaginal feeling can be facilitated by tensing and relaxing the pubococcygeous (PG) muscle. The easiest way to locate the PG muscle is to stop the flow when urinating. The muscle you use is the PG. You can practice exercising this muscle by tensing it for three seconds, relaxing, and repeating this for ten times in succession. This will take less than a minute.

As you look at and touch your vulva, be aware of the comfortable, pleasurable sensations. The area between the vagina and the anus is called the perineum, which many women find a pleasurable area. The anal area, like other openings of your body such as your ears, mouth, and vagina, is sensitive to pleasurable touch. Body and genital self-exploration is a nondemand, non-goal-oriented experience to enhance comfort and openness to your body and pleasurable sensations.

A logical extension of the self-exploration process is to integrate genital exploration and genital touching. Some women are intrigued by the concept of nondemand genital pleasuring while others find it incongruous. Yet the difference between a touch that is highly pleasurable and exciting as opposed to one that is uninteresting might only be a matter of an inch or two or a little bit more or less pressure. Genital stimulation is focused on

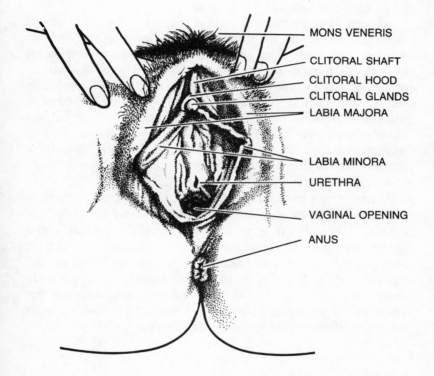

MONS VENERIS

CLITORAL SHAFT
CLITORAL HOOD
CLITORAL GLANDS
LABIA MAJORA

LABIA MINORA

URETHRA

VAGINAL OPENING

ANUS

A clinical view of the vulva showing the features of the external female genetalia.

discovering pleasurable and erotic sensations. You are the expert on your body. The more you learn, the easier it will be to share this with and guide your partner.

How does self-exploration merge into masturbation? Masturbation involves more rhythmic, focused genital stimulation, and the woman allows herself to let go and experience higher levels of arousal, which naturally culminates in orgasm. Self-exploration is not goal-oriented; masturbation is.

Women have different "orgasm triggers," thoughts or actions that allow the increasing levels of arousal to result in orgasm. For many women the key trigger is to engage in multiple stimulation with the arousal building until orgasm arrives. For other women, the trigger is to shut off other thoughts and activities and to focus all her sexual energy on one form of stimulation. Some women find the role of fantasy is critical. As she reaches heightened arousal during the fantasy, it triggers orgasm in reality. There is no "right" or "proper" way for a woman to be orgasmic. Each woman has her own masturbatory and orgasmic pattern.

Some women experience multiorgasmic response with masturbation. These women find subsequent orgasms are easier and more fulfilling. Other women like to lie and daydream about life, partner sex, or pleasant images after reaching orgasm. Some women prefer not to masturbate to orgasm, but enjoy the self-exploration and find it of value to continue whole-body touching and "come down slowly." Do what is comfortable for you and helps you acknowledge and feel good about your self-exploration and masturbation experience.

CLOSING THOUGHTS

Women have come a long way in accepting and enjoying their bodies and their sexuality. The body-exploration/masturbation process is experienced and enjoyed by more women than ever before. In assessing your attitudes and experiences, be aware how you can use self-pleasuring to enhance your image as a woman, your sexual self-esteem, and your experience of partner sex.

3

SEX AND THE UNMARRIED WOMAN

Being a single woman in the 1990s is dramatically different from being single in the 1950s. In the 1950s the rules about sexual behavior were clear, simple, and *wrong*. Yet you knew where you stood. The man was not to be trusted; he was out for sex, to use and then discard the woman. The woman's role was to protect her virginity and, if she couldn't do that, at least protect her reputation. Women learned that men and sex were the enemy. Only romance and marriage could justify sexuality.

The 1950s' double standard of premarital sexuality had innumerable difficulties. The chief one was that you wound up marrying young and marrying the first man you had sexual intercourse with. For some women this worked out well, but for many it was a poor choice resulting in an unsatisfying marriage. Negative attitudes toward sexuality acquired during adolescence did not magically go away with marriage. The double standard proclaimed that the young woman in love would be swept away with passion and that love was the only justification for sex. This is not a healthy basis for an ongoing sexual relationship. The double standard blocked clear, honest communication with men, including the special man in the woman's life. It was very difficult for the woman to view her partner as a loving, sexual friend and it was impossible for the man to view the woman as a sexual person and not a sexual object. One major consequence was the high rate of unplanned pregnancies—one of four brides was pregnant at the time of marriage. In the revered "sexual good old days" many marriages (most for people under twenty) were "shotgun weddings," brought about by the woman's pregnancy. The nostalgia for the days before the "sexual revolu-

31

tion" is misplaced—those were not good days for unmarried women. Going backward is not the answer for the 1990s.

Being an unmarried woman in the 1990s is not a great joy either. The rules regarding sexuality are unclear and confusing, and the feared consequences of sex—unwanted pregnancy, syphilis, and gonorrhea—have been joined by AIDs, chlamydia, and herpes. One in three women have a premarital pregnancy—a higher rate than in the 1950s. A new fear is the growing problem of infertility, especially among women in their mid to late thirties. The old "bad girl/good girl" categorization has broken down, but its replacement is neither clear nor helpful. The two biggest changes are that women are marrying later (the median age for women to marry in the United States is now twenty-three, and for college-educated women it is twenty-five) and they are beginning to have sexual intercourse at a younger age (nineteen is now the median age to begin sexual intercourse and a significant number of women are having intercourse as young as fourteen and fifteen). Some parents, educators, and ministers view the changes in premarital sexual patterns with great fear and trepidation.

A NEW MODEL FOR PREMARITAL SEXUALITY

The message for women about premarital sex has always been a fearful one. In this chapter we would like to present a positive learning model for being a sexually aware and responsible unmarried woman. We will try to deal clearly and directly with issues of unplanned pregnancies, sexually transmitted diseases (including AIDS), and sexual trauma (including rape, child sexual abuse, and humiliation and rejection). These are real fears; far too many young women are victims of harmful sexual incidents.

The best way to conceptualize premarital sexuality is as a learning experience to establish a solid base for healthy sexuality throughout later life. Premarital sex is not a proving ground; it is best thought of as a learning or training experience for adult sexuality. Premarital sex does not guarantee healthy adult sexuality, but neither does abstinence.

What are the most important lessons for a young woman? The

prime factor is attitudes toward yourself and sexuality. We suggest the adoption of the following three attitudes:

1. Sex is a good thing in life, not a bad thing.
2. Sexuality is a positive, integral part of your personality.
3. The crucial choice is how to express your sexuality so that it enhances your life and an intimate relationship without causing guilt, confusion, or trauma.

These cognitions are equally relevant for a sixteen-year-old adolescent, a twenty-six-year-old woman, a forty-sixty-year-old middle-years woman, or a sixty-six-year-old senior citizen. You are a sexual woman from the day you're born to the day you die. It is in your best interest to be aware of yourself as a sexual woman, be accepting of your body including your genitalia, be knowledgeable about sexual health, be comfortable with touching and affection, and choose to be sexually expressive. You can own your sexuality and express sexuality so that it adds to your self-esteem and intimate relationship.

It would be ideal if females and males could relate in respectful, trustful, and caring ways. Relating as sexual people in an honest, nonexploitative manner is an ideal to be striven for, but very different from the reality of adolescence. Thus, it is important to learn how to communicate clearly and assertively about sexuality. The young woman has to develop a clear sense of what is in her best interest at this point in her sexual development, and not be coerced by peer pressure or by the young man. By age sixteen, over 90 percent of males have masturbated to orgasm while fewer than 30 percent of females have. We do not adhere to the avant-garde view that all women need to learn to masturbate, but we do believe that self-exploration and masturbation is a healthy, normal step in a woman's acceptance of her body and sexual awareness. We also believe enjoying affectionate touch, with clothes on or off, is a crucial learning experience for young women.

Love has traditionally been used as the justification or permission to be involved sexually, including petting to orgasm and sexual intercourse. Crushes and romantic love can be experienced and enjoyed by adolescents. However, mature love is an adult emotion and is not likely to exist in a healthy manner before age nineteen at the earliest. This will certainly disappoint the moviemakers and record stores since love and sex are the main themes of movies, records, novels, and TV soap operas. Yet it is true. Love is magic and as a justification for sexual intercourse is a massive con game on adolescent women.

A third important lesson is unfortunate, yet vital. By age twenty-five, 95 percent of women can identify at least one sexual incident (and usually more) that causes them guilt, confusion, bad feelings, or trauma. Accept and deal with these incidents so they do not control your self-esteem and life. Women need to be involved socially and politically to change the culture so that these sexual events will not occur in their daughters' generation. The first healing step is in your own life.

The fourth area is learning to have positive relational and sexual experiences. Ideally, an adult married couple is composed of a woman and a man both of whom have integrated intimacy skills and sexual-expression skills. According to the traditional double standard, the woman learns intimacy skills and the man learns sexual-expression skills. In our model of female sexuality we encourage women to develop intimacy skills and sexual-expression skills in the context of maintaining her sexual health (protecting against pregnancy and sexually transmitted diseases) and having a satisfying and mutual relationship.

One of the most important lessons is that sexuality is best experienced in the context of a respectful, cooperative, pleasure-oriented relationship. Sexual expression, at a minimum, should exist in the context of a sexual friendship. As in any other friendship, the two people enjoy being with each other and try not to be hurtful to the other. Coercion, performance demands, threats of "if you don't do this sexually I'll abandon you" have no place in a sexual friendship. Positive intimacy skills include being open and self-disclosing, maintaining clear and honest communication, being able to make sexual requests, being vulnerable and expressive, and feeling valued. Sexual-expression skills include comfort with your body, enjoying the pleasurable sensations in giving and receiving nondemand touching, comfort with nudity, being receptive and responsive to genital stimulation, being aroused by multiple stimulation (which may or may not include intercourse), and being able to let go and enjoy the special pleasure of orgasm.

The question for women in the 1990s has changed from "Do

I keep my virginity until marriage," to "How and when is it in my best interest to be sexual?" Even in the mythical "good old days" over 90 percent of women engaged in genital stimulation and over 50 percent engaged in premarital intercourse. We strongly advocate three guidelines regarding premarital intercourse. The first is to refrain from intercourse until you have a comfortable relationship that allows you to discuss contraception *before* introducing intercourse into the relationship. Only about one-third of women use any contraception at their first intercourse, and the younger the woman, the less likely she'll use contraception. Effective contraception includes the birth control pill, the IUD, the diaphragm, condom, cervical cap, sponge, and foam, although the latter three are only moderately effective. Ineffective contraception includes the rhythm method, coitus interruptus (withdrawal), and douching.

The second guideline is to engage in sexual activities as a lesson for yourself not to please, placate, win over, or hold the man. So much of adolescent and premarital sexuality is male-oriented—that's not a good lesson for adult sexual awareness. Sexual expression should meet your needs and be congruent with your feelings.

The third guideline is that we are in favor of adolescent sexuality, but not adolescent intercourse. The data clearly demonstrates that the health and psychological risks of adolescent intercourse are too great. The traditional dangers of pregnancy, sexually transmitted diseases, and early marriages are well known. However, just as dangerous is the premature breaking of emotional bonds with family and friends by the adolescent woman who becomes too involved with and dependent on the man. Equally dangerous is losing a sense of herself as an independent person with developing competencies and goals. You need to have a clear sense of autonomy and self-esteem before entering into an emotionally and sexually intimate relationship. Too many adolescents become intensely involved, which leads to destructive relationships as well as early marriage. Sexual intercourse artificially heightens the involvement in a relationship. The evidence indicates that marriages are more stable and successful where the woman is at least twenty-one, and not pregnant at the time of marriage.

CIRCLES OF INTIMACY

The circles-of-intimacy concept will help you think about males, relationships, and sexuality in a more rational way. The idea is to clarify your values and aid in making decisions. What you decide will be relevant not only immediately but more important it will have a long-term effect on your sexuality and intimacy in adulthood.

The "E circle" consists of people you have no real connection with—you don't even know their names. They can include the clerk in the store, someone who sits next to you on the bus, a man you say good morning to on the street, or the temporary employee at school. It is important to treat such people respectfully and considerately, but there is no real personal connection. In a day there might be dozens of people in the E circle.

The "D circle" refers to people who are acquaintances. In this category are people whose names you know, who you might talk with about neutral topics like the weather, but who know little of importance about you. You might occasionally have a cup of coffee with such a person and talk about present job concerns or current events, but it is unlikely you will have an ongoing or personal contact with someone in the D circle. People typically have several acquaintances and particularly extroverted people might have a hundred in this category.

The "C circle" of friends is the first with whom any real emotional intimacy exists. You share your feelings and experiences with C circle friends. You enjoy them and have special moments and activities with them. You might work with a C circle person, have classes with him, live in the same dorm or apartment complex, be on the same team, or just enjoy each other's company. As long as the friendship lasts you trust your friend will not purposefully hurt you. As life and circumstances change these friendships end. At a given time some women have only one or two friends, others who are more gregarious might have ten or even twenty friends. Throughout a lifetime some will have thirty friends, others might have a thousand. When a friendship ends with anger and bad feelings, you will be hurt and disappointed, but this is temporary and you are not likely to be devastated.

"B Circle" relationships are best characterized as close friendships. You like and trust these friends and share your hopes, dreams, and personal feelings with them. Their opinion of you matters and you share good and bad feelings and experiences. When circumstances change, you go out of your way to write, call, visit, and try to maintain the bond of close friendship. Their feelings toward you are important to your self-esteem. If a close friendship is terminated angrily it will shake you and cause you to consider what went wrong and what that says about you as a person. Some women only have one close friendship at a time and in their whole life might have less than ten, while other women have five or six close friendships at once and might have over a hundred in their lives. Close friendships are an important, positive part of life. They provide a social network and enhance your self-respect. Letting someone know you intimately helps you know and accept yourself. Close friends will be there when you need help and will care enough to confront you if something is wrong in your life (you're drinking too much, you're in a destructive relationship, you've made a foolish decision). Level B friendships are to be nurtured and valued.

"A circle" relationships are the most intimate. These intimate relationships allow you to really be yourself, no holds barred. You disclose feelings and experiences you would keep secret from others. You feel strong trust and acceptance in a level A relationship. This is the type of relationship you have with a spouse, best friend, mentor, in a particularly close parent-child relationship. At some point in life (often in adolescence or young adulthood) there is no one in the A circle. In one's whole life there might be only one or two people, while others have up to ten. When such a relationship ends badly, for instance, in divorce, the feelings of hurt and grief last for many months or even years. Intimate relationships bring out the best in you, and hurt the most when the intimacy stops. The sense of trust and acceptance is particularly crucial. You need to choose carefully and wisely the people you let into your circle A.

Let us translate this theory into sexual relationships. In the traditional double standard, the man was supposed to have sex with any woman, any time, in any situation—thus it didn't matter if their relationship was circle E or A. The woman, on the other hand, was only to have sex with a man in her A circle—husband or at least fiancé. The abstinence standard said neither women nor men were to engage in premarital intercourse regardless of age or type of relationship. The sex-regardless-of-intimacy standard is very much like the abstinence standard, except the opposite side of the coin. You are encouraged to have sex with anyone regardless of age or degree of intimacy. Neither of these standards make any sense to us psychologically or sexually; they do not promote a good basis for adult sexuality.

The new cultural standard is called "sex with affection." This says that age and level of intimacy is crucial in making healthy sexual decisions. It provides a model to learn about oneself, men, relationships, and sexuality. The danger with the sex-with-affection standard is it's hard to be clear and specific, and is subject to misuse. Yet it offers a way of thinking about men and relationships that can promote learning for the single woman. In examining your attitudes and experiences concerning premarital sexuality, it is important to be honest with yourself. A prime guideline of mental health is "Do not bullshit yourself," and it's particularly relevant for sexual relationships.

In considering sexual involvement, a good guideline is that the relationship should be at least a level C—a sexual friendship. We do not believe there is much to be gained from one-night stands or from having sexual affairs with acquaintances because there is nothing better to do or no better relationship around. The risks and consequences are greater in level E and D affairs because they tend to be impulsive and manipulative. There are health risks if you have multiple partners. As well, many women become disillusioned and cynical about men and sexual relationships.

Ideally, most women would prefer a stable level A relationship that is both emotionally intimate and sexually satisfying. However, to get there you need learning experiences, and it's naïve to believe that all of them will be positive. If most of them are positive, you are a lucky woman indeed.

We believe that the trend toward delaying marriage is a good one. You are likely to choose better in your mid-twenties because you have a better sense of yourself. You are less vulnerable to being swept away by romantic love and powerful sexual urges. You can more clearly view the man, the relationship, and the sexual experience. Rather than feeling hurt by affairs that terminate or feeling guilty about being sexual, be aware and grow.

Jeanne

Jeanne is a twenty-six-year-old air traffic controller who is engaged to be married in three months. In looking back at her premarital sexual experiences there was a great deal she learned and felt good about as well as some things she regretted, but accepted.

Jeanne grew up in a middle-class suburb of Cincinnati and was eight when her parents divorced. Although she wanted to stay in contact with her father, he moved to California to start a new life and family, and Jeanne was estranged from him. Her parents had married before twenty when her mother had become pregnant with Jeanne's older sister. Her parents had a passionate, romantic affair, but found the realities and responsibilities of marriage and a family overwhelming, and the marital bond was broken. Jeanne's mother felt devastated, not so much by losing the personal relationship with Jeanne's father, but with the difficulties of being a single parent with limited financial resources. Her mother did not enjoy being a divorced woman in the dating scene. She was an active member of Parents Without Partners and enjoyed the support of other divorced women, and she became increasingly distrustful of men. Jeanne is convinced that her mother remarried not out of love, but for stability and convenience. Jeanne was thirteen when her mother remarried and she had a very difficult relationship with her stepfather. Jeanne's feelings were reinforced when her sister got married at nineteen (also pregnant) because she wanted to escape their unhappy home.

Jeanne found it easier to postpone marriage than to postpone sex. She felt she could not turn to her mother or older sister for advice or help, so she called a teenage hotline and talked to the telephone counselor twice. She was referred to Planned Parenthood where she received three sessions of group counseling and then was examined by a gynecologist and received a prescription for birth control pills. In retrospect, Jeanne regretted beginning intercourse at age sixteen. However, she was proud that she had prevented an unwanted pregnancy.

The young man Jeanne dated was nineteen, worked, and had his own car. She felt older and more independent than her peers. This relationship continued throughout her senior year and did not reach crisis proportions until the senior prom. Jeanne had gone out mostly with his friends or as a couple. When she saw him in the context of guys whom her high-school friends were dating, several of the young men college students, she was chagrined to discover her boyfriend was domineering and boorish. It was not a pleasant prom night. Jeanne felt he wanted to isolate her from friends in order to avoid joining in the postprom weekend activities. They had one of their worst fights that next day, and Jeanne realized she'd outgrown the relationship. As are many young males, her boyfriend was an early ejaculator and emphasized quantity of sex, not quality. He wanted to have sex at every opportunity and since she was on the birth control pill assumed she should be willing to go along. Her sexual feelings and needs were given short shrift.

Jeanne decided to continue her schooling at the community college. She could work enough to support herself, share a house with friends, and be a part-time student. Not surprisingly, this plan was not acceptable to her boyfriend. He wanted her to move in with him. Although he didn't say it directly, he didn't want her to have more education than he did. A sexually involved, early love affair is difficult and painful to break up. He thought of Jeanne as his possession, and there were several ugly scenes, two of which involved hitting and pushing. These were followed by tearful periods, using sex to make up and promises to "love each other forever." Each incident resulted in Jeanne feeling more disgusted with herself. It took until mid-July to extricate herself from what was an increasingly destructive relationship.

So at eighteen, Jeanne was back on her own. She found the young-adult dating and sexual game to be particularly hard on women. You had to justify why you didn't want to have sex with a new date. Jeanne had enjoyed sexuality, but she disliked the sense of being on the sexual defensive. Jeanne would get involved in ongoing dating relationships as much to avoid feeling "hit on" as from a desire to be sexually active with this particular man. Her pattern was to date men who were three to five years older, and to focus her social life around their friends and activities. Although it was not a terrible two and a half years, she would not like to relive them.

Jeanne was saving money and, with help from her mother and stepfather, enrolled full-time at the state university. Three months before she left the town she'd grown up in Jeanne had to deal with a sexual incident that was to profoundly change her sexual pattern. She developed chlamydia, the most common sexually transmitted disease in females. She was embarrassed by having a sexual disease, and she did not find the gynecologist who treated her to be particularly helpful or supportive. He told her the man needed to be treated but did not emphasize it enough. So Jeanne was treated and then reinfected. Her boyfriend's reluctance to be treated first frustrated her and eventually enraged her. Jeanne wanted more respect and consideration from a man she was sexually involved with. Instead of merely complaining, she took decisive action and broke off the relationship. She was pleased and proud of herself. Jeanne determined to manage her dating and sexual life in a more respectful manner at the university.

Jeanne decided to date only college men, either seniors or graduate students. Most important, she'd be active in choosing a partner rather than hooking up with whoever was available and interested in her. At twenty-one it was time to take control of her dating and sexual life. She was tired of her sexual feelings and needs being secondary to the man's. She was especially tired of males who "worked on her" to be ready for intercourse and then ejaculated early. She wanted a man who was more sensitive, who would talk about feelings, and who would listen to her needs and how *she* wanted to make love rather than only doing it his way.

The first six months at the university were the most social Jeanne had been since her sophomore year in high school, although paradoxically the most lonely. She reestablished a pattern of socializing with female friends and in groups (joining a tennis group and an aviation group). For the first time in five years she did not have a boyfriend. Jeanne missed the predictability of a Saturday night date but frankly did not miss the sexual relationship. The two one-night affairs she had convinced Jeanne that was not the way to go.

One night she was sitting around with girlfriends discussing males and dating, and she was surprised and pleased to hear other young women admit to their dissatisfactions with sex and relationships. They discussed how it was easier to be orgasmic with masturbation or with partner manual stimulation. These were two experiences she had not had, but she was very interested listening to the others' discussion. That night in the privacy of her room in the house she rented with four other women, she began her first genital self-exploration and touching. She was not orgasmic that night, but she continued with her self-exploration and three weeks later was orgasmic. Jeanne understood a crucial element that had been missing in her sexual life, the pleasure of orgasm. As she continued to masturbate on a twice-weekly basis, she would be orgasmic almost each time and found out more about the kind of touch she was responsive to.

Jeanne was open to a new man in her life but this time was more careful in making her choice. The man she became involved with was a graduate student in literature. An intellectual man who wanted to be a writer was a different and intriguing possibility for Jeanne. They did a number of things together before going on a "real date." Jeanne thought it was good to have had a friendship before beginning a romance. They talked about sex before they had it. Jeanne resumed taking the birth control pill, but she emphasized that because she was safe from pregnancy did not mean she was always ready for intercourse.

For the first time ever, she requested more time spent on pleasuring her, especially using manual clitoral stimulation. Jeanne learned intercourse was much more enjoyable if she was aroused before beginning. As the sexual relationship progressed, so did her involvement and arousal. Jeanne had not read that most women have their first orgasm in nonintercourse sex, but she had the intuitive sense that she'd be orgasmic if they could stay with her rhythm of manual stimulation. She found it hard to say this directly, but with a combination of guiding his hand, emphasizing taking more time, and his being sensitive enough to follow her rhythm, the result was orgasms with manual stimulation. As Jeanne hoped it would, this increased her responsiveness during intercourse, and she found it easier to be

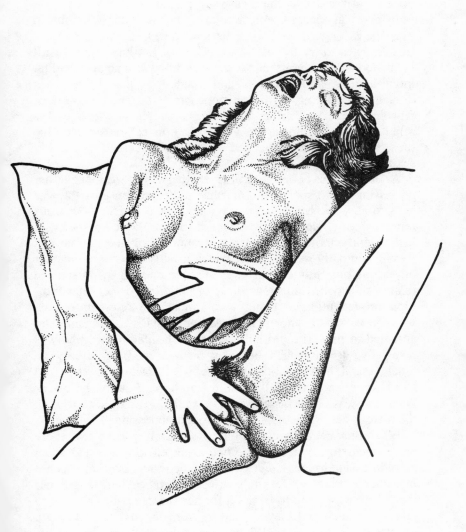

The pleasure of self-exploration and masturbation can lead to a better awareness of the kind of touch the body is responsive to.

orgasmic with intercourse. This was especially so if she had been orgasmic during the pleasuring period.

Jeanne was pleased with the development of the relationship over the prior year, but when he announced he was moving to Los Angeles to try to write for television, she knew she wasn't interested in pursuing that dream with him. Jeanne was feeling more assured about herself and wanted to pursue her own dreams of working in air traffic control, but not in the Los Angeles area. It was an amicable, although sad, end to the affair. Jeanne had no regrets about this connection, enjoyed the time they spent together and what she'd learned about her sexuality.

As Jeanne felt better about herself, her ability to manage her professional and social life, and had a clearer sense of the role of sexuality in her life, she felt ready to pursue a serious relationship. Craig was a managerial trainee, her own age, who had recently moved to the area. Jeanne's only hesitation was they'd originally met in a bar, which usually is a poor indicator of serious possibilities. She was flexible enough to pursue the relationship with Craig regardless of how they'd met. Her intuition proved reliable. Craig was a man she felt comfortable with, attracted to, and trusted. Although she was romantically attracted to him, she did not want to rush intercourse. She was responsive to his touch but was put off by how rapidly he touched and how goal-oriented he was. Each time they did touching, even if she did not stimulate him genitally, he ejaculated. He was embarrassed by his ejaculations and tried to hide them from her, something Jeanne found endearing.

When they began having intercourse, Craig was an extremely early ejaculator, which Jeanne had expected. She worried when he didn't want to talk about it and avoided touching that was not intercourse-oriented. Jeanne's prior experience had taught her that if sex was going to be good for her she needed to be able to talk to the man and they needed to work together to develop a satisfactory sexual style. When she told him this was important, Craig took a big gulp and said he'd never done that with a woman because he'd felt so bad about his early ejaculation. Yet if they communicated and tried new things sex would be more fun and more satisfying. They purchased *Sexual Awareness* and although they didn't rigidly practice ejaculatory control exercises, they did slow down and gradually built a sense of comfort. Jeanne enjoyed the process of Craig opening up to her, and this allowed her to be more open with him. It usually takes about six months to develop a satisfying couple sexual style. For Jeanne and Craig the process extended over a year. Successfully dealing with sexual problems had the effect of building a more intimate bond, which resulted in their decision to marry on the second-year anniversary of their first date.

GUIDELINES FOR THE UNMARRIED WOMAN

You do not have to be married (or even in love) to justify having sexual feelings and being in a sexual relationship. For young adults (nineteen and over) including sexual intercourse in the relationship while using appropriate contraception is the norm in our culture. This does not mean that women should be pressured to have intercourse when they don't feel comfortable with it. A key element in healthy sexuality is to be aware and responsible and express sexuality in a manner that enhances your life and an intimate relationship. It is perfectly acceptable for a young adult woman to choose not to have sexual intercourse or to delay intercourse until she feels committed to the relationship.

Perhaps the most important guideline is to view premarital sexuality as a training ground for later adult sexuality. You need to be aware of both positive and negative insights about yourself, men, sexuality, and relationships. Although there are incidents and relationships that you might regret, it is not in your best interest to feel guilty about them. You survived and learned—acknowledge that. Most important, you deserve to feel good about yourself now as an adult sexual woman.

4

CONTRACEPTION: AVOIDING UNWANTED PREGNANCY

The birth control pill was a major breakthrough in allowing women more control over their bodies and their sexuality. Women have been concerned with family planning and birth control for centuries, but until the advent of the pill they couldn't do much about either. The condom (rubber) was the man's domain. The diaphragm has been in existence for almost one hundred years, but had not been widely used, even by married women. Although there have been difficulties and controversies surrounding the birth control pill (especially the type originally prescribed in the 1950s), it revolutionized women's attitudes toward family planning and sexuality. For the first time the act of intercourse and the process of contraception were separate. Contraceptive use became acceptable for unmarried as well as married women.

We are strong advocates, both personally and professionally, of birth control and family planning. We used birth control rigorously until Barry had his vasectomy. We have three children, two biological and one adopted.

It is essential that children be planned and wanted. Very few pregnancies of nonmarried women, especially teenagers, are planned and wanted. The United States has one of the highest rates of premarital pregnancies in the world. One in three women has an unwanted, unplanned premarital pregnancy. There is growing public concern about "children having children." For the sake of the child, it would be preferable if there was a cultural guideline that twenty-one was the minimum acceptable age for motherhood.

Traditionalists urge a return to the rigid no-sex-before-marriage standard. The reality is that will not happen. Whether adults

46

approve or not, nonmarried young women will engage in inter-course. The stance of sex educators is to recommend against adolescent intercourse, but if the adolescent woman is having intercourse to provide her with education, counseling, and access to birth control. This stance is realistic and makes sense. The trend among women, especially those who are better-educated and career-minded, is to delay marriage until the mid or late twenties. These women are having sexual intercourse and are in need of contraceptive protection. Marriage is no longer the sole justification for sexual expression.

IS THERE A PERFECT CONTRACEPTIVE?

Students look forward to the lecture on contraception in Barry's college-level Human Sexual Behavior class with the naïve expectation that they'll learn there is a perfect contraceptive or one just about to be marketed. They leave the class with a roaring headache. The truth is we are a long way from a perfect contraceptive. A perfect contraceptive would have the following characteristics: 1) totally effective, 2) no immediate or long-term side effects, 3) separate from sexual activity, 4) easily reversible, 5) require little or no effort on part of user, 6) could be used by male or female, 7) inexpensive. Nothing we now have comes anywhere close to meeting those criteria. The closest is sterilization, especially vasectomy, which will be covered in a separate chapter. However, the major disadvantage of sterilization is a devastating one for a young woman—it is a permanent form of birth control that is difficult and sometimes impossible to reverse.

Unfortunately, for a number of political and cultural reasons, there is not a large amount of research being conducted on contraception. We are not likely to produce a perfect contraceptive in the near future. So women of the 1990s will need to carefully evaluate their contraceptive options and choose the contraceptive that best meets their needs at the time. Let us examine six classes of contraceptives: 1) birth control pill, 2) diaphragm, 3) IUD, 4) condom, 5) foam and spermicide, 6) natural family planning. Each woman, hopefully in consultation with her gynecologist and partner, needs to decide which contraceptive is best for her.

BIRTH CONTROL PILL

The birth control pill is the most effective form of contraception presently available. Significant modifications of the pill have reduced side effects and make it safer with little to no reduction in efficacy. The major change is that pills now contain much lower levels of estrogen. This has resulted in a dramatic decrease in immediate side effects and even more important reduced the risks of long-term usage.

The birth control pill functions by preventing ovulation. Since no ovum is released, conception is not possible. On most regimens, the woman takes the pill each day at approximately the same time. Twenty-one of the pills have active hormonal ingredients, the other seven are inert but are used to reinforce the habit of taking the birth control pill daily.

A major advantage of the pill is that it separates the contracep-tive act from the sexual act. The pill prescription is relatively inexpensive, although a new set of pills must be obtained monthly. It is convenient and easy to use. For the great majority of women it is a medically safe procedure with few side effects. Most women can stay on the birth control pill indefinitely—there is no need to take a break from its use.

Drawbacks are that some women, especially those with a family history of blood clotting and stroke, are not good candidates for the birth control pill. In order to obtain a prescription for birth control pills, you need to consult a gynecologist who will then monitor your use on at least a yearly basis (we suggest six-month follow-up appointments, especially for younger women). A major disincentive for using birth control pills is smoking, especially when the woman is over thirty. Smoking is not a healthy behavior in any case, but it is particularly unhealthy in conjunction with the use of birth control pills. Some women complain of weight gain, headaches, water retention, or a sense of malaise as a result of using the birth control pill. Other women report lower sexual desire. These side effects have been lessened by lower doses of estrogen in the pill.

If a pill is forgotten or missed, you should take it as soon as possible or take two pills the next day. If over twenty-four hours has elapsed, it is strongly advised that the woman utilize a back-up contraceptive for the *entire* pill cycle. That means using a diaphragm, condom, or foam each time you have intercourse that month. The reason for such a rigorous backup procedure is that the lower-estrogen pills must be used with more care than the pills of ten years ago, which had almost ten times as much hormonal content. If you are taking penicillin or other medications you should consult your gynecologist about its effect on the efficacy of the birth control pill. You might need to use another contraceptive while using medication to ensure safety from an unwanted pregnancy.

Contrary to popular myth, the birth control pill does not increase risk of cancer for most women. In fact, risk for certain cancers is decreased. For most women the pill is a safe and effective contraceptive.

DIAPHRAGM

The diaphragm is one of the oldest and still most effective forms of birth control. The famous feminist and birth control pioneer Margaret Sanger was a strong advocate of the diaphragm. She rightly maintained that the diaphragm gave the woman control over the conception process and had minimal interference with sexual expression.

Recently the diaphragm has made a major comeback in popularity. It has two major advantages—it is highly effective when used properly and there is no threat of medical side effects. A woman must be examined by a gynecologist to be properly fitted for the diaphragm, which is a rubber-based ring that is inserted inside the vagina. The diaphragm blocks conception in two ways. The device itself serves as a barrier covering the cervix so sperm cannot penetrate. Just as vital, a spermicidal jelly is put around the diaphragm and serves to kill sperm.

Misuse of the spermicide is one of the major reasons for diaphragm failure. It needs to be placed on the diaphragm no sooner than two hours, and preferably closer to an hour before beginning intercourse. The diaphragm must be left in place at least six hours after intercourse. If you desire to have a second intercourse, you must use a special inserter to apply a second dose of spermicidal jelly while the diaphragm remains in place. Common mistakes that reduce diaphragm efficacy (and can result in pregnancy) are to put the diaphragm in at the beginning of the evening and not have intercourse until five hours later, or to take the diaphragm out to insert the jelly for a second inter-course, or to wait less than six hours before removing the diaphragm because you feel uncomfortable keeping it in. The most common cause for diaphragm failure is that in the passion of the moment the device remains in the drawer, the partners have been unable to interrupt the sexual excitement to insert the diaphragm. The key to successful diaphragm use is the commit-ment to use it on every sexual occasion and to do so no matter what the partner says or how late it is or how aroused you are.

The diaphragm must be kept clean and dry when not in use. If you gain or lose ten or more pounds, your gynecologist should refit you for a new diaphragm. You should also be refitted after giving birth.

The diaphragm need not be an impediment to sexual satisfac-tion. Some women prefer to put the diaphragm in an hour prior to beginning sexual activity. Some couples use diaphragm inser-tion as part of the pleasuring (foreplay) sequence. Some males even take responsibility for the insertion. Other women prefer to engage in nonintercourse sexual activity, then take a break and go into the bathroom and insert the diaphragm. The scenario we are most ambivalent about is the most common one—being highly aroused and then breaking to insert the diaphragm. There is a tendency to go with the moment and not stop for the diaphragm. Another potential problem with the diaphragm is that when the couple are having intercourse in the woman-on-top position, especially when the woman is orgasmic, the dia-phragm might "float" from the cervix and increase the risk of pregnancy. In those situations, we advise use of another contra-ceptive or altering the intercourse position.

The cervical cap is similar to the diaphragm, but does not offer as reliable protection. The advantage of the contraceptive sponge (which contains a measured amount of spermicide) is that it can be purchased over the counter without a doctor's prescription. It can be a good backup contraceptive, but it is not as efficacious as the diaphragm.

IUD

The IUD (intrauterine device) is one of the most controversial contraceptives. It was a popular contraceptive in the 1970s—touted as effective, safe, and maintaining a boundary between sexual expression and contraception. In an attempt to provide the advantages of the IUD to women who never had children, the Dalkon shield—a smaller IUD—was developed. Unfortunately, this particular IUD caused infection in many women, leading to blockage of the fallopian tubes and resulting in infertility. There were literally thousands of lawsuits and manufacturers took almost all IUDs off the market.

Now newer and safer IUD models are being introduced. It is important to work with a gynecologist who is current on IUD research and is skilled at inserting the IUD. Perforation of the uterine wall upon improper insertion of the IUD is a rare but devastating complication. The side effect most women complain about is heavy menstrual bleeding. The IUD strings that extend into the vaginal canal should be checked once a month to ensure that the IUD has not spontaneously been expelled from the uterus. This is most likely to occur within a few weeks or months after IUD insertion, and women who have never had an IUD are more likely to experience this. The newer IUD models include copper material that increases the contraceptive effectiveness, but the IUD needs to be replaced every two or three years. No one has established precisely how the IUD works, but it appears to interfere with the implantation of the ovum in the uterus.

Few women are neutral about the IUD. Those who have had success with no side effects rave about how trouble-free it is. They don't have to take a pill each day or insert a diaphragm each time they want to be sexual. They need only check the strings once a month. Other women have found the IUD the worst of the contraceptives. Complaints are heavy cramping and bleeding, painful IUD expulsion, and infections.

CONDOM

Another contraceptive having renewed popularity is the condom. The major reason is fear of AIDS. The surgeon general emphasizes the use of condoms as a preventative. Condoms do not provide total safety against the AIDS virus, but they do significantly decrease the risk of AIDS transmission as well as gonorrhea and other sexually transmitted diseases. Traditionally, males objected to the condom (the only male-oriented contraceptive) because of loss of sensation—the line about "taking a shower with a raincoat on."

In the past few years the quality of condoms has greatly improved. They come in various colors, lubricated as well as nonlubricated, and even have a small receptacle to catch the semen. Condoms are now available at drug and grocery stores and are out in the open rather than hidden. Don't try to economize, you are better buying quality latex condoms, which are more effective. People who test condoms by blowing into them or putting water in them are reducing rather than improving their safety. Obviously, reusing condoms is inappropriate.

Women are becoming more assertive in insisting that their partners, especially new partners, use condoms. This is perfectly appropriate. The proper use of condoms includes insisting that the condom be put on before inserting the penis into the vagina, leaving a small space at the end to catch the semen, and being sure the male withdraws soon after ejaculation and holds the base of the penis so the condom doesn't slip off. An advantage of the condom is that you don't need a prescription or a doctor's visit. Nor are there side effects. The biggest problem is the misuse or lack of use of the condom. Although it is a very good contraceptive, it is not as effective as the pill, diaphragm, or IUD. Some women us spermicidal foam or jelly along with the condom.

OTHER CONTRACEPTIVES

Spermicidal foams, creams, and jellies are acceptable backup contraceptives, but not as effective as condoms, diaphragms, and birth control pills in preventing conception. They have the same advantage as condoms—you can purchase them over the counter. They are utilized right before beginning intercourse. Ideally they would only be used with a condom or other contraceptive. Spermicidal creams, jellies, and foams have major disadvantages. These include being messy, preventing oral-genital sex, interfering with sexual spontaneity, and being only moderately effective.

Natural family planning is a Catholic procedure to help religious people plan families without using artificial birth control. Some of the techniques have appealed to feminists, especially the woman's awareness of her menstrual cycle and examining her vaginal mucus. This technique is much more rigorous than the haphazard system of rhythm, which is based on the calendar and prayer. Couples who are highly motivated to maintain records of the menstrual cycle, examine the mucus, and are able to abstain from intercourse for over a week during the high-probability period can use natural family planning with some success. Yet it is not for most women, especially not for single women.

Judy

Judy is a thirty-seven-year-old married woman whose husband, George, had decided to have a vasectomy two years after the birth of their last child. It was a hard decision, but one Judy was glad they'd made. During the past twenty years Judy had utilized almost every type of contraceptive known. She'd been a conscientious and effective contraceptive user, but freely admits she is glad to no longer have to deal with it.

Judy reached adolescence during the turbulent 1960s when the emphasis was on sexual experimentation. Like most adolescents, Judy began intercourse before beginning contraception. Judy's first intercourse was at seventeen, and her partner engaged in coitus interruptus (withdrawal) almost each time. Judy was aware that even if he did pull out before he ejaculated, she still risked becoming pregnant. There is a discharge well before ejaculation that contains enough sperm to cause conception. After two months of anxiously worrying when her period started late, Judy went to Planned Parenthood. She was given a prescription for birth control pills and over the next three years was a successful pill user.

She switched to the diaphragm which she did not like because it required her to carry the device and spermicide with her. She did use the diaphragm for a year without incident, but about once a month because of overconfidence she would have intercourse without it. One out of three women has an unplanned, unwanted premarital pregnancy, and in her fourteenth month of diaphragm use Judy became one of those statistics. Judy ultimately did want children, but not at this time, and certainly not with this particular male. Although she found it a very difficult decision, Judy chose to have a therapeutic abortion.

After the abortion she decided to try the IUD. Although Judy enjoyed the freedom she'd missed with the diaphragm, she did not like the cramping and bleeding that occurred with the IUD. She stayed with it until she began the relationship with George. George had always used condoms and was willing to continue. Judy found that having to stop while George put the condom on interfered with her sexual pleasure. After discussing it with her gynecologist and reviewing recent research on the pill, she returned to the pill for the next four years until they chose to get pregnant. For the three months between stopping the pill and before starting to try to get pregnant, George used condoms.

Judy and George very much enjoyed the freedom from birth control. Trying to get pregnant served as an aphrodisiac and Judy was almost disappointed to find herself pregnant after only four months of trying. She chose to breastfeed so was not able to return to the birth control pill. While she breastfed she was a dedicated diaphragm user. However, she was glad to return to the pill. After the birth of their second child, they could not decide whether to stop at two. During the next two years they used the condom, diaphragm, and then returned to the pill. Finally they resolved that two children was best for them and George had a vasectomy. Judy stayed on the pill until George had a follow-up sperm sample that ensured there were no sperm in his ejaculate. They had a celebratory burying of all leftover pills, diaphragm, and condoms. Judy looked forward to sexuality free of contraceptive concerns.

FEMALE-MALE COMMUNICATION ABOUT CONTRACEPTION

Traditionally contraception has been the woman's domain. Other than the condom, all contraceptives are used by the woman. This is a source of growing resentment for women, but the reality is not likely to change in the foreseeable future. Researchers emphasize how difficult it is to develop usable contraception for men. Yet one cannot help but believe that if it were men who became pregnant contraceptive research would receive a much higher priority.

Even when it is the woman who uses contraception, it does not follow that the man has no role or responsibility. Women, especially those who are married or in ongoing relationships, appreciate the man's active involvement in contraception whether that means being committed to use the diaphragm every time, checking IUD strings monthly, reminding her to take the pill, or paying half the cost of the gynecologist visit. Conversely, women are irritated by men who ignore contraceptive issues. The single man who doesn't even ask about contraception, but just assumes it's her responsibility, or the married man who views conception, contraception, and children as outside his domain are not the respectful, trustworthy partners most woman desire. Ideally contraception would be a joint responsibility of women and men. At a minimum the man needs to be aware of and appreciative of the woman's taking responsibility for contraception.

Ultimately it is the woman who must act in her best interest because it is she who becomes pregnant and bears the child. It is the woman rather than the man who will commonly be the custodial parent if the marriage ends. Don't be so caught up in "the way things ought to be" that you put yourself or a child in an untenable position. The world would be a better place for both adults and children if the decision making and responsibility for conception, contraception, and parenting were shared equally by women and men.

THE ISSUE OF ABORTION

The legality and morality of therapeutic abortions has been argued vociferously for the past twenty years. It is almost impossible to have a rational, objective discussion of this value-laden issue. We will give it our best effort but are sure it will not satisfy certain readers.

Therapeutic abortion is distinguished from spontaneous abortion (miscarriage) on one hand and illegal (back-alley) abortion, on the other. Approximately one in three pregnancies ends with a spontaneous abortion, usually in the first trimester—some women do not even realize they were pregnant. Spontaneous abortion is an example of the "old wives' tale" explanation being true. It is nature's way of dealing with a fetus that is not developing in a healthy manner. Illegal abortion refers to those performed in a non-medically-safe manner. Often these are done by quacks and result in medical damage to the woman and in some instances even her death.

A therapeutic abortion refers to a legal abortion performed by a physician in a safe manner. There are two major types of a therapeutic abortion—the suction curettage procedure and the saline or prostaglandin procedure. Approximately one and a half million therapeutic abortions are performed in the United States each year. Approximately two-thirds involve single women— the majority under twenty-five. Over 80 percent of therapeutic abortions involve the suction curettage procedure, which is performed at outpatient clinics for women who are less than twelve weeks pregnant. This is the medically safest, most inexpensive, and least psychologically traumatic procedure. More intrusive, less safe, and more psychologically traumatic is the saline or prostaglandin procedure, which entails an injection of a solution that causes the fetus to abort. It is typically performed on a one-day hospital inpatient basis, usually between fourteen and twenty-two weeks of fetal development.

We strongly support the concept of planned, wanted children. When an unmarried woman has an unplanned pregnancy she needs to be aware of the range of alternatives and discuss them with the man, friends and/or family, or a minister or counselor. Alternatives include having the child and keeping it herself, marrying the father, having a therapeutic abortion, and carrying the pregnancy to term and placing the child for adoption. People who love and care for the woman can and should offer their support and advice. The man, especially if married to her, has an integral say in the decision making. However, since the fetus develops in her body and she is ordinarily the one responsible for child care, the ultimate responsibility and decision should be hers—not the man's, or her parents', or doctors', ministers', judges', and certainly not politicians'. This is a very important personal decision and should not be approached lightly. Abortion is not a form of contraception, but a backup when contraception fails or was not used.

Antiabortion advocates point to the guilt and regret that some women have. This is very important to consider—the woman has to make a decision she can live with both at the time and in the future. What these advocates have not considered is the impact of an unwanted child on the child, woman, family, and society. There is a good deal of evidence that unwanted children fare more poorly than wanted, planned children. The woman needs to carefully consider her values and her options.

More unmarried women are keeping their babies and raising them alone or with family help. The danger is that these women and their children grow up in a life of poverty, lack of educational and vocational opportunity, and abusive relationships. One in four women is pregnant at the time of marriage. These marriages involve greater risks of divorce, especially if the woman is under twenty-one and/or was not planning to marry that particular man. Many women choose abortion with a commitment to have a planned, wanted child in the future. Those who choose to give up a child for adoption may realize that the waiting list for babies in most communities is at least two years. Such a woman has given another couple a much-wanted child.

We do not not believe there are easy right-wrong answers to the complex question of unwanted pregnancies. For those women who choose abortion, it is now a legal and medically safe alternative. The research evidence suggests that the great majority of women who choose to abort believe that it was the best decision for them.

CONTRACEPTION—A WAY OF TAKING CARE OF YOURSELF

Contraception is not an easy issue. There is not a perfect contraceptive available nor is there any reason to expect one to be developed in the foreseeable future. It is up to the woman, in consultation with her partner and with a gynecologist, to choose a contraceptive that is the best match for her needs at the time. Consideration must be given to issues including efficacy, safety, comfort of use, motivation, side effects, expense, and the state of her relationship and sexual life. You are the expert on your sexuality and can decide what is in your best interest. If you do not want an unwanted, unplanned pregnancy, the best answer is prevention—using effective contraception.

5

MARRIAGE: INTIMACY AND COMMITMENT

Traditionally getting married was the most important thing that a woman did in her life. Marriage was viewed by her family, friends, and the culture as a symbol of success. Phrases describing single women, "old maid," "spinster," "alone and lonely" are clearly derogatory. Lyrics in popular songs talk about how crucial love is for a woman, without it life means nothing. Pop psychology books ask whether a woman without a man has any worth. In our culture there is a strong "marriage mandate" for women. In some other cultures, one of the greatest burdens on the father is to arrange a marriage for his daughter. He puts the family's savings toward a dowry to convince a suitable man to marry his daughter; having an unmarried daughter is a sign of failure.

Marriage has traditionally been the demarcation point for female sexual expression. To have intercourse premaritally was to put the woman's future in jeopardy. Would a man want "used goods" when he could marry a virgin? Some cultures even had the newly married couple hang out their bloody bedsheets as a sign that the woman had been a virgin. Women needed the state of marriage for permission to be sexual. It was not sexuality that was of value, but the status and security offered by marriage.

The sophisticated young adult American woman reads this and says, "How old-fashioned, it has nothing to do with me." In our culture, where 80 percent of women have intercourse premaritally and where the median age of marriage is now twenty-three, and older for college-educated women, these notions would not appear relevant. However, on closer examination we find these traditional concepts are very much alive today.

58

Our questioning attitude toward marriage and sexual expression is not to deny the importance and value of marriage. Our promarriage bias is reflected in our own marriage begun in 1966, which we view as a strong and satisfying one. However, the "marriage mandate" and "romantic love" motivation for marriage in our culture are problematic for women. We want to directly confront these influences. We will propose an alternative model of marital choice and an approach to developing and maintaining the marital bond.

MARRIAGE AND SEXUALITY

Historically there was a strong double standard for women and men. Women were to remain virgins until marriage or if they had intercourse it was a result of love with the understanding that this was the man they would eventually marry. On the other hand, the man was permitted to have as much sex with as many different partners as he could. This macho attitude is best exemplified by the phrase. "So many women, so little time." In practice, the premarital experiences of women and men are not as dramatically different as the model would lead us to believe. Women did engage in necking, petting, and nonintercourse sexual activity beginning in adolescence. The majority of women had intercourse by age twenty-one, although they had fewer intercourse partners than men. Women had longer, more involved premarital relationships and were more committed to the concept of marrying. Premarital sex was seen as more for the man than the woman. She was concerned with the consequences of unwanted pregnancy, sexually transmitted diseases, sexual humiliation or rejection, and damage to her "reputation." The man who had fifty partners in a year was admired. The woman with fifty partners was scorned and labeled "promiscuous."

It has been said that female sexuality thrives on marriage, and there is empirical support for that view. As the woman feels greater comfort being in a committed marriage, she gives herself permission to let go and be more sexually expressive. The clinical observation that women experience higher levels of desire, arousal, and orgasm in their thirties has more to do with psychological factors than with biological changes. A marital bond of respect, trust, and intimacy is a solid base for female sexuality. This does not mean that the woman has to be married to enjoy sex or that marriage is the justification for sexuality. Nor is marriage a guarantee of sexual satisfaction. There are many married women with unsatisfying sexual lives. What is true is that a stable and satisfying marital relationship integrated with a comfortable and sexually expressive style is a goal to strive for.

There is an adage in sex therapy that when sex goes well in a marriage it is a positive, integral component and accounts for 15–20 percent of the marriage. The functions of sex in an ongoing marriage are as a shared pleasure, a way to build and reinforce intimacy, and as a tension reducer to help you deal with the normal hassles and frustrations of life. When sex is problematic it is a drain and subverts the marital bond. Sexual problems can become 50–70 percent or more of the marriage. Marriages can survive sexual problems, but poor sex robs the marriage of special feelings. Good sex in a marriage is an energizer for you as a woman and your marital bond.

THE DECISION TO MARRY

The quality and stability of marriage would be much improved if it were viewed as a genuine choice, not a "should" or mandate. Over 90 percent of women, and even a larger portion of men, will marry at least once in their lifetime. Marriage is the most popular voluntary institution in our culture. That's not likely to change, even with our high divorce rate. A good marriage meets the woman's needs for emotional intimacy and a sense of security better than any other kind of human relationship. From a cultural viewpoint, marriages and families promote stability and continuity. From a social viewpont, it is easier to organize activities as a couple and to promote social connections and combat loneliness and alienation.

So, if the outcome is ordained, why consider it a choice? It is a belief in psychology that positive motivation promotes positive behavior, while negative motivation promotes negative behavior. The woman who affirmatively chooses to marry as a way to enhance her life is more likely to make a good choice. Realizing you are a complete person as you are and that you don't need a man to validate you reduces the fears and pressures that have such a deleterious effect on women and distort their decisions.

So often women marry for the wrong reasons, and this burdens their view of themselves and the relationship. For example, one in four women is pregnant at time of marriage, a figure that is much higher for younger women. Ideally a couple would be married at least two years before the birth of a child. This time allows the couple to solidify their life together. This does not mean couples who are pregnant at time of marriage are doomed to problems, but it does mean they'll have to communicate more and work to set aside couple time if their marriage is to thrive.

Fear of not marrying is one of the most insidious motivators. Friends and family say, "All the good men are taken and you're getting older," so the woman desperately seeks out a mate. She convinces herself this is a good man to marry when an objective observer would say he's too passive, or drinks too much, or is too immature, or is still dependent on his family. Fears do not promote clear thinking and good decision making.

A common motivation for marriage is the woman is not satisfied with her life and doesn't know what to do next. The woman who has graduated from college and doesn't want to go back to living with parents, or the woman who is working as a computer programmer and finds she doesn't like computers, or the woman who has moved to another city to start a new life and finds it lonely are all vulnerable to marrying for the wrong reasons. It's the "Cinderella Complex." Looking for a man to rescue you and take you away. Marriage is not a rescue operation. Marriage cannot give you self-esteem or a way to organize your life. That's your responsibility, not the man's. You need to know who you are and what you value before choosing a marital partner.

Some women choose men who need help or rescuing. The idea is that once married, the woman will be able to change the man. Individual change is the man's personal responsibility, perhaps with the help of professional therapy. Wives do not reform husbands no matter what the self-help books say. You change for yourself, not for your partner. If the male is motivated to change, having a caring and supportive spouse can be of great help. However, the process has to start with the man—he has to want to be more fiscally responsible, want to stop using cocaine or gambling, want to be more social instead of introverted. Women who marry men with the plan to reform them are doomed to failure and bitterness.

Another common myth involves marrying a man to change his attitudes toward sex, commitment, or children. The man whose self-definition of masculinity includes seducing women will not change because of marriage. The male who cannot make an emotional commitment will not do any better if he's tricked or coerced into marriage. The male who has no interest in children or assuming responsibility for them will not be changed by marriage, and probably will not change even if he has children. What you see is what you get. So it behooves you to talk about what you want and need with your prospective partner, and if he says no, believe him.

CHOOSING A MARITAL PARTNER

We are opposed to arranged marriages and we are equally opposed to "romantic love" marriages. The decision to marry a specific man is not the most important decision of your life, nor is it irrevocable, but it is one of life's prime decisions and commitments. There are no hard and fast rules that guarantee marital success, but we would like to present guidelines that have been of value to clients, students, and friends.

The key guideline is the belief that the bond of respect, trust, and intimacy will grow and be stronger five years into the marriage. We choose the five-year period because it's long enough for the woman (and man) to think about a realistic life plan including living arrangements, planning children, career decisions, and how the couple will organize their life. It's short enough so that they can talk in specifics and practicalities rather than indulge in fantasies and dreams.

In romantic love, you idealize the partner and the relationship. You believe love is enough—in reality, love is never enough. In realistically assessing the bond between you, carefully examine each component. Respect means that you objectively view your partner and are aware of personal characteristics you value and admire; you can recognize his weaknesses and problems without losing your respect for him. You also need to respect the way you handle yourself in the relationship. When a marriage works well it brings out the best in each person.

There are two major factors in the trust bond. You believe your partner will not purposefully do something that will harm you. The second is that you trust your partner has your best interest in mind and will be there to help and support you. Trust is usually thought of as marital fidelity, but it is much broader than that. In regard to extramarital sexuality, we suggest the couple clearly state their feelings about sexual fidelity and reach an explicit agreement about sexual trust (for the consequences of not doing this, you might consult the chapter on a cost-benefit analysis of extramarital affairs). Trust involves emotional and attitudinal components in addition to sexual commitment.

Intimacy is the motivating force that draws a couple toward marriage. Being in love is a transitory emotion and not a good basis for a marital decision. Emotional and sexual intimacy is a longer-lasting and more solid basis for a stable and satisfying marriage. Emotional intimacy includes the ability to share the whole range of feelings, be vulnerable with your partner, and deal with each other in constructive, problem-solving ways. Sexual intimacy involves having an attraction and desire for your partner, being receptive and responsive to his touch, and a sense of sexual satisfaction. It takes most couples at least six months before they develop a comfortable and satisfying sexual style. There is an initial charge which comes from entering into a sexual relationship. The question is whether, when this charge inevitably decreases, it will be replaced with an ongoing sense of attraction, comfort, and satisfaction.

Making a good marital choice includes both rational, objective components and emotional, intuitive components. The typical female trap is to be "swept away" by romantic love and later say this was not the man I thought I married. We are not saying marital choice is solely a rational decision, but it must be based on loving feelings and emotional attraction and it must have a rational base. Without the emotional pull, you would not take the risk to involve yourself in the relationship. Loving someone and being loved is one of life's genuine special experiences. Yet love does not and cannot conquer all. If you need stability in your life, you will not have a happy marriage with a man who travels three days a week or who works away from home for months at a time. Similarly, if you are committed to living in the area you grew up in, you will not be happily married to a foreign service officer or someone in the military. The more dissimilar you are from your partner in background—education, religion, social activities, political values, etc.—the more difficult the marriage is likely to be. Difficult does not mean impossible, but it does mean the couple will have to work harder to bridge the differences if they are to have a satisfying marriage.

It is important the couple discuss and reach agreements about the major elements of their life together—about whether to have children and if so when, where they will live, how they will manage careers and money, relations with extended family, the role of sex and intimacy in their marriage, how they will communicate and problem solve. A marriage does not just happen, it requires time and psychological energy to develop individual growth and couple satisfaction.

Ruth and Nigel

Ruth and Nigel have been married three and a half years and have a ten-month-old daughter, Kara. Ruth is an excellent example of a young woman who had to fight against feminine and cultural stereotypes to choose a marital partner. She is committed to developing a marital bond she respects and derives emotional satisfaction from.

Ruth was the youngest of three children from a traditional background and a complex, yet loving, extended family. Ruth's older sister married at nineteen; a boy from her neighborhood and ethnic background whom she'd known for five years. Her brother married at twenty to an eighteen-year-old young woman who was pregnant. Ruth was the first person in her family to go to college, although several of her younger cousins were to follow her example, Ruth lived at home the first two years, and was a resident hall counselor the last two so she could live in the dorms for free. She was committed to having a more educated, independent life than her parents had, although she respected their life and especially their marriage. They had the best marriage of any couple she knew, and she felt lucky to have such a model.

After college, Ruth decided not to pursue secondary education, her major, but instead entered a bank-manager training program that allowed her to take graduate management courses on a part-time basis. It was while working at the bank that she met Nigel. Nigel was employed by a management consulting firm and was a very ambitious young man. He had left England at eighteen to study in the United States and the previous year had become an American citizen.

Ruth's dating and sexual history was in the mainstream for college-educated women growing up in the 1970s. She began dating in high school, went steady twice, and engaged in "heavy petting." She did not begin having intercourse until she was twenty and living in the dorms. Ruth was a conscientious and effective contraceptive user, but she was embarrassed and upset when she contracted chlamydia. Ruth did not think of herself as the type of person who would get a sexually transmitted disease (STD). She was surprised and reassured when she learned that more than one in three women do contract an STD, that chlamydia is the most common STD, and that effective treatment was readily available.

Ruth had dated males from backgrounds similar to hers, and she was intrigued by dating someone with Nigel's "exotic" background. Although Ruth had received two marriage proposals, she had not taken them seriously. She was committed to establishing her professional credentials and a career, although she was distressed by the warnings from her older sister and aunts that all the good men were being taken and she'd be left with the "dregs." Her parents supported her personal and career plans, and her mother reassured her "the right man will come along." The idea that the woman actively chooses a man was not in Ruth's conceptual framework. Yet that is what happened with Nigel.

Nigel had three goals in life: become a U.S. citizen, be a partner in his management firm, and save enough money to buy a house. Marriage was not in those plans. Nigel was confident professionally, but shy. Although two years older than Ruth, he had less social and sexual experience. Ruth saw in Nigel a man she could respect and care about, a man who would promote her strength and independence. Nigel valued Ruth as someone who would broaden his life and would bring out a more sensuous and fun-loving part of him.

After dating nine months, they moved in together. Ruth made it clear to Nigel that this wasn't simply a trendy or convenient thing to do. She considered their living together to be a trial marriage—to see how viable a couple they were. It gave them more time and privacy to develop their emotional and sexual relationship. Nigel was an early ejaculator, a problem he'd had all his life. He had not thought of it as a problem; sex was meant to be short and intense and focus on intercourse. Ruth had taken an elective human sexuality course in college and had a different view of emotional and sexual intimacy. She endorsed the concepts of touching inside and outside the bedroom, that sensuality was the basis of sexual responsiveness, of nondemand pleasuring and multiple stimulation (multiple stimulation was the basis of Ruth's orgasmic response), and that intercourse was an integral part of sexuality but not the whole of sexuality. Ruth wanted Nigel to realize that her sexual needs were as important as his.

Living together was good for the relationship but raised strong parental opposition. Ruth's father, who had been very support-ive, told her she was twenty-five and it was time to marry, not live with a ''foreign'' man who was not an appropriate marital partner. Her father wanted Ruth to come home, which would have been a disastrous regression. It is usually not a good idea for adult children to return to a dependent relationship in their parents' home. Her mother was less condemning, but concerned that Ruth had made the wrong decision.

That fall Ruth and Nigel traveled to England to meet his family. They had their most emotionally draining argument because Nigel insisted that his family not be told about their living together. Ruth had downplayed cultural differences be-tween them until she met his parents. Nigel's parents had a very different marriage from the one she imagined for herself. They were cold and formal with each other and slept in different bedrooms. Ruth was put off by a number of things, from the cooking to the lack of emotional openness to the rigid female-male roles. Seeing his family allowed Ruth to understand Nigel in a deeper way and to be aware of how difficult it would be for him to provide what she wanted in a marriage.

Ruth and Nigel took a three-hour walk in the beautiful English countryside and talked honestly and in great detail about how hard they would need to work to establish a life and marriage that would make them happy. Nigel listened and perhaps for the first time realized what being married to Ruth would mean. Usually parental support and friends' approval is a good indicator for a marriage. Their friends were very supportive and Ruth and Nigel decided to plan the marriage without parental approval. They realized what the problems would be and believed they could devote the time and energy to make their marriage happy and satisfying.

Returning home was like a honeymoon period for Ruth and Nigel. The quality of their emotional intimacy and their lovemaking improved markedly. However, they did not allow themselves to be swept away into marriage. There were a number of important things to discuss and agree upon before committing to marriage. Chief among these were careers, the issue of children, and where to live. Ruth wanted to finish her degree before moving and wanted veto power as to where they would live (she did not want to move across the country from her family, although she knew that for Nigel's career they would have to move). She wanted at least one child, but told Nigel her career was important and she was not willing to be a full-time homemaker. He did not want the children raised by a nanny. For this marriage and family to be successful, both would need to be actively involved in parenting. Nigel had not been around babies, but he wanted to be a more active parent than his father had been. At present, this is one of the most difficult issues for Ruth. Although Nigel does love and care for Kara, Ruth is the primary parent and she is stuck with the feeding and diapering chores while he takes the fun jobs like giving her a bath and reading to her.

Ruth and Nigel are in their third year of marriage. At times Ruth finds it difficult to juggle the balls of work, marriage, a child, and now looking for a house. Despite this, Ruth is basically satisfied with her life and her marriage. The bond between them is solid and growing, and Kara has added a wonderful dimension to the family. Ruth's parents and family have come to love Nigel and to affirm the marriage, although his parents maintain emotional distance. Sex plays a strong energizing role in the marriage. Although it's less frequent than two years ago, the quality of their sexual expression has become more satisfying. Working together to develop ejaculatory control served to strengthen their emotional bond and communication. Ruth is aware that the marriage and marital sex cannot rest on its laurels. She is looking forward to sharing her life with Nigel and to their growth as individuals and as a couple.

DEVELOPING AND MAINTAINING A MARITAL BOND

When we emphasize the importance of the marital bond, we are talking about the components of respect, trust, and intimacy. Marriage is a process. If taken for granted (treated with benign neglect) the marriage stagnates and becomes unsatisfactory. Sex is not the most important element in the marital bond, but it is an integral component that serves to energize the couple. Marriage is like a garden; you need to choose a good spot, carefully plant the vegetables and flowers, and provide consistent care and upkeep. A satisfying marriage means choosing a man you can share your life with, putting in the time and energy to establish a cohesive and flexible bond, and continuing to grow as a woman and as a couple.

Psychology and marital self-help books emphasize the importance of communication in marriage. Certainly we are in favor of communication—especially communication in which you clearly state your feelings and needs; are open and vulnerable in exploring feelings, perceptions, and alternatives; where you problem-solve and reach satisfactory agreements; and you feel valued and cared about by your spouse. So much of what passes for communication is poor-quality talking that is more like gossip or complaining than genuine communication.

In our view, the marital bond is anchored by self-respect and respect for the partner. People who are in the midst of divorcing will sometimes look back at an incident (the spouse being drunk and hitting his child, or lying about an extramarital affair, or pretending to have accomplished something when in fact he was incompetent and couldn't admit it) and say that when they lost respect for the spouse the marriage began to unravel. When you lose respect for yourself in the marriage (accepting being hit or called stupid in front of friends, or going along with a hurtful sexual scenario), you give up a vital ingredient, your self-esteem. Ideally, marriage brings out the best in you as a person and promotes psychological well-being. A marriage that decreases self-esteem and destroys psychological well-being is not worth preserving.

Trust is a vital ingredient not only in choosing a partner, but in maintaining a satisfying marriage. All marriages go through difficult times. It is perfectly normal to be disappointed or angry with or hurt by your spouse. However, when you see your partner as your worst critic, see him as out to undermine you, believe he is pleased when you fail, or see him as purposefully humiliating the children, then your marriage is in great jeopardy. Loving someone includes trusting him and his intentions. You might be upset by a specific behavior, but that problem is multiplied when you believe his intention was to purposefully hurt. For example, the discovery of a spouse's extramarital affair can cause a major crisis in a marriage. It is easier to deal with if you learn that he was impulsively attracted to the woman and has been trying to disengage from the affair. However, if you learn that it was a well-thought-out comparison affair, that he purposely deceived you and told the other woman intimate things about you, the trust bond is seriously ruptured. Trust is a reassuring element in a marriage. Both partners need to be aware of and protective of trust.

Emotional and sexual intimacy are vital elements in nurturing a marital relationship. This is what makes the hassles and compromises inherent in a marriage worthwhile. Feeling good about yourself as a sexual woman and good about the role of marital sex is much more than being orgasmic. Sexuality is more than genitals, intercourse, and the few seconds of orgasm. Sexuality is an affirmation of your attractiveness as a woman and desire to be sexual with your husband. It includes affectionate, sensuous touching, both inside and outside of the bedroom, both as a pleasure in itself and as a prelude to intercourse. It includes abandoning inhibitions, being open and comfortable, becoming involved in sexual pleasure, and letting go and being orgasmic. Sexuality energizes the marital bond, reinforces intimacy, and validates your choice of this man as your husband.

Preferred approaches to sensual touching vary widely from person to person and strongly reinforces a sense of intimacy.

Emotional intimacy exists apart from sexuality as well as being integrated into sexuality. Some of the most important emotional experiences have nothing to do with sexuality, e.g., celebrating your child's birth as an affirmation of your love. Other experiences represent an integration of emotional and sexual intimacy—talking and touching resulting in an arousing sexual experience. Emotional intimacy includes an impressive array of emotions—positive as well as negative. In an emotionally intimate marriage you can share your sadnesses and frustration as well as your joy and happiness.

CLOSING THOUGHTS

Much of what is written about women and marriage is either too idealistic or too cynical. We have tried to state a position that is positive and optimistic, yet realistic, while pointing out pitfalls (both the traditional and newer ones). Marriage is not a mandate nor is it the pass-fail test of a woman's life. A good marriage is one of life's special joys, and a bad marriage one of life's most burdensome realities. In the latter, the woman has the opportunity to change by either improving the marital relationship or opting to divorce.

Traditionally women have given more in marriage than they've gotten back. They've been burdened by the responsibility to take care of the husband, the children, and the house. We propose a model of marriage that is based on equity between the woman and the man: Marriage works best when it's an equitable partnership. The marital bond of respect, trust, and intimacy needs to be consistently nurtured. In our culture there are more divorces, but there are also more high-quality marriages. Sexuality is not the most important component in a marriage, but it is a positive, integral part. You will feel better about yourself as a woman, better about your husband, and better about the marriage if both of you put in the time and psychological energy to make the marriage a living, growing, satisfying partnership.

6
PREGNANCY AND CHILDBIRTH

Is there a biological mandate for women to be mothers? Unequivocally, no! Pregnancy and child-rearing is a choice for a woman, not a given. Having a child or children is central to the feminine self-concept of many women. Other women feel perfectly feminine and comfortable without having children.

We strongly advocate planned, wanted children. Choosing to have a child is one of the most important decisions a woman makes in her life. It is also one of the most difficult to reverse. You can switch your career, marriage, and house more easily than children. Having a child is not just taking care of a baby, but an eighteen-year commitment to physically, emotionally, and financially parenting a human being. It is a decision to consider with great thoughtfulness and care.

But when we examine pregnancy and childbearing in our culture we find a very different reality. There is a growing trend for adolescents to have babies—the specter of children having children.

There are few things in life that are as emotionally complex as the decisions to have children, when to have children, and how many children to have. We have talked to competent, successful female executives who have no trouble making multi-million-dollar decisions, but absolutely wilt under the stress of a decision about children. A movie like *Baby Boom* pokes fun at the dilemma, but it is a very real one for many, if not most, career-oriented women. Traditional women are confronted with different practical and emotional questions of how many children to have and how to space them.

THE DECISION WHETHER TO HAVE A CHILD

Why is it so hard to plan children? It seems obvious that an unmarried young woman would not plan to become pregnant. It would appear easy for married couples to engage in a logical discussion about whether to have children and if so when. Although we are in favor of rationality and logic, that is not the reality of planning children. The decision to have a child is fundamentally an emotional one. If people decided only on the basis of financial, practical, and logical factors, hardly anyone would choose to have a child and the human race might disappear. Just the opposite is happening—this planet is faced with a population explosion that threatens our resources—our ability to house and feed the rapidly growing world population, especially in urban areas. The population of the United States is growing at a slower rate than that of Third World countries, but it does continue to grow. We have one of the highest rates of premarital pregnancies in the world, and the highest of any developed country.

The primary emotional reason women have children is to experience the process of carrying a fetus and watching a baby grow to be a person. Pregnancy and childbirth is one of life's wonderful experiences, and the majority of women choose to become mothers. Biologically, the major difference between women and men is the woman's ability to become pregnant, deliver a baby, and engage in breastfeeding. In our increasingly sophisticated and technological world, the process of impregnation and childbirth is still one of life's most basic experiences.

If you were to consider only finances, you would never choose to have a child. The cost of raising a middle-class child from birth to age eighteen (which does not include the extremely high expenditures for college) exceeds two hundred thousand dollars. Even more than the financial burden, a child requires a dramatic time commitment and a major change in adult life-style. Especially difficult is coordinating career plans with being a mother. Where you live is strongly influenced by the school system, availability of parks and planned children's activities, a neighborhood that has other children, and access to babysitters and child care. You no longer can spontaneously go to a movie or jump in the car for a weekend trip. The planning necessary to take a child on a trip tests the ability of a seasoned military logistics expert. Arranging a weekend away without children requires detailed planning, backups, and emergency contingencies that remind one of preparing for a presidential convention.

There are few commitments in life that are as binding as having a child. If you are unhappy with your career choice after two years, it is difficult, but possible, to change careers. It is extraordinarily difficult, and done with great community stigma, to revoke the role of mother. From a career, financial, and practical viewpont, the decision to have a child is a daunting one.

In saying this we do not want to appear to be ogres who are advising against having children. We have three children, two boys and a girl, two of whom are biological children and one adopted. We do not regret our life choice to have children, and would do it again if given the opportunity. What we are saying is that this is a complex, crucial decision that should be thought out in the context of your life, values, and relationship. There is not a ''right'' answer or an answer that fits all women and all circumstances. It is a decision for the woman and her husband (or partner) to make based on their life circumstances. It takes two people to create a child, and ideally, a child should be raised in the context of a stable, loving family. We are practical enough and feminist enough to realize that having and raising a child falls primarily to the woman so that her vote (and especially her veto) deserves special weight.

There are subcultures and religious groups where there is not a personal choice. For example, in the Indian culture and the Mormon or Roman Catholic religion, the commitment to marriage assumes a commitment to having children. These ethnic and religious values strongly reinforce the desirability of children and the primacy of the family. However, this mandate is not applicable to most American women. The decision whether to have children is a personal one governed by a woman's values and emotional commitments. This decision is usually, but not always, made in consultation with her husband.

Women promote the desire for pregnancy and children with the assumption that once it is a reality the man will accept it. We find this a questionable assumption. In fact a relationship is most likely to be terminated three months before or three months after the birth of a baby. Ideally, having a child is an affirmation of the couple and a symbol of continued caring. The decision to have a baby should come as a commitment, not as a way to save a relationship or coerce a man into marriage. The most likely outcome of having a child for poor reasons is greater stress on the relationship and hastening its termination. The woman is left with the responsibility to care for the child with limited resources. The fastest growing poverty group in the United States are female-headed households with unplanned children.

NONMARITAL PREGNANCY

With few exceptions, single women are surprised and upset to hear they are pregnant. They did not want or plan to be pregnant. Contraception either was not used or used haphazardly. Of course, some women are conscientious contraceptive users, but the contraceptive fails. Condoms, diaphragms, and IUDs have a failure rate of 5–20 percent.

When the woman discovers she's pregnant, she has a very difficult decision to make. She can carry through with the pregnancy and marry the man, or she can place the baby for adoption (there are thousands of infertile couples who desperately want a baby), keep the baby herself, or have relatives raise the child. The other alternative is to have a therapeutic abortion.

The majority of therapeutic abortions are performed on unmarried women, during the first trimester of pregnancy, and in a medically safe outpatient clinic under a local anesthetic. Philosophers and theologians argue the morality of prolife versus prochoice. When it comes to an individual woman and her personal choice, decisions are never easy. Each woman, in consultation with her partner, family, friends, minister, or professional counselor, has to reach a decision based on her values, feelings, and life circumstances.

Pregnancy counseling is complex and emotionally laden, and yet must be done under a time limit. If the woman chooses therapeutic abortion, she must usually decide and act before the twelfth week of the pregnancy in order to get the safest type of abortion (a suction curettage abortion) in the first trimester, although the legal limit is twenty weeks. There is not a right answer for all women (no matter what the ideologues say). We have seen pregnancies that were unplanned turn into solid marriages and wanted children. More often we have seen "shotgun weddings" that end in divorce and neglected or abused children. We, ourselves, have adopted a child. However, we have seen children shuffled from foster home to foster home because the mother could not make a decision. We have seen women successfully have a child, take care of it, and later marry when it was the right person and the right time. We have seen women who have had to give up their education and life plans to take care of a child and resent it. Although we have seen women racked with guilt and regret over an abortion, we have seen many more women relieved that they made the right decision for them at the time. Each woman must decide how best to deal with her unwanted pregnancy.

A different example is the older single or divorced woman who desires a child, and is concerned about her biological time clock. She is not in a committed relationship, but if she does not get pregnant soon, she will miss the opportunity to have a child. Rather than entering a nonintimate marriage, she tries to get pregnant through a dating relationship or with a male friend who is willing to provide "stud service." This solution is fraught with serious perils. The woman has to be committed to "going it alone" in raising a child. The woman has to have a clear agreement with the man about what, if any, his emotional and financial responsibility will be.

MARITAL PREGNANCY

You may assume that most marital pregnancies are planned, and you would be right, but just barely. Approximately 40 percent of children born to married women are unplanned. One of our central guidelines is that the couple should strengthen their marital bond before becoming pregnant. We suggest married couples wait at least two years before having a child. The birth of a first child is a major stress and transition in a marriage even when the child is planned and joyously wanted.

The same decision that faces unmarried women also faces

married women who have an unplanned pregnancy. About one-fourth of therapeutic abortions are obtained by married women, often older women who already have children. Some of the women do not possess the emotional or financial resources to have one more child. Other married women find this is not the right time for a pregnancy, either because of the state of the relationship, or career issues, or they want to wait for a better time and planned pregnancy.

The majority of married pregnancies start as planned and wanted, and most pregnancies of married women, even if unplanned, do not remain unwanted. The decision to create a baby is a positive commitment to the marital bond and the desire to become a family. Having children is a highlight of many women's lives and a central element in their self-esteem and sexuality.

The decision to get pregnant and becoming pregnant is a positive experience for most couples. They have spent much of their adult lives avoiding pregnancy, and it's really fun to have sex with the intention of getting pregnant. Many women find the three to six months it typically takes to become pregnant is a time of great sexual desire and responsiveness. Creating a baby is a special motivation.

INFERTILITY

Approximately one in five women has difficulty conceiving. Infertility problems put inordinate stress on the woman and the relationship. Most people assume that they will have no trouble becoming pregnant. It is very upsetting and frustrating to discover that what is easy and natural for so many women is difficult and could prove impossible for you. If you are faced with an infertility problem, do not blame yourself or question your femininity.

There are a host of causes for fertility problems in the woman including failure to ovulate, blocked fallopian tubes, an incompetent cervix, high vaginal acidity, endometriosis, and vaginismus. About 40 percent of fertility problems involve male disorders, which include low sperm count, erection problems, poor sperm motility, and ejaculatory inhibition. A fertility problem is best viewed as a couple problem. It can put enormous stress on each person's sense of well-being, on the couple's bond, and on the sexual relationship. Referral to a fertility specialist is obvious: not so obvious is a referral to a marital therapist or infertility support group to help you deal with the psychological and relational stress.

About 55–65 percent of couples with fertility problems do successfully have a biological child. A number of medical techniques are currently available to improve the likelihood of pregnancy, including drugs to promote ovulation, microsurgery to open the fallopian tubes, surgery or hormonal treatment to improve sperm functioning, as well as sex therapy and fertility-enhancement suggestions. Artificial insemination with either husband or donor sperm has been successful. There are a number of new and expensive technological breakthroughs such as in vitro fertilization, which have some success. However, at some point couples have to ask themselves if it is in their best interest to continue to pursue the fertility process or to pursue adoption. Some couples decide it would be better to remain childless and focus their energy in some other productive manner. There are no easy answers in the complex area of infertility. The woman and the couple must choose what is in their best interest.

THE JOY OF PLANNED, WANTED PREGNANCY

The birth of our two biological children and the adoption of our daughter were among the highlights of our life. Emily was the last of three children, thirteen years younger than her middle brother. She grew up around children—her nieces and nephews. Emily wanted to have children in her twenties so she could have the time and energy to keep up with and enjoy them. Barry was the oldest of two, had never babysat, and was hesitant around children, especially babies. Our decision to become pregnant with Mark was talked out, but was emotionally heavily influenced (as these decisions often are) by the fact that our best friends from graduate school were pregnant. Emily was twenty-three and Barry twenty-five at Mark's birth—fairly young by today's standards, but a decision we have no regrets about and would repeat. We adopted Kara almost exactly two years later and Paul was born two and a half years after that. Although we hate to admit it (especially in print), Paul's pregnancy was a result of a diaphragm failure. However, once we realized Emily was pregnant, Paul quickly turned into a wanted child.

The key elements in planned, wanted pregnancies are confidence in the viability of the marital bond and an emotional and rational belief that this is the right time to start a family (or add to it). In other words, the motivation for the pregnancy is a positive and shared one. This does not guarantee an easy pregnancy nor transition to parenting, but certainly facilitates the process. Making a personal commitment to having a child allows you to talk out hopes and concerns beforehand, and aids the transition to parenting a baby. It reinforces the idea that conception, childbirth, and parenting are a shared venture.

Amelia

Amelia is thirty-three years old with a five-and-a-half-year-old daughter and four-month-old son. Her husband, Joe, had a vasectomy a week earlier. As Amelia rocks and breastfeeds Trevor, she finds herself thinking back on the experiences and emotions she'd had concerning conception, contraception, abortion, and prepared childbirth.

Amelia was the youngest in a family of five. Her mother's whole life centered around children and grandchildren. Amelia hated being thought of as the "baby" and fought against her mother's overprotectiveness. As a twelve-year-old, Amelia liked the hustle and bustle of an extended family and taking care of nieces and nephews. Amelia especially enjoyed babies and toddlers, but did not like the games and manipulation that occurred as they became four and five. The kids would play mother against grandmother and Amelia thought this was too much a child-centered household. In her junior year of high school, she had a history teacher who waxed on and on about the advantages of traditional extended families, and Amelia remembered thinking it sounds better in a class than it is in real life.

Amelia wanted a more independent and career-oriented life for herself. Her second oldest sister had planned to go to medical school, but an early pregnancy dashed those hopes. Amelia's goal was to obtain a Ph.D. in French and be a university professor. She was determined that nothing, especially not an unplanned pregnancy, would interfere with those goals. As a seventeen-year-old, Amelia was sure she wouldn't marry until thirty at the earliest. She was not impressed with the marriages of her siblings nor with the high divorce rate among her friends' parents. Amelia had grave doubts about the whole subject of marriage. She did want a child, but was certain that with a two-career marriage, one was all she'd like. If she wanted more children around, she could always invite her siblings' children. Remembering those strong opinions, she smiled as she contentedly rocked Trevor. Life experiences can shake the most rigid of adolescent opinions.

Amelia started using contraception about a month after beginning intercourse. She was proud that, with one exception, she had been a conscientious contraceptive user. Amelia had gone to Planned Parenthood and received a prescription for the birth control pill, which she'd used faithfully throughout college and into graduate school.

In graduate school, she'd become involved in a living-together relationship with a law student who was enrolled in a special international law program. He invited her to come to the Middle East for a year where he'd been awarded a fellowship. Despite the advice of her academic adviser and the anguish of her parents, Amelia agreed. Amelia had traveled to France for a summer language program, but this did not prepare her for being an unmarried woman in a Moslem country. She felt harassed and unrespected, and the man she was so involved with in the States had little time or concern for her welfare. He was interested in his fellowship and making professional contacts, and he wanted her primarily as a sexual companion.

It was exceedingly difficult to get refills for birth control pills. Amelia switched to the diaphragm, which she never became comfortable with nor did she believe was fitted properly. Her lover did not like to interrupt sex to put in the diaphragm.

Four months into the Middle East adventure, Amelia found herself pregnant. After a good deal of arguing, her lover helped her arrange transportation to France where she obtained a therapeutic abortion in medically safe conditions (this was not easily available in the Middle East country). Amelia was relieved to have the abortion. This was not a good relationship nor the right time for her to have a baby. She would not have her present life if she had a baby at that time.

A sign of psychological maturity is the ability to admit mistakes and make changes. Amelia returned home and was given permission to enroll late and reenter her graduate program. She was more motivated than ever to complete the courses and begin work on her dissertation.

Joe come into Amelia's life about a year and a half later. It was he who pursued the relationship. Joe was an assistant professor of biology and one of the best-liked young professors on campus. He was enthusiastic about his work and enjoyed social and athletic events on campus. Amelia had no desire to be a "groupie" or sexual companion for Joe. He was impressed by her frankness and sense of self-respect.

Six months into the relationship he suggested they move in together and Amelia declined. She told him that moving in would signify a commitment to eventually marry and she was not prepared at present to make such a commitment. This launched them into a series of important conversations about their lives and future plans. Joe was more optimistic and dedicated to the concept of marriage than Amelia. She raised hard issues he'd not thought through. Joe agreed that if they were going to be a two-career academic family he'd have to be more involved with parenting than his father had been. Joe felt he'd had an excellent relationship with his father, but recalled that while growing up when something difficult had to be done it was his mother he always turned to.

Amelia was twenty-six when they married. They'd lived together eight months and she was as sure as she could be that the bond of respect, trust, and intimacy would continue to grow. They were a sexually active and functional couple, although the romantic love glow of the first few months was fading. It was replaced by a solid sense of desire, attraction, arousal, and emotional intimacy, which is a better basis for an ongoing marriage.

Amelia found the first year of marriage one of the best years of her life—she completed her Ph.D., they moved into a small house in a pretty, rural setting fourteen miles from campus, and they made a successful social transition from the singles world to couple activities. At the beginning of their second year of marriage, Joe raised the issue of timing of their first child. Amelia feared it would disrupt their lives. She suggested an academic tour of Europe the next summer that would end in Paris. Amelia thought of herself as a hardheaded pragmatist, but after discussing it throughout the trip she loved the symbolism of creating a baby in a Left Bank hotel in the City of Light. Even now, Amelia looks at her five-year-old daughter and remembers making love in Paris.

Pregnancy was a real "trip" for Amelia. The first trimester was as bad as people said it could be, but once symptoms of morning sickness abated the pregnancy was relatively tranquil. The gynecologist she had liked so much was not helpful as an obstetrician so she switched to an obstetrician who had a more open attitude and was supportive of husband-coached prepared childbirth. Amelia's biggest struggle was with her weight—she did not gain as steadily as the doctor wanted her to. She disliked having to reduce her exercise program. Amelia was awed by the experience of a human being growing inside her, but she did not enjoy the physical experience of the pregnancy and weight gain. Joe was an active participant in the prepared childbirth classes and encouraged practicing the skills between classes. Joe was overly upbeat for Amelia's taste. She wished she could share more fully with him her doubts and fears.

First births are the longest and most difficult. Amelia's labor began three weeks later than the predicted date, but when the time came she didn't feel ready. The labor was more difficult than she had expected and lasted over sixteen hours.

In comparison, her new son's birth four months before had been an easier experience. Amelia was more sure of herself and felt that the pregnancy was really hers. She knew Joe desired a second child, but he assumed she only wanted one so hadn't pushed. When Amelia was granted tenure, she stopped taking the birth control pill without telling Joe. She did joke about children to be sure he hadn't changed his mind. Amelia was grateful they had an easy time getting pregnant (a colleague in the department had one child, but was unable to become pregnant again). When she told Joe she was pregnant he was ecstatic. Throughout the pregnancy and childbirth, Amelia experienced an inner glow—this was to be her last pregnancy and one she enjoyed to the fullest.

THE PREGNANCY PROCESS

There is no time in life when the woman should treat her body better than during pregnancy. The changes occurring in her are awesome. A woman who is planning to get pregnant is advised to quit smoking, stop drinking or drastically reduce her alcohol intake, and consult with her physician about all prescription and over-the-counter drugs she is taking. She is advised to exercise regularly and to reduce her sugar, salt, and caffeine intake.

You should establish a comfortable relationship with a gynecolgoist/obstetrician before getting pregnant. Ideally, you will have a gynecological checkup and discuss any potential problem areas before trying to become pregnant.

A woman's reaction to the first trimester of pregnancy is extremely variable. Some experience tiredness but no other symptoms, while others are extremely symptomatic. The most famous symptom is morning sickness, but people don't tell you it can just as easily occur at night. Nausea and vomiting are not uncommon. Some women develop sleep disturbance, special food hungers, and irritability. Sexual desire is lessened, especially during the first and third trimester. Many women experience a nagging fear of a miscarriage (spontaneous abortion), especially during the first trimester. Although women blame themselves if there is a miscarriage, in reality a miscarriage is nature's way of dealing with the fetus that is not developing healthily. Although you need to consult your gynecologist after a miscarriage, typically the advice is to wait two months before trying to get pregnant again.

Women report the second trimester of pregnancy to be the most satisfying. The pregnancy begins to "show" physically and as the baby moves and kicks you become more aware that a living being is growing in your uterus. There's relief from the symptoms of the first trimester. Women report greater sexual interest and arousal during the second trimester and feel more emotionally bonded to their husband. For older mothers (thirty-five or older) or those with genetic concerns, the amniocentesis procedure can be performed at this time. The great majority of women receive positive results and are reassured that the baby is healthy.

We strongly believe in prepared childbirth, which can be

focused on in the third trimester. This is a time when the couple should be talking about and preparing for the birth of the child. Traditionally the woman became very involved with the pregnancy and the man felt he had no role and that his needs, especially sexual, were ignored. This was a time men began extramarital affairs. We strongly believe this is a time for couples to be together, not alienated. Practicing childbirth exercises and talking about the baby are one way to strengthen the couple bond. Another is to discuss the role of sexuality during this period and after the birth.

This is not the time for the man to withdraw, emotionally or sexually. From a physiological viewpoint, the woman can have intercourse right up to the delivery room as long as there is no pain or bleeding, her amniotic sac (bag of waters) has not broken, and the physician has not instructed her otherwise. This does not mean intercourse in the man-on-top position. Couples can experiment with a side rear entry position or with the male kneeling and the woman sitting. The key element is to avoid pressure on her abdomen. Some women enjoy intercourse through the entire pregnancy, but the majority report somewhere in the eighth or ninth month the sense of heaviness or discomfort becomes too great. Typically, neither saying anything, sex just fades out. We suggest the couple talk about sexual alternatives, which can include the woman stimulating her partner to orgasm, to her caressing him while he stimulates himself, or his masturbating in private. The fact that she doesn't want to have intercourse does not mean she doesn't want to be held, cuddled, or perhaps stimulated to orgasm.

After childbirth, gynecologists suggest a three- to six-week prohibition on intercourse to allow the vagina to heal and to avoid the risk of vaginal infections. It is important to discuss sexual alternatives during this time. Ideally, sexuality is broadly viewed to include affectionate and sensual touching as well as intercourse and orgasm. During the crucial transition to becoming a family or adding to a family, it is important to continue being sexual friends. Traditionally, the male was seen as demanding intercourse and the woman had to accommodate him or run the risk of his having an affair. This is a self-defeating

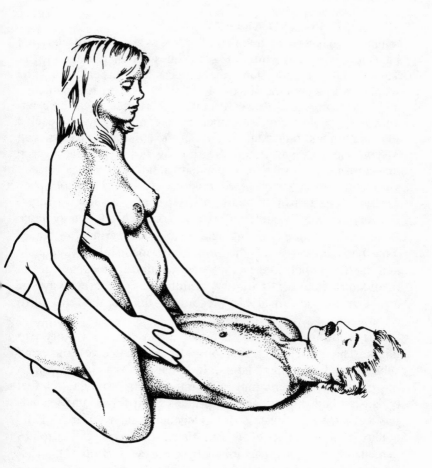

Intercourse during pregnancy. Except in rare cases, it is a myth to suppose that the fetus can be damaged by intercourse during pregnancy.

view of sexuality. The couple can be open to meeting each other's need for affection and sexual expression, which need not be limited to intercourse.

CHILDBIRTH AND AFTERWARD

No one has ever claimed childbirth was easy, but it need not be as terrifying and painful as sometimes depicted in the media. The more you understand the process the easier it is. The woman who learns the stages of childbirth will be less panicked and better prepared. Prepared childbirth classes have three advantages: 1) you work together as a couple, 2) you receive information and understanding about the childbirth process, and 3) you and your partner practice coping skills. You learn deep muscle relaxation to relieve pain, breathing techniques to help with contractions, stimulated practice on the stages of labor especially the transition phase, and see a movie showing actual delivery to build your comfort and confidence. You practice these skills in the meeting and with your partner at home. You become aware of the variety of medications available and their optimal usage. Prepared childbirth does not mean medication-free or "natural" childbirth. You are aware of and can use all available, resources during the childbirth experience.

The childbirth process can take from two to twenty-two hours. The average for first births is about twelve hours and subsequent births eight hours. It is hard work—some women have equated it to running a marathon. The woman can feel exhausted and discouraged—a prime reason for an understanding and supportive mate/coach. Depending on your area of the country and practice of obstetricians, as many as 20 to 25 percent of births are performed by cesarean section. This disturbing trend reflects the growing fear of medical malpractice suits. We suggest the woman have a frank talk with her obstetrician about her or his policy concerning use of medications and cesareans. It is important to give permission to exercise medical judgment if there is a medical crisis, but not to practice defensive medicine.

The woman need not feel like a failure if her delivery is

difficult or requires anesthesia or cesarean. Perfect deliveries happen only in the movies. As much as possible, be aware and involved in the process of childbirth.

Once the child is born, you enter an entirely new chapter of life, as a woman, mother, wife, and sexual person.

7

SEX, YOUR CHILDREN, AND YOU

Few women are satisfied with the sex education they received as children. Instead of complaining, you can take a proactive stance and be a better sex educator for your children than your mother was for you. One of the things we find objectionable about "pop psychology" is its preoccupation with blaming parents, especially "mother bashing." We are not interested in finding fault, producing guilt, and certainly not mother bashing.

As an adult you can objectively look at your own mother and identify the positive attributes you would like to adopt in your life. As well, be aware of the negative attributes that can be considered "traps" to avoid in your life. What was the quality of parenting your mother received, what was happening in the culture when she was growing up, and what were the educational and sexual resources available to her? Being aware of her background will allow you to be more empathetic with your mother and less critical of her. As a woman today you have more knowledge and resources to draw on. You are raising your child in a much different sexual culture from the one you or your mother grew up in.

Being a mother is a very special experience. You never really master parenting because as a child grows, each stage requires a different set of skills. Parenting a baby is different from parenting a three-year-old, which is different from parenting a six-year-old, first-grader, which is different from parenting a fifth-grade ten-year-old, which is dramatically different from parenting a junior-high adolescent of thirteen, which is different still from parenting a sixteen-year-old sophomore who drives, or a twenty-year-old young adult away at college, or

Many women find breastfeeding an enjoyable, even erotic way of developing the parent/infant bond.

a twenty-eight-year-old who is married with a child of her own. Mastering such a complex process deserves a Ph.D. in parenting.

BEING AN ASKABLE PARENT

The key concept in being a sex educator for your children is being an "askable parent." This means more than giving lectures and facts to your children. It means being available for them to answer a range of questions and discuss topics from the abstract to the concrete. Be open to talk about what they want to know, which is often different from what you would like to be discussing with them. It means being tolerant of their giggles and "Oh, Mom" comments. Most of all it means integrating sexuality topics into general communication with your children.

WIFE-HUSBAND AND MOTHER-FATHER RELATIONSHIP

According to family systems theory, the single most important relationship in a family is the wife-husband bond. If the bond is respectful, trusting, and caring the whole family is likely to benefit. A good marital relationship provides your children with a healthy model for a female-male relationship.

Women wish they could relate more as a person and wife instead of mothering the children. They feel they shouldn't because it would be cheating the children. When you are being good to yourself as a person and are maintaining a positive marital relationship, it's of real value to your children. One of the best things you can do for your children in the long run is to feel good about yourself as a woman and provide them with a model of a well-functioning person and marriage.

When children see their parents relate in a respectful, loving manner they receive a lesson about being a woman or a man. Conversely, if the man treats the woman in a denigrating manner or the woman ignores or belittles the man, the child is receiving a very poor message. When the woman is a competent partner and so viewed by the husband, female and male children learn to view women as competent.

The traditional role assigned to women is that of caretaker.

This is a vital role, especially for babies and young children. But should it be the woman's alone? Where both the woman and man are involved in child care (we are not advocating a fifty-fifty equality policy, but rather an equitable level of involvement), it is to the child's benefit. The woman's involvement in family finances, repairing things, and disciplining children all contributes to a positive model of child rearing. Instead of women and men leading separate lives with separate roles, we recommend women and men relate in a more flexible and equitable manner as people, spouses, and parents.

Theorists argue whether children should see affectionate touching between parents. We believe it is good for parents to be affectionate with each other in front of children as well as each parent being appropriately affectionate with each child. What is inappropriate and harmful is being sensuous or sexual in front of children. Women need to give themselves permission to be more affectionate with their husbands in front of their children. This can include kissing, hugging, and holding as well as doing family hugs. What is inappropriate is breast stimulation, genital touching, or foreplay/pleasuring kinds of stimulation.

Obviously, it is inappropriate for an adult (and especially a parent) to be sensual or sexual with a child. Females are much less likely to sexually abuse children than are males. In over 90 percent of the cases of incest, the perpetrator is a male.

Another controversial topic is the question of nudity in front of children. Our guideline is that a child needs to accept the human body, including genitals, as normal and natural. This includes a comfort with nudity. However, we have several reservations in terms of appropriateness and age-related factors. For example, it is perfectly appropriate to shower with a two- or three-year-old child, while it is clearly inappropriate to shower with an opposite-sex thirteen-year-old child. A child of two or three can run around the house nude, while the same behavior is inappropriate for a child of seven or eight. A two-year-old child touching her or his genitals in public would be normal, but not so a six- or seven-year-old. Children learn the value of privacy as they become older.

Children should not be punished for touching their genitals. What kind of learning is it for a child to be touching herself and having her hand slapped and told it's "dirty"? Tell her that touching her genitals is normal and natural, but not in front of other people. Genital play and sexuality are good things, but are best practiced in the privacy of the bedroom. This is a positive lesson about privacy and sexuality. Parents can explain why their bedroom door is locked by saying they need private time in the bedroom to express their love for one another.

Children should not see their parents having sexual intercourse, but it is a good thing to know that their parents are a sexual couple. Especially with adolescents, being aware that there is sex during adulthood has a stabilizing emotional effect. There is evidence that adolescents who believe their parents are sexual are more likely to delay beginning sexual intercourse. The point is that in a variety of ways and for a variety of reasons, you do yourself, your marriage, and your children a favor by building and maintaining a strong marital bond, including affection in front of the children and with the children.

MOTHER-DAUGHTER RELATIONSHIP

The closest parent-child relationship is between mother and daughter. Having a good relationship with your daughter is rewarding for you and crucial for her development as a person. This relationship begins even before birth. One of the advantages of prepared childbirth classes is to build a positive anticipation of the child joining the family. Whether or not you believe in a "maternal instinct," it is clear that if the child is unwanted and the woman is not prepared either practically or emotionally for the birth, the outcome can be devastating for all. Deciding to have a child is one of life's most irrevocable choices, so you need to be sure it is a commitment you want to make. Timing is of great importance. Is this the right time to begin a family?

You can use the pregnancy period to prepare yourself for parenting. This is an especially good time to talk to your mother about what you were like as a child. The focus is on information seeking, not guilt or criticism. Getting information about what it was like parenting you can help you decide what you want to keep the same and what you'd like to change in parenting your daughter. You might be especially interested in what you were like as a baby, how you felt about touching, and what you did as a young child. What kind of sex education did you receive and how inquisitive or reserved were you when discussing sexual issues?

A major decision is whether or not to breastfeed. There is no right or wrong; it depends on the woman, the child, and the circumstances. There is clinical and research evidence that breastfeeding is of value both in building a mother-child bond and for the health of the child. If you decide not to breastfeed, be sure the child is held and comforted when bottle feeding. An advantage of bottle feeding is that the father can take a more active role in the feeding and holding process.

One of the joys of watching a baby develop is when she begins to examine and explore her body. At about six months she will discover her genitals and have a special fascination with them. Some mothers become anxious about this and worry that their daughters will become sexually fixated. This is an irrational parental fear—it is perfectly normal and natural to include genital touching in body exploration. Genitals have more nerve endings than other parts of the body so naturally there will be pleasant sensations with genital touch.

As little girls develop, they play games like "house" and "doctor"—sometimes by themselves, sometimes with siblings, sometimes with friends. These games can include same- as well as opposite-sex playmates. Some parents may be concerned that their daughter is growing up too fast or emphasizes sexual games too much. Our experience, both in reviewing child development literature and observing our three children when they were young, is that these fears are usually unfounded.

Focus on the positive things you want your daughter to learn and experience about her body and sexuality during the preschool years. The most important elements are comfort with her body and enjoying receiving and giving affectionate touching like hugs and kisses. You want her to know that she's a girl and not a boy. That's a crucial understanding and needs to be firmly established by age two or two and a half. You want her to be comfortable with her genitals and to use proper terms such as "vagina," "penis," and "breasts" rather than silly words like "whatsit" or "down there." You want her to feel loved and valued for herself.

In many cultures, males are preferred to females, especially the first-born child. In some cultures, if the first-born is female, she is killed—a truly shocking cultural aberration. Our culture does follow the tradition of celebrating male children more than female. You need to be sure you don't fall into that trap. Some parents say to the child, "You don't have a penis, so that means you're a girl." You would be better to say, "You have a vulva and that makes you a girl, your brother has a penis and that makes him a boy."

Daughters are particularly interested in pregnancy and where babies come from. There have been more than enough "stork stories." A good guideline that applies to most elements of parenting is to be open and honest with your child. This is especially true when it comes to sexual issues. Discussing pregnancy, especially if you or one of your friends is pregnant, is an excellent vehicle for sex education. You don't need to give a complete lecture on sperm and eggs, but you can discuss with the child what she wants to know and speak at her level. This will help establish that you are an "askable parent"—the most important attribute in the entire sex education process. Above all, do not lie to or laugh at your child—her questions and concerns, even if silly to an adult, are not silly to her.

As she enters elementary school and has contact with other adults you need to discuss a difficult topic with her—trust and sexual abuse. One of the most frightening statistics in our culture is that by age fourteen, one in three females will have some sexual interaction with an adult. About half the time, this involves "hands-off" abuse, which includes being exhibited to, peeped on, or verbally harassed. The other half is "hands-on" abuse, which is typically nonviolent and nonintercourse and includes having breasts, vulva, or anal area fondled, being manipulated into touching a man's penis, and/or being rubbed against. A minority of cases of child sexual abuse are violent (which is considered sexual assault) and involve oral, anal, or vaginal penetration. The more violent and the more sexually invasive, the greater the trauma to the child and the greater the need for professional assessment of the impact of the trauma on the child.

Make sure your child receives positive sexuality education before discussing sexual abuse so that she does not see sex as primarily a frightening part of life. In talking about sexual abuse emphasize that no one, whether stranger, teacher, neighbor, or relative, has the right to touch her body and genitals in a manner that is frightening or uncomfortable. Give her rules for what to do. Emphasize that she can say no to the adult. If she has any questions, she can come to you. Adults should not tell children to keep secrets from their parents. The child can ask questions and express concerns that will be listened to and believed.

Sex educators would prefer having integrated programs of education from kindergarten through college that would include parents as sex educators of their children, formal classes in the schools, and values about sexuality taught in Sunday school. But if there was just one grade to focus on, it would be fifth grade when the child is ten or eleven years old. The child's cognitive development is such that she can understand a great deal about sexuality before she has had a range of sexual experiences. She can develop a solid intellectual understanding of sexuality. Since most school systems have poor to mediocre sex education programs, you need to take a proactive stance and have her read and discuss sexual information with you. This is much preferable to giving her a pamphlet on menstruation and asking if she has any questions (the most common form of mother-daughter sex education). Focus sex education on attitudes, values, and feelings, not just biological facts. Approach menstruation as a positive event, an exciting step in becoming a woman, not a frightening and embarrassing experience when she whispers she needs Tampax.

As your daughter approaches adolescence, be clear about your values concerning boys, dating, premarital intercourse, and marriage. She probably won't agree with you, but it is worthwhile to state your beliefs and values. Fear is the prime motivation that governs parents of adolescents. Fears include their daughter having an unwanted pregnancy, responding to peer pressure to drink or use drugs, doing badly in school or dropping out, contracting a sexually transmitted disease, running away from home. The theme is losing control over your children— peers have become more important than family. The specific fear is that if a daughter acts out, it will include sexual acting out. Your adolescent can be vulnerable to a manipulative young man, can be raped, can be exposed to the AIDS virus, become pregnant, or contract a sexually transmitted disease.

These adolescent scenarios need to be seriously addressed,

but the best way to avoid them is not to lock your daughter in a nunnery. The best preventative is good sex education, encouraging a healthy sense of herself as a young woman, and open channels of communication in the family. If she has goals in her life and good values, she will not be as vulnerable to adolescent rebellion and high-risk or destructive sexual behavior.

Motherhood does not end with your child's adolescence, although it does get easier. You switch gears and become a consultant to your young adult daughter. One of our friends described young adulthood as when your daughter starts worrying more about her future than you do. This often begins around age eighteen when she is launched from the parental home whether to college, to the service, a training program, or to work. This does not mean your daughter doesn't need your love, support, and advice. This can be one of the most rewarding times in parenting because you begin giving up the sense of responsibility and fear and relate to her in a more open, realistic, adult fashion. It means frank talks about potential marital partners, contraception, protecting her health, sexual expression, and integrating sexuality into a relationship. The challenge mothers and daughters find most difficult is making the transition (beginning about age twenty-five) to a full adult, equal personal relationship. For those who do achieve a genuine adult relationship with their daughter, the rewards are worth the effort.

MOTHER-SON RELATIONSHIPS

Many of the same issues and concepts in mother-daughter relationships are present for those between mother and son. Rather than repeating ourselves, let us focus on the special challenges and special traps of the mother-son relationship. The mother-son dyad is the second closest (by the way, the third is father-son and the most distant is father-daughter). Mothers have a lot to offer their sons in terms of parenting generally, and sex education specifically. Parenting and sex education, whether for a daughter or son, is best done in conjunction with your husband. The man being actively involved in parenting is of benefit to the whole family. Although there is obvious value in same-sex talks (mother-daughter, father-son), the opposite-sex parent discussing issues is equally important. A son can learn from his mother's view of the world, especially her view of female-male relationships. The young man appreciates his mother's suggestions of how to talk to a young lady or ideas of what to buy her or where to go on a date.

We strongly endorse family sexuality talks. Allowing your son(s) and daughter(s) to converse with each other and with you gives a more complete picture of sex issues and values. The single most important concept in sexuality education is that there are more similarities than differences between women and men. This allows women and men to relate as people rather than enemies or sex objects. What better place to learn respect and caring than in the family?

Mother's greatest fear is babying her son and making him a "sissy" or a "mamma's boy." To guard against this mothers overreact and do not give their sons enough attention. Many mothers (and fathers) believe that to be a successful man you have to learn to be tough and independent, and this should start as a baby but certainly before you begin school. We take strong exception to that viewpoint. There are more similarities than differences in the needs of boys and girls, especially at a young age. Boys need nurturance, physical and emotional, from both mother and father. Psychological well-being requires developing a sense of balance. We would be foolish to hold that there isn't a danger of giving a boy too much attention so that he becomes passive and dependent. Nurturance is good, but smothering a boy (or girl for that matter) is not in the child's best interest. The truth is that boys get too little attention, especially from fathers, and mothers stay away because of irrational fears.

Boys are given cultural permission to be independent and explore, which includes sexual exploration, with self and others. It is crucial that by age two or two and a half the boy have a solid identity as a male. It is important that he be allowed to touch his genitals in the bathtub without his hands being slapped. Sexual exploration games with same and opposite sex are perfectly normal as long as they do not become obsessive or coercive. If it seems to be the major activity, acknowledge that sexuality is a healthy and interesting activity, but introduce other activities and games. If sex play is coercive, for example, taking someone's pants down and mocking him or her, we suggest you intervene and make a point about sharing and cooperating, not hurting. Sexuality is a good thing in life. Sexuality is not about forcing, humiliating, manipulating, or harming others.

Sexual abuse prevention is just as important for boys as girls—about one in seven boys has a sexual incident with an adolescent or adult man by age fourteen. These incidents are usually "hands-on" abuse. Boys are less likely to report it to parents or others because of the stigma of same-sex activity. The view is that boys are strong and not vulnerable to sexual abuse. There is some evidence that boys are more traumatized than girls by sexual abuse because of the secrecy and stigma.

Most boys begin masturbating to orgasm between ages ten and fourteen. This is a healthy, normal activity. It can cause the boy guilt and anxiety and the mother embarrassment when she finds dry semen or stains on underwear, sheets, handkerchiefs, or towels. She could say and/or have his father say that masturbation is a healthy sexual behavior and that he can clean up the semen with Kleenex rather than letting it dry on things.

When your adolescent starts dating, talk to him about seeing young women as people and treating them in a friendly, respectful manner, not as sex objects. Adolescent male development has traditionally focused on proving masculinity by using women and performing to some unrealistic image. Mothers can reassure sons that sexuality is integral to him as a person, not something that he has to prove. Teaching your son that a "real man" is not a macho user is one of the best things you can do for him and will foster healthy masculine development.

Doreen

Doreen is a thirty-two-year-old mother of two—a six-year-old daughter and a four-year-old son. Her husband, Taylor, had a vasectomy because he only wanted two children. This was Doreen's first marriage and Taylor's second. Doreen and Taylor had been a couple two years before marrying. Doreen resisted marrying until they received ten sessions of premarital counseling with the minister who married them. Doreen was committed to raising her children differently from the way she'd been parented and in a way dramatically different from the one in which Taylor had been raised.

Dorren's parents had divorced when she was eight. Doreen lived with her mother and had only sporadic contact with her father, a retired military man who cared more for adventuring than middle-class values and parenting. She had a lot of fun with her father but did not respect him. Doreen wanted to avoid the bitterness her mother continued to hold. Her mother had briefly remarried when Doreen was eleven, but had wisely extricated herself from the marriage when she determined her new husband was similar to her former one.

The best advice her mother gave Doreen was not to marry young (a common trap for children of divorce whose early marriage is often an attempt to compensate for the instability they faced growing up). The sexual advice her mother gave was scanty and negative. She did not approve of the young men Doreen dated. Doreen felt she could not have a personal talk with her mother. She very much wanted her daughter and son to be able to confide in her and to see her as an understanding and askable parent.

Taylor came from a family that said nothing to the boys about sexuality, but overprotected the girls. The double standard was strong in his family: his father had affairs and his mother took total responsibility for the children. Taylor married at eighteen when his girlfriend became pregnant, although she later miscarried. It was a marriage in name only—they dated other people, ran around with single friends, and were more like quarrelsome roommates than spouses. Taylor wanted more out of his marriage to Doreen and had matured a great deal in six years, but the kind of marital bond Doreen desired was foreign to Taylor. The premarital counseling helped, but it was not until the prepared childbirth classes and the birth of their daughter that Taylor felt fully married and committed.

Taylor proved to be a more active and involved father than even Doreen hoped. He was affectionate with both children, did not play favorites, could roughhouse with his daughter and hold and comfort his son. Doreen enjoyed both children, but especially liked being with them one on one. Her daughter was an active child, enjoying a range of activities—some that are considered typically feminine like playing with dolls and some that are considered masculine like playing soccer—she was a particularly fast runner.

Until a year ago, Doreen had bathed the children together. The daughter would make funny comments about her brother's penis and they would joke when he would play with it. She would touch and play with her vulva during the bath. Both children learned to use proper terms for their genitals. As they got older, it was a natural transition to needing more privacy and bathing alone.

Both children were quite talkative, and Doreen especially encouraged her son to verbalize his thoughts and feelings. Doreen wanted him to feel good about himself as a boy, but not fall into the traditional "traps" of being a male. In the past month his favorite bedtime story was a book about how babies were born. He loved talking about how it must have felt in his mommy's belly and how lucky he was to be born into this family.

Doreen and Taylor were determined to enjoy each stage of their children's development, but they wanted to plan ahead and anticipate potentially problematic issues. They enjoyed parenting together. As much as possible they hoped to raise their female and male child similarly. They wanted both children to be competent, both to feel good about their body image and sexuality, both to be responsible and caring people and to have positive relationships with the opposite sex. They realized that there would be good times and difficult times with their children, but vowed to persevere throughout.

Doreen and Taylor remembered their adolescent years and up to the early twenties as the most unhappy time in their lives. They realized they could not shelter their children from all the turmoil, but they believed if they established a good relationship when the children were young and were seen as askable parents it would provide an excellent base for the transition to parenting adolescents. Doreen was glad she had chosen to be a mother, was enjoying the present stage of parenting, and looked forward to the next challenges. She realized sexuality education was an integral part of the process. Doreen and Taylor provided a good example of a couple from problematic family backgrounds who were motivated to devote the time and psychological energy to build a positive marital bond and a happy family.

SPECIAL ISSUES IN PARENTING ADOLESCENTS

One of our favorite sayings is that parenting children is like building an emotional bank account. It's important to establish the account when the child is a baby and make regular emotional deposits. We view seven to eleven as the "golden years of childhood" where the child is developing her or his own personality, but still sees the family as primary. By the time the child enters adolescence you want to have a large balance because in adolescence there are not many deposits and sometimes there are big withdrawals. The adolescent years are the most unhappy in many people's lives. Not surprisingly, parenting adolescents is one of the most difficult phases in adulthood. Partly this is because you have less control, partly it's fear of peer group pressure, concern about success and future plans, concern about drinking and drugs, and a large part is the issue of sexual expression. Adolescents are sexual; this cannot be denied. The question is what kind of sexual expression is appropriate at what age? Will sexuality enhance their life or cause confusion, guilt, and trauma?

At a minimum, the role of the parent should be to educate with the hope of avoiding major problems. If a major problem develops, the adolescent needs to know she or he can come to the parent for understanding and help, not anger and rejection. Ideally, the mother would positively state her values about sexuality and establishing an intimate relationship. Adolescence is best viewed as a training period for later adult sexuality. As we have told our own adolescents, the trick is to survive adolescence without getting your life off track. Things get better in early adulthood because the person has more control over her life and better resources to direct her life. It gets better for the parents as well in that they don't feel as burdened and responsible.

CLOSING THOUGHTS

Parenting is one of life's most complex yet potentially most rewarding experiences. The typical motherhood trap is to feel overly responsible for your children and to base your self-esteem on their successes and failures. You will enjoy parenting more (and do a better job of it) if you attend to your needs as a person and set aside time to enjoy your couple relationship.

Ideally the marital bond will extend to active parenting with your spouse. A major element, although certainly not the most important one, of parenting is being an understanding sex educator for your child. The key is to be an askable parent. Give a clear message to the child that you will be there for her whether it's dealing with a sexual trauma or celebrating a newfound awareness about herself or about relationships. Enjoy your role as a mother—seeing it as a beneficial challenge will make it easier for you as well as for your children.

8
CHOOSING STERILIZATION

Women of our mother's generation looked on menopause with a great deal of ambivalence. Menopause was the feared "change of life," but it did have one positive side effect—relief from the fear of unwanted pregnancy. Few women desired to bear a child in their mid-forties. Our mother's generation could admit to no longer wanting a baby at that age, but seldom before. When the chief role and means of status for a woman was to be a mother, how could she say she didn't want any more children?

The status of women has dramatically changed in the last generation. Women have many sources of self-esteem—it no longer comes from being "a baby-making machine." Sterilization is now the most common birth control method for couples over thirty. Women are taking increasing control over contraception and family planning. It is culturally acceptable for a woman to say she doesn't want any more children. Rather than waiting until their forties, many women make this decision in their twenties and thirties. As women have developed career alternatives and new sources of self-esteem, it is both practical and psychologically appropriate to evaluate the financial, emotional, and personal costs of having and raising children.

The norm in our culture is the two-child family. After the birth of their second child, many women conclude that procrastinating and continuing to deal with the hassles and possible medical complications of birth control (not to mention the possibility of an unwanted pregnancy) is not worth it and opt for a permanent form of birth control, i.e., sterilization.

The most appealing thing about sterilization is also the most sensitive: It is permanent. Once a woman is sterilized it is difficult to reverse the process. This is less true for male sterilization, but whether it is the woman or the man who undergoes the procedure we strongly suggest that sterilization be viewed as a permanent commitment to not have more children. A well-thought-out sterilization decision can have a profoundly positive effect on the woman's life, sexual relationship, and marriage.

WHAT IS FEMALE STERILIZATION?

Many women confuse sterilization with a partial or full hysterectomy. A full hysterectomy involve surgical removal of the ovaries and uterus and is done to treat a gynecological illness. Partial hysterectomy involves the removal of the ovaries. A side effect of hysterectomies is sterilization.

Female sterilization can be performed in a simpler, safer, and less disruptive manner. In the past five years, there have been breakthroughs in the technology used for sterilization. Many sterilization procedures now involve local anesthesia rather than general. Most are conducted in an outpatients surgical suite thus reducing costs since there is no need for overnight hospitalization.

The most common female sterilization procedure is the tubal ligation. This surgical procedure involves cutting and closing off both fallopian tubes. After a tubal ligation, the ovum is still released, but because of the interruption of the fallopian tube the ovum and sperm cannot meet. The surgical modality involves cutting or cauterizing. Once severed, each fallopian tube is tied to prevent it from regrowing together. Tubal ligation surgery has improved in its technology and is a safe and effective procedure. One of the most professionally interesting experiences Barry ever had was visiting a sterilization clinic in Bombay, India. Although the physical circumstances were not on a par with American medical standards, the actual surgical procedures were very impressive. The gynecologist had performed thousands of tubal ligations, and did the procedure very efficiently and effectively.

A variant is to perform the tubal ligation right after the birth of a baby. The advantage of this method is the woman is already on the operating table and her fallopian tubes are easily accessible. If the woman (and her partner) are convinced that this is the last child they want it is an excellent procedure. Many women are wary of doing it at that time because they want to be sure their baby is healthy before going ahead with the sterilization.

POTENTIAL NEGATIVE SIDE EFFECTS OF FEMALE STERILIZATION

There are three types of potential negative side effects: 1) changing your mind and wanting to become pregnant, 2) physical side effects caused by the surgery, 3) psychological side effects that can interfere with self-esteem and/or sexual functioning.

Women who change their minds or whose life circumstances change so that they want to have another pregnancy are faced with a difficult dilemma. Female sterilization should be thought of as a permanent choice because it is difficult to reverse. However, where the couple want an additional child, or there is a divorce and remarriage with a desire for a second family, or if a child dies and they want another child, some options are available. One is microsurgery to restore the fallopian tubes. The fallopian tubes are very narrow and delicate, easier to cut than to restore. Even when microsurgery appears successful, it is sometimes not functional, i.e., a pregnancy does not result. Another intervention is in vitro fertilization, thus bypassing the fallopian tubes. Adoption is another possible option. Although easier to reverse than a decade ago, tubal ligation should not be undertaken unless the woman is sure she does not desire additional children.

Any surgical procedure, especially involving the abdominal cavity, involves potential medical side effects. Although the technology has improved and serious side effects are rare, they can occur. Most common are effects from anesthesia, internal bleeding, and uterine infection. It is important to procure the services of a competent gynecologist who regularly performs tubal ligations and who has access to a surgical suite in a well-run hospital.

Most women report positive psychological effects of sterilization. They are freed from concerns about unwanted pregnancy and the interference that comes from utilizing birth control devices. There is usually improved frequency and quality in their sexual relationship. Some women do report negative psychological and/or sexual side effects. The most common is a decreased sense of femininity since she's no longer able to conceive. Others report lessened sexual desire since there is no longer the possibility that sexual intercourse can result in pregnancy. A small percentage of women report regret or guilt and lower self-esteem. This should alert us that sterilization is a major life decision and needs to be carefully thought out in light of the woman's values, feelings, relationship, and life circumstances. You need to consider psychological and emotional as well as practical and financial factors. Sterilization is a major decision and needs to be carefully weighed by the woman and her partner.

MALE STERILIZATION COMPARED TO FEMALE STERILIZATION

If the decision was based solely on medical factors, men would get vasectomies instead of women having tubal ligations. The vasectomy is a fifteen-minute outpatient surgical procedure that requires only a local anesthetic and can be done at a urologist's office. There is a vas on each testicle that is identified, cut, and tied. Vasectomy requires minimal intrusion into the man's body and medical side effects are rare and minor. The vasectomy is a cheaper, safer, and easier sterilization operation. So why are there three times more tubal ligations than vasectomies? The answer centers on psychological factors. Males are more fearful and anxious about the sexual aspects of sterilization. Many confuse vasectomy with castration (the surgical removal of the testes). Males are afraid the vasectomy will affect their erectile functioning or sexual desire—both these fears are based on myths and misinformation. Additionally, males do not have the "biological clocks" that females do—they are able to conceive children in their forties, fifties, and even sixties, and some men prefer to keep that option open.

If the couple decide they do not want additional children, they need to carefully discuss the range of factors (medical, psychological, sexual, and motivational) to determine who should undertake the surgery. There is not a simple, right answer for every couple. For example, when the woman has definitely decided against having another child and the husband is ambivalent, it is probably best that she have a tubal ligation. If the woman has a history of uterine infections and/or poor results with anesthesia, the man should be the one sterilized. Males who are insecure about sexual functioning or have doubts about their masculine self-image are not good candidates for vasectomy. Conversely, women who view pregnancy as an integral part of their femininity are not good candidates for tubal ligation. The crucial determinants are which partner is more certain she or he does not want more children and which is more comfortable with and committed to the surgery.

Just because it is the woman who becomes pregnant and has the child does not mean that she should have the sterilization operation. However, the reality is that if the woman does not want more children and her partner is ambivalent or procrastinates, she will need to take the initiative. To avoid a power struggle, resulting in no action and the risk of an unwanted pregnancy, in this case, the woman may decide to have a tubal ligation since it is her body and likely the children will be her responsibility.

SEXUAL FUNCTIONING AND STERILIZATION

There is no direct link between sexual functioning and the female or male sterilization operation. However, there is an indirect relationship. When couples are initially trying to get pregnant, they experience more frequent and pleasurable sex. It is fun and exciting trying to make a baby for the 75 percent of couples who have no fertility problems. On the other hand, when you do not want to get pregnant, fear of unwanted pregnancy is a major sexual inhibitor.

Women in their thirties have been using contraception their entire adult lives and are tired of it. Whether it is remembering to take daily birth control pills, or check strings on an IUD, or insert the diaphragm each time before intercourse and leave it in for six hours, or reminding your partner to put on a condom each time, or rigorously charting your menstrual cycle, ten or more years of that is more than enough. No wonder sterilization is the most popular form of birth control for women in their thirties.

A positive side effect of sterilization is a more spontaneous and enjoyable sexual relationship. Freedom from the fear of unwanted pregnancy and being unburdened from the inconvenience and worry about birth control devices can be a powerful stimulus to sexual desire.

A PERSONAL NOTE

Emily and Barry enjoyed the pregnancies and births of their two biological children. In between those births, we adopted our daughter. Before the birth of our younger son, we discussed whether this would be our last child. We had a series of complicated and at times highly emotional talks. A prime factor was our dissatisfaction with the birth control alternatives and worry about an unplanned pregnancy since we were an easily fertile couple. Emily was committed to breastfeeding the baby so the birth control pill could not be used. We had previously utilized the IUD, condom, and diaphragm and were not enthusiastic about using them again. Even more important, we felt that two biological children were sufficient. We believe in population control and wanted to practice what we preached. If we were to have additional children, we could adopt a child. Although Emily agreed with the sterilization decision, Barry was more committed to it so it fell to him to have a vasectomy. The fact that the vasectomy was cheaper and safer (especially fifteen years ago) made it the deciding factor. Barry was thirty when he received his vasectomy, and it is a decision we never regretted. Raising three children, from both an emotional and financial standpoint, has been a challenge. Our life and sexual relationship has been improved by sterilization, which eliminated the risk of an unplanned pregnancy and allowed for increased sexual spontaneity.

DECISION MAKING

Sterilization is not just a simple, rational, medical decision and procedure. The choice of whether to have children is one thing, but the decision of how many children to have and when to stop is more difficult. The major reason people give for not choosing sterilization and waiting is the inability to make a decision concerning the number of children they want. They simply cannot make a proactive decision, and the path of least resistance is to do nothing. Of course, sterilization is against the religious or moral beliefs of some people.

People are governed by fears of what could happen. The "what if" questions make a permanent sterilization decision difficult. The most common "what ifs" are if a child would become ill or die, if a marriage would end in a divorce or death, if you have a midlife crisis and decide to have a late-life child, etc. There are no guarantees in life. Only you can decide what risks are prudent for you. However, leading your life in fear of "what ifs" is a very difficult way to live.

You need to make decisions based on what you believe is in your best interest and your best assessment of what will happen in the future. For example, a woman who chooses a tubal ligation at age thirty-two after having two children is expecting both children to stay healthy and her marriage to continue. If the marriage is tenuous, it is extremely unwise to have a third child as a way to rescue the marriage. An additional child or children are more likely to have a deleterious effect on the marriage than save it. If the woman feels she might divorce in the future and wants to keep open the possibility of another child in a subsequent relationship, having a tubal ligation would be a poor decision.

Practical matters can and do influence the decision to limit family size. For example, a woman who wanted five children, but decided to stop at two because of financial factors, might choose to remain on birth control rather than be sterilized because she is hopeful her family's financial status will improve in the future.

Eileen

At thirty-three, Eileen chose to have a tubal ligation after consultation with her husband, but only with his halfhearted agreement. Eileen had married Arthur eight years earlier—it was her first marriage and his second. Arthur wanted Eileen to become pregnant right away. She wanted to complete her accounting degree and pass the licensing exam before beginning a family. Arthur equated having children with marital stability, a view Eileen did not share.

Eileen wanted two children approximately two years apart so they could be companions for each other. She enjoyed being pregnant and staying home when her children were babies. She began working part time in accounting when her younger child was two. Eileen planned to return to full-time employment and develop her professional practice when her youngest was five. Arthur was a successful small-business owner who would have preferred that Eileen remain at home and have another two or three children. Eileen enjoyed her life and felt good about her marriage, but she wanted a career to provide balance for her life. Although she did not admit it to herself at the time, Eileen wanted a source of income in case the marriage were to deteriorate. Arthur did not say it, but Eileen believed his view was that having a "barefoot and pregnant" wife was his best marital insurance policy. Eileen was afraid if she were financially dependent on Arthur he would be more likely to take her and the marriage for granted. Most important, though, was Eileen's motivation. Eileen enjoyed her two children, her growing professional practice, and her marriage. She was ready to make the commitment to sterilization, and she did not need Arthur's permission to go ahead with a tubal ligation.

Eileen investigated and found an excellent doctor and facility to obtain her tubal ligation. She consulted her family practitioner and obstetrician for references and decided on a gynecologist who performed tubal ligations at the outpatient surgical suite of a well-respected hospital. She had an appointment with the gynecologist, emphasized she wanted it done under a local anesthetic, and discussed her concerns about possible side effects. She invited Arthur to come to the appointment, but he declined. Eileen did request that Arthur pick her up after the operation.

Eileen fasted for twelve hours before the surgery and checked into the surgical suite at 7:30 A.M. Surgery was at 9 A.M. and lasted less than half an hour. Eileen remained in the recovery room until one, and Arthur took her home. A friend stayed with her through the afternoon, and the children were taken care of at another friend's home. Eileen felt tired and disoriented, with some discomfort over the next three days. She was relieved that the procedure was over and that there were no complications or side effects. Although she had to take things slow and easy for the next week, she could look forward to a full recovery.

One advantage of a tubal ligation over a vasectomy is that it is immediately effective. After a vasectomy a backup contraceptive must be used for at least fifteen ejaculations and then a semen sample must be tested to ensure it is free of sperm. You can return to intercourse after a tubal ligation without having to use a backup contraceptive.

Eileen was pleased with the result of the operation. She enjoyed the spontaneity of intercourse without worrying about putting in her diaphragm. Sexually she felt they were on a second honeymoon. Although Arthur had been ambivalent about the sterilization, he was extremely pleased with the sexual results.

A year after the surgery, Eileen was happy with her decision. She was enjoying the freedom and spontaneity of sex, her burgeoning career, and her two children. The marriage was more solid, contrary to Arthur's fears. There are no total guarantees in life about a marriage or children, but Eileen was convinced that she had made the right decision for herself and her family.

CLOSING THOUGHTS

Women are taking more control over their lives. It is perfectly understandable that a permanent solution to the birth control dilemma should have great appeal to the 1990s woman. It's a way to be responsible and assume authority over your body. Sterilization is the most popular form of birth control for couples over thirty and more women get tubal ligations than males get vasectomies. This is not ideal, but since many males are irrationally concerned about vasectomies it is necessary that females take the initiative. The choice of a tubal ligation should be made freely by the woman. She can feel comfortable with her sense of feminity before and after the surgery. Sterilization is a positive way women can assert control over their bodies and their lives.

II. ENHANCEMENT—MAKING SEXUALITY A POSITIVE PART OF YOUR LIFE

9
NEW CHALLENGES:
FEMALE AND MALE ROLES IN THE 1990s

Sometimes it appears that the anger and disappointment in the "war between the sexes" will never abate. The 1960s saw the rise of the feminist movement and a frontal assault upon the double standard. The 1980s experienced a backlash against the unfulfilled promises of the women's movement, with men complaining about increased powerlessness. Many books have recently been written for women warning them against men who are untrustworthy, hateful, and destructive in their relationships. There is another host of books telling women how to choose a man and convince him to marry you. The assumption is that the prime responsibility for developing and maintaining relationships lies with the woman. The traditional view is that the woman is supposed to be passive and accepting, while the feminist view is that women should be empowered to be more active and in control.

Our belief is that the key to a genuine, healthy change in female-male relationships is the focus on equity. This requires both women and men to adopt a respectful, trusting, and caring approach. Women alone can not bring about positive change; it must be a cooperative venture between women and men.

We are unequivocally opposed to the traditional double standard. It is not in the best interest of women, nor in the long run is it in the best interest of men. The double standard creates a climate of misunderstanding and miscommunication between the sexes. It fosters attitudes of disrespect, distrust, and lack of emotional and sexual intimacy. The only advantage of the double standard is its rules about female-male roles are clear—wrong, but simple and clear. We need a new model to help rethink and redefine female-male relationships and subsequently enhance the psychological and sexual well-being of both sexes.

FEMALE-MALE SIMILARITIES AND DIFFERENCES

So much of the discussion and writing concerning female-male roles has been ideological, moralistic, and/or highly emotional. It generates much heat, but little light. Let us approach this most complex subject from a more objective point of view. There has been a great deal of scientific research during the past twenty years about female-male similarities and differences in a number of areas—physical strength, intellectual ability, behavioral characteristics, health status, sexual response, emotional reactions, and interpersonal traits. The objective evidence of this research is overwhelming—there are many more similarities than differences between women and men in all these areas, including sexual response. The same phases of desire, arousal, orgasm, and emotional satisfaction are experienced by women and men. The same psychological process of positive anticipation, the same physiological process of arousal by vascongestion and myotonia, the same rhythmic contractions of orgasm, and the same gradual resolution period occurs for women and men. Of course there are differences, but the similarities—physical, psychological, and emotional—vastly outnumber the differences.

The differences involve latency of response and variability of orgasm. Women require a longer period of time and more direct genital stimulation for arousal than men, although these differences decrease with age and experience. Female orgasmic response is more flexible and variable in comparison to male orgasmic response. The male has a single orgasm, which is accompanied by ejaculation and occurs during intercourse. The woman might be nonorgasmic, or singly orgasmic, or multiply orgasmic. Her orgasm may occur in the pleasuring/foreplay period, or during intercourse, or in the afterplay period. Female sexual response is neither better nor worse than male, rather it is more complex and variable. The important similarity is that both women and men are sexual people with the ability to give

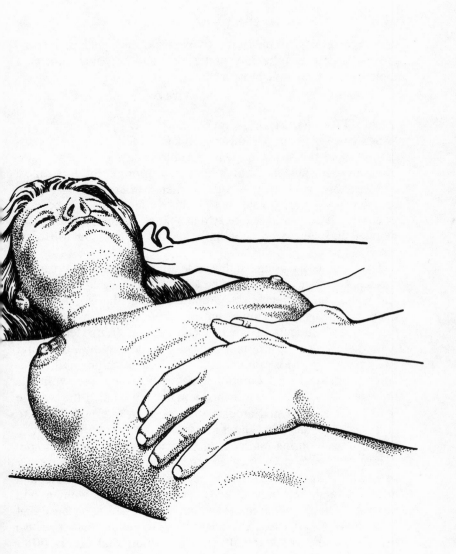

"Pleasuring" is an essential way to maintain a healthy intimate relationship. Sensual massage is one of many ways to do this.

and receive sexual pleasure, to be orgasmic, and to experience sexuality as a healthy part of life and an enhancement of their intimate relationships.

TRADITIONAL MALE-FEMALE ROLES

Sexuality is an important component of femininity and masculinity, but not the dominant or controlling part. In the traditional double standard, which has ruled in our culture and most cultures throughout the world, women and men are assigned dramatically different roles with little overlap. This is especially true when it comes to sexuality and sexual expression. It is as if women and men were not both human beings, but different species.

The woman is assigned the role of the weaker, dependent person. Her focus in life is to be a caretaker—she has to nurture and watch out for her husband and children. She is not to have goals and a life of her own, but to derive her self-esteem from the accomplishments of her husband and children. Her domain is the home, and her life is organized around cooking, cleaning, and caretaking. Most important, the ultimate responsibility for others' practical and emotional needs rests on the woman's shoulders. Sexual pleasure is his domain, not hers. If the woman is to experience sexual arousal it is the man's responsibility to give her this and she should respond just like him—have a single orgasm during intercourse. If she works outside the home, it is only for extra money for the family, not to pursue her personal needs or career. She is not expected to have intellectual interests, and her only friends are to be other women and relatives. She is in charge of the couple's social life because that is her area of expertise. She is not to have male friends because such friendships undoubtedly lead to extramarital affairs (after all, why would a man want to have a friendship with a woman other than to have sex with her).

In the stereotypic double-standard socialization, the man plays the strong, dominant role. He is the leader, the provider, the achievement-oriented person. The entire responsibility for the family's financial success rests on his shoulders. He makes decisions, especially about his career and the family's style of living. His role with children is to be the disciplinarian and to be sure they succeed in the world. He prepares his boys for the rigors and competition of the adult, male world. For daughters, his role is protector against predatory males who only want "one thing." He will strive to make a good marriage for his daughter so she will produce grandchildren and look after him in his old age. The man has male friends whom he drinks with, plays cards with, and watches sports with. He depends on the woman to take care of his clothes, food, health, most important, his sexual needs. Being married is necessary for him. His wife takes care of him, home, and family, and he is free to put all his energy into his career.

These rigid stereotyped female-male roles have a destructive effect not only on the couple's emotional and sexual relationship, but even more important, they inhibit the psychological well-being of the individual. Everyone, including children, lose out in relationships based on these rigid, irrational roles.

It is always easier to tear down an old system than to develop a new one that is more rational, functional, and satisfying. We are not suggesting the model we're presenting is perfect, or the only one, or that it is appropriate for all women or all couples. The model is based on equity between women and men, and has the potential to enhance personal, emotional, and sexual satisfaction for both sexes.

A NEW MODEL OF FEMALE-MALE RELATIONSHIPS

The foundation of the model is the woman's self-view of being a respectful, competent, and sexual individual. The woman cannot look to the man to give her this. She empowers herself to develop this view and to insist that the man treat her accordingly.

The model is not one of fifty-fifty equality in every aspect of life (which is overly idealistic and doomed to failure). A more solid and realistic base is a sense of equity between women and men. One person can have prime responsibility and/or skill in one area of life while the other has prime responsibility and skill in a different area. The crucial element is that the woman and man relate as respectful human beings who value each other's competence and share power in an equitable manner. Relating as fair-minded and caring partners serves as an excellent model for children to learn about female-male relationships. An added bonus is that people who treat each other well outside the bedroom will treat each other well inside the bedroom.

The second dimension involves trust between women and men. Instead of women and men being at war, seeing men as the enemy trying to dominate women, in a trustful relationship you have confidence the man would not do something to purposely undercut or harm you. You view him as acting in your best interest, as your friend and supporter. We are not suggesting women return to the traditional naïve view that as long as you love a man you back him no matter what. Too many women have been hurt and victimized by men who they naïvely believed and who took advantage of them. The woman has to choose a man who deserves her trust. She needs to be clear and assertive in stating her needs and the importance of maintaining trust in the relationship. Trust is not something you can take for granted, it needs to be clearly established and its importance maintained. For trust to be genuine, it must be reciprocal. The man needs to have that same degree of trust in your motivations and behavior.

Trust does not guarantee there will not be problems, disappointments, and anger in dealing with issues and disagreements. Each needs to communicate and problem solve to reach an agreement both can live with. In dealing with difficult issues, it is important to act in a trusting way and not to intentionally hurt your partner. You can state your feelings and positions in a clear and forceful manner without breaking trust. Negotiation and problem solving does not break trust as long as you are not trying to intimidate or hurt your partner.

The third building block is a genuine sense of caring and intimacy. This is a more solid and mature basis for an ongoing relationship than the romantic love glorified in movies and fiction. Romantic love is passionate, all consuming, and irrational. It is the seductive goal offered women as the justification for letting go and being sexual. Romantic love promises total bliss, "never having to say you're sorry." Unfortunately, rather than living up to its billing, romantic love often ends in bitterness and resentment. Romantic love makes great drama, but is a difficult and disrespectful way to conduct your life.

Our model of intimacy and caring views the choice of a committed love relationship as based partly in emotion, but more on a mature view of the man (in terms of respect, trust, and ability to communicate about a range of issues). Caring for one another would be deep as well as passionate. You believe you can plan and develop a life together. Intimacy includes sexuality as well as sharing thoughts, feelings, beliefs, and values.

Sexuality is an integral part of an intimate relationship. Sex serves to energize the relationship by reinforcing and deepening intimacy, being a shared pleasure, and serving as a tension reducer or safety valve. Contrary to the male-generated cultural myth, sex is not the most important element in a loving relationship. Sex does serve as an important expression of emotional intimacy and as a bonding experience. A favorite saying is "a marriage can tolerate bad sex, but it's hard to survive the absence of sex." The couple need to view each other as sexual people with sexuality being integrated into a respectful, trusting, and intimate relationship.

The ability to listen and respond emphatically to each other's thoughts and feelings is necessary to a satisfying relationship. Clearly and directly stating your feelings and making requests (not demands) of your partner is important. Dealing with problems, not avoiding them, is crucial. Developing and utilizing problem-solving skills (clearly stating your feelings about the problem, developing alternatives, objectively evaluating the pros and cons of each, committing yourself to trying a specific solution, implementing the solution, and monitoring the results) and acting in a constructive, goal-oriented manner is important to a successful relationship. The importance of problem-solving is downplayed in traditional female socialization, which emphasizes love conquering all and the woman standing by her man. A relationship needs to include humor and tolerance to get past the difficult situations and hard times that occur in even the best of marriages.

Elements of our model of female-male relationships are relevant to a range of interactions in work, friendships, and family. It is especially relevant for a marriage, the most intimate and stable relationship between a woman and a man. Marriages in which these attitudes and skills are practiced are the most satisfying and secure.

Jackie and Don

We have a great deal of respect and admiration for women who take responsibility for their lives and overcome family and cultural barriers to establish the kind of life, marriage, and family that promotes a sense of well-being. Jackie was the middle child in a working-class family with five children. Her parents had a traditional, Catholic, double-standard marriage that Jackie vowed she would not repeat in her life. Jackie did treasure memories of the extended-family Sunday lunch and activities, enjoyed having an older brother and sister as well as a younger brother and sister, and felt lucky to have had a caring mother. She was extremely dissatisfied with the role her father played in her life and with the limited options available to women. Her father was a responsible, stable provider who was minimally involved with the family. Jackie vividly remembers that her father stopped being affectionate with her when she reached ten. It was as if she was then a "young woman" and her dad's only roles were to discipline her and protect her from predatory males. Her parents were not affectionate in front of the children. They seemed to get along, but there was little romantic or feeling-oriented communication. Her mother and father had totally different roles. Although their system worked and was stable, Jackie felt it was terribly unsatisfying, especially for her mother. Dad was in charge of work, money, cars, outside chores, and discipline. Mom was in charge of everything else. She was given the responsibility of "mothering" making sure that everyone was okay, and if they weren't it was her fault. She was constantly keeping score—four were doing well and two were doing badly. Mom never counted herself and didn't take care of her needs.

When her father died at sixty-two of a heart attack, Jackie felt cheated that she never really knew him. Jackie was much closer to her sisters than brothers and was alienated from her older brother, who acted more as her protector than her sibling friend. Jackie was athletic and wanted to play basketball and soccer, but in those days there were very few women's teams. The only sport she was encouraged to pursue was track. Jackie was angry at her missed opportunities and is committed to the idea that her daughter will have equal opportunity to be a "jock."

Starting in junior high school, girls and boys became more

and more separate; it was as if there were a war and they were enemies. The name of the game was "boys chase and conquer girls." The boys most admired by other boys were those who bragged about "scoring" with many girls. Girls who were sexually active had a "bad reputation" with both sexes. Jackie realized that the male-female game, as it was played in her community, was exciting but stupid.

Being Catholic didn't make it any easier. The Catholic prohibition against petting to orgasm and premarital intercourse was one thing, but the prohibition against sexual thoughts, masturbation, and kissing and caressing seemed outrageous. Jackie knew that males masturbated; her older brother would joke about masturbating. At fourteen, Jackie engaged in self-exploration and by the fifth or sixth time continued masturbation through to orgasm. Jackie's reaction to her first orgasm was pleasure mixed with guilt. The next day Jackie went to confession. Unfortunately, the priest was from the "old school" of Catholicism and berated her for "abusing herself" and said if she kept it up she would become a "whore." Jackie felt victimized by the priest's rantings, but she was intelligent enough to know that what he was saying did not make objective or rational sense. She knew that priests did not say the same thing about masturbation to adolescent boys. These dire warnings and threats did not stop Jackie from masturbating, but they did undermine her confidence in the Catholic church and its teachings. By the time Jackie left home for college she no longer attended church. It was not until after her daughter was born and at her husband's urging that she returned to church attendance. She became an activist Catholic dedicated to changing her religion's stance on women generally and sexuality specifically.

Jackie had maintained good grades during high school. Through the support of two teachers and her guidance counselor she planned to become the first person in her family to attend college. Her father was helpful, although he wanted to be sure she majored in something that would guarantee her a job—like teaching or nursing. Jackie was particularly good at math and interested in business. She expected to begin at the local community college, but with a combination of good advice, getting admissions information and financial aid, and some luck she was accepted in a work-study program at the state university with a partial scholarship.

Senior year of high school was the most difficult time in Jackie's life. Not only did she have to face hard decisions, but the fact that she was taking a different life path made her feel alienated from friends and her two older siblings. Jackie had the support of her mother, teachers, and college-bound friends, but she felt stigmatized by others, particularly boys. Jackie had dated extensively sophomore and junior year and enjoyed it, although she was not comfortable with the heavy petting boys desired at the end of the date. It was not that Jackie didn't like the sensations and feelings of the touching, but the guys were very goal-oriented and would rub their erections against her. She was aware that on several occasions boys had ejaculated during petting and she felt "funny" about it. Jackie was not ready for intercourse. Several of her friends worried about late menstrual periods, and she knew at least two girls in her class had gotten pregnant. During senior year, several girls Jackie was friendly with became engaged. Guys who were not intending to go to college mocked and hassled her. Jackie felt humiliated that she went to the senior prom with a guy she didn't like.

Transitions are difficult at any time in life, but one of the most important and arduous is your first year away from home. It can be a time of great personal growth or a major disaster. Jackie's first year in college had characteristics of both. For work-study she chose to be a student assistant in the accounting department. This turned out to be an excellent decision. She was well liked and well respected by the professors in the department, and since at that time accounting was a male-dominated profession it provided unusual opportunities for Jackie. She majored in accounting, eventually received her CPA and became the first female partner in a seven-person accounting firm.

Socially and sexually freshman year had been difficult for Jackie. The freedom from home and broadened social opportunities were exciting. Jackie was determined to be liberated and at nineteen to "lose her virginity." Sexuality can be negative when used to "prove" something to yourself or anyone else. Jackie's first intercourse was everything she promised herself it wouldn't be. Her partner was a junior she'd known a little over a week. It was unplanned, contraception was not used, and it did not feel particularly good. The relationship lasted six weeks, but that was because Jackie did not want to admit it was a mistake. Jackie wanted an involved connection, he wanted a sex-focused affair. After the initial two intercourses, Jackie insisted he use a condom and went to the local Planned Parenthood clinic for a diaphragm, although she only used it twice before the relationship broke up. During her freshman year, Jackie had four less than satisfactory sexual relationships.

Jackie committed herself to organizing her social and sexual life with men in a more respectful, positive manner. She decided that unless she was comfortable with the man, attracted to him, and trusted that they could form a longer, more involving relationship she did not want sex. Jackie was pleased to discover that being more assertive and discriminating had a number of positive results. She formed friendships with males and joined group activities with female friends and coed groups, including a Sunday afternoon volleyball league. Another benefit was spending more time on her academic and vocational pursuits. In March of her sophomore year she became involved in a more satisfying relationship that continued for one and a half years. Jackie felt valued as a person as well as for her sexuality. Eight months into the relationship she started being regularly orgasmic. She switched to the birth control pill, which served her well throughout young adulthood.

Don came into Jackie's life when she was twenty-two, and they married just as Jackie turned twenty-four. When Jackie explains how they met and why she was ready to pursue a more serious relationship, she emphasizes that she was not desperately seeking a man to marry, but that she had tired of the singles dating scene.

After college Jackie decided not to return to her hometown, but to pursue job opportunities in a larger city. Although her family did not like the decision, Jackie was convinced it was a responsible choice. Jackie was committed to making the transition to the work world better than to college; she had learned from past mistakes. Jackie rented an apartment, and she established a group of female and male friends before looking for a dating relationship.

Jackie met Don through friends who had organized a day hike. He struck her as a nice guy who shared many of her values. Don was her age, an architect who had broken up a two-year relationship three months ago. Don was interested in Jackie, but neither wanted to rush into a romantic affair. For the next two months they did things with friends and had weekly lunches and several long walks. Jackie learned Don's father had left his mother for another woman when Don was twelve. His father was a moderate drinker, but the woman was alcoholic, and much of their life centered around alcohol and boating. Don was terribly disappointed in his father, and over time became alienated from him. His mother had been devastated by the divorce, and she was angry and distrustful toward males. On the other hand, the divorce had been the impetus for her to return to work and she became the office manager of a law firm. Don had a history of longer-term relationships and had a number of female and male friends. The friend who had set up the hike told Jackie that of all the males she knew Don was the most solid person.

You can learn a lot about people by observing the small things in their behavior. Jackie was impressed by how responsible Don was with the niece and nephew he babysat for one weekend. Jackie went with them to a children's museum, and instead of turning them over to Jackie, Don took prime responsibility for their care. Two weeks later, Don asked her to go shopping with him to buy a chair for his apartment. Don did not know as much as Jackie about furniture and decorating and he valued her advice, but he didn't play the role of "helpless male"—he made the final choice.

One evening Don invited her to his favorite music club, and through the medium of discussing music revealed a good deal about his feelings and experiences. He was more affectionate, and Jackie felt open and receptive to his touches. She was impressed and pleased that he cared enough to ask her about contraception before moving toward intercourse. She was assertive enough to request that they come back to her apartment where she had her diaphragm. Jackie preferred being sexual in her own apartment, at least for the first time (which is a good guideline for women since it allows them to feel more in control).

Once they began as a romantic and sexual couple, it was a passionate coupling. Jackie and Don did the special things lovers do—stay up hours talking, spend the next day in bed making love, eat popcorn for breakfast, kiss and touch while walking in the rain, make love at midnight on a deserted beach, and dream of the perfect love, marriage, family, and life. Romantic love is an experience not to be missed, but at best it lasts only a year or two. Romantic love gives you the courage to risk and get involved deeply in a relationship, but it is not a basis for marital decision.

In discussing their relationship and whether to marry, they needed to deal with hard issues as well as indulge in romantic plans and dreams. Perhaps the best indicator of a successful marriage is the couple's ability to develop a joint life plan that respects their individual requirements and still meets couple needs. The plan is not set in concrete and cannot be foolproof, but it involves agreements on the crucial issues of children, sex, money, where a couple will live, and how they will nurture and maintain respect, trust, and intimacy in their relationship.

The second indicator of a successful marriage is the ability to clearly see your partner for his strengths and weaknesses and feel respectful and intimate. Jackie had no desire to fall into the traditional female trap of believing that love would conquer all and that once married it was her role to change Don and make him a better person. Don was a competent architect who was committed to providing them a middle-class life, but he was not ambitious enough to own his own firm or be rich. She was aware that he would not be an "Alan Alda" sensitive man. Don would be respectful and caring, but not a sentimentalist or someone who would bring flowers every week. Jackie realized Don was capable of committed, intimate feelings and most of all Don was someone she could respect and trust. She and Don had shared dreams for their life, and Jackie believed in them as a couple.

Jackie and Don, like many couples, found the first three years of marriage both the most satisfying and the most diffi- cult. Satisfying because of the thrill of seeing their dream start to become reality in having their first child and buying their first house. It was a period of personal and couple growth, a really exciting time. Difficult in that they had to grapple with hard issues and reach agreements on the way they would organize their life together. It is one thing to talk about basing a marriage on female-male equity, and more difficult to successfully live out the model. One of the hardest issues was that Jackie was more professionally successful than Don, and through much of their marriage made more money. Jackie did not want her accounting career to dominate her life nor to base her entire self-esteem on it, but she was proud of her successes. She did not want to downplay her competence to protect Don's ego (although that was the advice from friends and family). Dividing household chores was difficult; sharing everything fifty-fifty simply didn't work for Jackie and Don (nor does it for most couples). Jackie realized Don was a better cook than she, but she had to accept that if the house was to be clean and kept in the manner she desired, she would need to do the housework and not depend on Don. Some of the tasks were assigned in the traditional sex-role manner such as Don mowing and taking care of their yard, some as a role reversal such as Jackie managing the checkbook and retirement investments, and some tasks, such as child care, were shared.

A major crisis occurs when a child is sick or the child-care system breaks down (school vacation, snow day, absent sitter). Jackie and Don had to negotiate who stayed home and who had a trip or meeting that couldn't be changed. Both of them, but especially Don, complained that it would be easier if they had the traditional arrangement of the working husband and the housewife. Jackie knows she wouldn't be happy without her career and the benefits of two good incomes. Being a two-career family makes life hectic, but more satisfying. There were periods (at the birth of their two children, while Don's mother was dying of cancer, and when Jackie had abdominal surgery) where she cut back to two-thirds time. Jackie appreciated the fact that she was able to alter her work schedule without jeopardizing her career, but she resented the fact that males could not make similar adjustments. Business still stigmatizes males who reduce their work commitments for the sake of their families. Women's careers are less hampered by that stigma, but women do find it harder to advance, especially to senior positions.

In deciding to marry, Jackie and Don made a firm commitment to putting in the time and energy to make their marriage work. They agreed not to stay together for tradition, dependency, or for the sake of the children. Jackie was not willing to tolerate a poor or destructive marriage; she had seen its effects on family and friends. Don surprised and pleased Jackie by saying he would not accept a marriage that was a lukewarm compromise; he also wanted a viable, loving relationship. This agreement about the importance of marriage served to maintain the commitment to make their marital bond a respectful, trusting, and intimate one. They would attend to their marriage and nurture it, not take the marriage for granted and allow it to stagnate.

A marriage (and especially martial sex) cannot rest on its laurels; there needs to be a sense of growth and development. Sexuality plays an integral role in energizing the marital bond. Setting aside couple time to be sexual, including special events such as weekends away without the children, are vital. Jackie and Don enjoyed parenting their children, but they knew they also needed time alone as a couple.

As Jackie and Don changed and grew as individuals, their marital relationship needed to be emotionally cohesive and flexible to accommodate personal and situational changes. For an emotional and sexual relationship to thrive, both people have to be empathic listeners and responsive to each other's feelings, be clear and direct in stating their opinions and making requests, look at a range of alternatives when facing a problem, and problem solve in a respectful manner so they reach an agreement both can live with. The latter skill is vital in balancing personal, career, and parenting decisions.

In his mid-forties Don discovered he had a flair for writing, and since his career was stable but not satisfying, he wanted to indulge his fantasy of being a writer. Jackie encouraged his interest because she knew he got tremendous satisfaction from having a short story published. She gave him the time and space to pursue writing as an avocation, but she could not agree to his writing fiction as a vocation because so few writers were financially successful. She argued with herself that if she were a traditional loving wife she would agree to anything that made him happy, but she realized her resentment over the financial changes and giving up her dream of a phased retirement starting at age sixty would poison the relationship.

Jackie and Don are aware as they look toward the future that life will continue to be filled with challenges and change. They set aside time to talk, plan, and develop goals for the second part of their life. They enjoy their children as young adults (much more than as adolescents). The "empty nest" has resulted in a more satisfying personal and sexual life. They enjoy having their adult children visit and look forward to being grandparents, but value being a couple again. Contrary to cultural expectation, Jackie has particularly enjoyed this stage, which has allowed her more time to pursue friendships and professional activities such as being elected president of the local accounting society. Jackie especially enjoys the freedom to be sexual in other areas of the house instead of sex being relegated solely to the bedroom.

GUIDELINES FOR FEMALE-MALE RELATIONSHIPS

Jackie and Don are not the perfect pair, but they have achieved as individuals and as a couple much that is admirable. In part that comes from following guidelines about female-male relationships that can serve to enhance the lives of both sexes.

1. Basing the relationship between females and males on respectful attitudes that promote, and even demand, equality.
2. An open and flexible attitude toward female-male roles.
3. An acceptance and security about yourself and your femininity so that you do not need the approval of males nor are you intimidated by males.
4. A realization that intellectually, behaviorally, emotionally, and sexually there are more similarities than differences between women and men.
5. Personal and/or professional friendships with males are encouraged, but resist the pressure to sexualize these relationships.
6. Be comfortable and confident in your femininity so that the activities or interests that have traditionally been labeled "masculine" can be integrated into your life.
7. An intimate sexual relationship will be more satisfying if both the woman and man can initiate, say no, request, and enjoy a range of sexual pleasures.
8. Conception, contraception, and children are as much the responsibility of men as women.

9. A marriage based on respect, equity, trust, and intimacy is most satisfying for women and men alike.

10. A communicative, sharing, and giving relationship between a woman and a man promotes emotional and sexual satisfaction.

It is not solely the woman's role to advocate these guidelines. Women and men must share the responsibility. It is the woman's right to choose a male who believes in and lives out these guidelines. Women need to avoid men and relationships that promote a view of female-male relationships that are not in the woman's best interest. Women and men who accept and live out these guidelines can avoid the ongoing war between the sexes and enjoy a mutually enhancing life together.

10
PLEASURING, INTERCOURSE, AND AFTERPLAY

This chapter, and its title, reflects the special viewpoint of women. Males would call it "Foreplay, Intercourse, and Going to Sleep." In male sexuality, intercourse is the end all and be all of sex. In fact, "sex" and "intercourse" are used as synonymous terms. Foreplay is the period in which the man gets the woman ready for intercourse. Sex ends when he ejaculates. Simple, straightforward, and wrong!

The sex-therapy concepts and procedures developed by Masters and Johnson constituted the first major challenge to the male-defined sexual scenario. Their "sensate focus" exercises serve as the underpinning for our broader concept of "pleasuring." Pleasuring includes affectionate and sensual touching, as well as sexual stimulation. The major concept underlying pleasuring is that touching occurs in a nondemanding atmosphere. In other words, there is no pressure or demand that the touching result in intercourse and orgasm. Affectionate, sensual, and/or sexual touching is important in its own right; it does not require intercourse to justify it.

Affectionate touching usually involves clothes on, can be done inside or outside the bedroom, is not genital (i.e., does not involve breasts, the vulva, or the penis) and is a way of communicating warm or playful feelings. The most common types of affectionate touching are kissing, hugging, and hand holding.

Sensual touching can be partially clothed or nude, is mostly nongenital but can include light genital stroking, can occur inside or outside the bedroom but requires privacy, and is meant to communicate pleasure and enjoyment of your partner's body, as well as your own. The most common forms of sensuality are whole body massage, bathing or showering together in a sensual manner (not just to get clean), and caressing or stroking the partner's body in an exploratory or playful manner.

Sexual touching can be clothes on or off, in the bedroom or outside, and requires privacy. It includes manual and oral stimulation of the breasts, vulva, or penis. It is meant to communicate sexual interest and pleasure. It is often a prelude to intercourse, but need not be. Unfortunately, most couples never engage in genital touching unless they plan to have intercourse. Genital touching can be exploratory and playful, or it can be focused and erotic. The latter is more demanding of sexual arousal and orgasmic release.

PLEASURING, NOT FOREPLAY

What is the difference between foreplay and pleasuring? Foreplay is a defined prelude to the "real thing"—sexual intercourse. Foreplay involves a demand behind the touching, it is goal-directed, and there will be unfortunate consequences if the performance demand of intercourse is not met. Negative consequences can vary from mild irritation to rageful anger. Pleasuring is a nondemand, non-goal-oriented activity in which the focus is on giving and receiving pleasure. It involves a broader concept of what sexuality is all about. Sexual pleasure is much more than genitals, intercourse, and the few seconds of orgasm. Affection can lead into sensuality but doesn't have to, sensuality can lead to genital touching but doesn't have to, genital touching can lead to intercourse but doesn't have to. Affection, sensuality, and genital touching are parts of the pleasuring process that can serve as a bridge to intercourse, but they are positive expressions of communication and intimacy in and of themselves. Traditionally, women have not felt the freedom to express themselves in a broad-based sexual manner. Males would use derogatory terms like "tease" or "flirt," which said to the woman, "If you don't want to go all the way to intercourse, don't even start." Pleasuring gives both women and men more freedom to express their affectionate, sensual, and sexual feelings.

INTERCOURSE AS PART OF PLEASURING

In the traditional male approach, intercourse was the "real sex" and everything else was unnecessary or devalued. In our broad-based approach, intercourse is viewed as a special pleasuring technique. Like other pleasuring techniques, intercourse is as much for the woman as the man. Intercourse is not something the man does *to* the woman. Intercourse is a pleasuring experience the woman does *with* the man. Intercourse is not a separate part of the sexual experience, it is a continuation of the entire lovemaking process. Affection, sensuality, and genital touching (i.e., multiple stimulation), can continue during intercourse. Intercourse is a positive, integral part of sexual expression, but sexuality is much more than intercourse. Intercourse is part of the pleasuring process, not apart from it.

Women have varied patterns of sexual arousal and different ways of reaching orgasm. The male model of sexuality holds that the "one right" way is to have a single orgasm that occurs during intercourse. Female sexuality is more variable and complex. There is not one right pattern. Each woman develops a sexual response style that is comfortable and pleasurable for her, and she should not try to meet a rigid male performance criterion. Being comfortable with and enjoying intercourse is the important thing, not whether or not you are orgasmic during intercourse.

AFTERPLAY

The afterplay (also called afterglow) phase is the least appreciated part of the sexual experience. Again, women are cheated by male standards. The typical male pattern is for sexual contact to end after he gives her a perfunctory hug and goes to sleep or gets up and goes about his life. The woman's typical reaction is to be frustrated but shrug her shoulders and say that's the way men are. You just had an intense physical and emotional experience. It is perfectly natural to need and desire to close that experience in a positive manner, which is what afterplay is all about.

Before discussing afterplay scenarios, let us begin by challenging the assumption that sexual activity must end with the man's orgasm. What about the woman's sexual needs? Perhaps

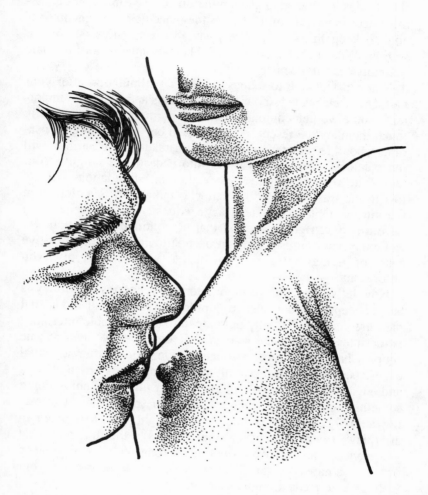

Breast stimulation need not necessarily be the "foreplay" that leads to orgasm. It can also be "afterplay."

she desires further genital stimulation to orgasm. You can almost hear males saying that after they ejaculate it is uncomfortable to keep thrusting and anyway the penis slips out of the vagina. What about their hands? There is much more to male sexuality than the penis.

You can feel free to request additional stimulation after your partner has ejaculated. Your sexual feelings and needs are important. Some women complain that their partner will mechanically touch them and be resentful. Arguing in bed and trading accusations about sexual technique is a mistake—your partner will react defensively and you'll get into a destructive fight. Your legitimate request that he give additional stimulation will get lost in the fray. It would be better to talk about this clothed at the kitchen table and state it as a request, not a demand. You have a perfect right to request that he continue stimulation. He can enjoy your arousal and approach stimulation with a positive sense of giving, not a resentful duty to mechanically give you an orgasm.

Now let's talk about positive afterplay scenarios. Afterplay is best conceptualized as a sharing process. You just shared sexual pleasure and arousal, why not extend that pleasurable interlude? After intercourse many women feel emotionally open. Some couples have their most intimate conversations after a sexual experience. Others feel playful and silly after sex and tell jokes and engage in tickling or a pillow fight. Still others enjoy doing something physical like taking a walk, or showering, or throwing a Frisbee. There is not just one right way to engage in afterplay; it is dependent on your feelings at the time and what you want to share. There is nothing wrong with going to sleep or taking a nap as long as it's agreeable to both people and your feelings and needs are not being ignored.

Some couples develop rather elaborate afterplay scenarios that can include having a dessert or glass of wine in bed, looking at favorite pictures or reading poetry. Most couples have a simple pattern of lying and talking or putting on a pot of coffee or sharing for two or three minutes and then going off to sleep. Be aware of your feelings and needs as the sexual experience is ending and close it in an enjoyable manner.

TOUCHING OUTSIDE THE BEDROOM

Sexual desire develops outside the bedroom. This is true for nonmarried couples and couples without children, and is of special importance for couples with children. For many couples, sex is what you do at eleven at night after you've done all the important things in life—paid the bills, put the children to bed, done the dishes, returned phone calls, and watched the news. If American businesspeople put as little time into their businesses as American couples put into their marriages (and marital sex) we'd have a bankrupt country. You have to attend to and nurture the marital and sexual relationship, especially outside the bedroom. Sexual intercourse generally occurs in the bedroom, but developing the conditions for sexual desire and expression occurs outside.

The kiss before going to work that includes a playful caress on the inner thigh is a powerful sensual message. A call at noon saying not to work late because this would be a good evening to get together is a nice invitation. Not putting clothes on after a shower, but taking five extra minutes to play will provide a fun fantasy to use during the day. Planning and anticipating a weekend away without children can build sexual desire. Curling up watching TV or listening to music serves to reinforce affectionate bonds that nurture sexual desire.

TOUCHING INSIDE THE BEDROOM

The great advantage of being in your bedroom is privacy. We strongly suggest that, if you don't already have one, you should buy a lock for your bedroom door. Because you've locked your door does not mean you are committed to having intercourse. Pleasuring concepts and nongoal orientation extends into the bedroom. Pleasuring and sensuality are as important as intercourse and orgasm.

One of the advantages of pleasuring is that the variety of pleasuring positions and techniques are greater than for intercourse. If you and your partner are interested in experimenting with pleasuring techniques, be sure to give yourself at least half an hour free of interruptions. Lock the door and turn off the phone (or take it off the hook). Set a mood that is comfortable and sensual. Turn the lights in your bedroom down if you wish (but not off—you'll want to see what you're doing) or light a candle. Put on your favorite music and/or use a pleasant-smelling water-soluble body lotion. We have a scented candle in our bedroom that creates a sensual atmosphere, but the choice of such paraphernalia depends entirely on individual tastes.

PLEASURING EXERCISES

A good way to begin pleasuring exercises is for one partner to start as the giver and the other as recipient. Since women traditionally have not been given permission to initiate, in the first exercise the woman can initiate and be the giver. The giver's role is to explore and learn about her partner's body. Experiment with a variety of nongenital touches. Instead of trying to second guess your partner and please him, do touching for yourself. The recipient closes his eyes, lies back and passively receives (for many men, this is much harder than it sounds). If the touch is painful or uncomfortable, he can tell her. Otherwise, he should lie back and take in the sensual feelings of being touched. Later the recipient will get a chance to guide his partner and make requests for the kind of touching that is most pleasurable for him. Take in sensations without being critical or judging. Accept the touches and feelings. When the giver feels she has finished exploring and pleasuring her partner's whole body, switch roles. Women have to get over the feeling of being selfish or too hedonistic. Allow the pleasurable sensations to sweep over your entire body.

During the next pleasuring exercise, try guiding your partner. This can be particularly tricky if you have fallen into the traditional trap of the woman never guiding or making requests and the man assuming any request is a put-down of him as a lover. He views guidance as a threat and reacts defensively or angrily. The way to avoid this trap is to view the pleasuring exercises as enhancement; you are learning to increase pleasure. The emphasis is on openness not defensiveness, on learning not performing, on developing a couple style of pleasuring not on proving something. The giver-recipient format will facilitate these lessons.

It might be easier for the man to start as recipient. Instead of being passive, he can guide her by making verbal requests.

Even more effective is to use the hand override technique in which he puts his hand over hers. He can show her what kinds of touch are most pleasurable. Sometimes the difference between blah and pleasure is less than half an inch or a minor adjustment in strength of touch.

Sexual communication is dependent on keeping channels of emotional communication open. Sexual communication involves requests, whether verbal or nonverbal, to make touch more comfortable, pleasurable, and erotic. Although we're allowing the male to go first, the skill of making sexual requests and guiding is even more important for women. You are the expert on your body and your sexuality. Men pretend to be sexual experts, but he cannot know how to turn you on unless you tell or show him. At first it might seem awkward and you might feel self-conscious, but sexual requests need not be cold and clinical. It is a personal sharing of yourself and your sexuality; you are doing this as an "us" experience, not for him to service you.

Pleasuring exercises are spelled out in specific detail in our book *Sexual Awareness* for those women who prefer to use a more structured approach. Let us highlight some of the concepts and techniques for those women who prefer to "wing it."

As both people become more comfortable with the pleasuring process, as they learn each can initiate, and as they explore the roles of giver and recipient, you can move on to a more mutual give-and-take touching. Although it's nice to be a passive receiver, most women find it more involving and pleasurable to touch as they are being touched and to initiate as well as respond. Women appreciate the concept of nondemanding touching both inside and outside the bedroom. It is validating to realize that affection and sensuality are worthwhile in themselves.

Incorporating genital touching entails going back to the giver-recipient format. The most important concept is non-goal-oriented genital exploration. When people think of genital touching they immediately think of focused genital stimulation in preparation for orgasm and intercourse. We suggest genital touching be exploratory, with a focus on learning what kind of genital stimulation you find pleasurable and the type of genital stimulation your partner is receptive and responsive to. This process is facilitated by placing a temporary prohibition on orgasm during the exercise.

A major mistake men make is to immediately focus on breast and vulva stimulation to try to quickly arouse the woman. If she's not open to breast stimulation or receptive to vulva stimulation at that time it can be an irritant rather than an arouser. We suggest initial genital touching be light, exploratory, tender, playful, and that it be intermixed with nongenital touching. As the woman responds, more focused, erotic, rhythmic genital stimulation will build arousal. The timing and sequencing of genital stimulation is crucial. The woman can feel free to guide and request rather than assume he's the expert. Stay with your rhythm of arousal, don't feel you have to keep up with him.

A common male mistake is being too rough. Some men tend to overly focus on the areola rather than general breast stimulation. They may employ intra-vaginal finger stimulation instead of gentle, rhythmic stimulation around the labia and clitoral area. They don't mix nongenital and genital stimulation, but focus only on genital. Each woman has her own preferences for genital touching and her own pattern of sexual response. Be aware of your preferences and share those with your partner.

Women can become more comfortable stimulating the man's penis and testicles. Younger males have automatic and autonomous erections so many women make the mistake of believing this is natural and will always continue. They believe if he already has an erection it is indulgent to want more stimulation or that additional stimulation will cause early ejaculation. In truth, males can enjoy and respond to additional genital stimulation as much as women. Accepting and enjoying penile stimulation will lead to better ejaculatory control. Most important, as a male ages, beginning in his thirties, he needs the woman's stimulation to obtain and maintain erectile functioning. Learning this before it's needed will enhance sexual pleasure and inoculate the man against fears of erectile difficulty as he ages.

Contrary to popular myth, almost all males are occasionally unable to achieve an erection sufficient for intercourse. This can be caused by a number of factors including stress, drinking, not feeling in a sexual mood, distracting thoughts, side effects of medication, anger, lack of sleep, anxiety, etc. What often causes continuing erection problems is performance anxiety. Couples who have learned to view sexuality as mutual pleasure rather than performance and to enjoy a range of sensual and sexual expression are less likely to be plagued with erectile problems.

The ABCs of sexual satisfaction are: a) an emotionally open and intimate relationship, b) nondemand pleasuring, and c) multiple stimulation to build sexual arousal. In developing multiple-stimulation scenarios, the woman is open to higher levels of erocticism and passion. People think of stimulation as something a woman does for a man or something a man does for a woman. Sexuality is most satisfying when both partners are involved and aroused—their arousal plays off each other's. The woman being active in receiving and giving stimulation heightens arousal. Examples of multiple-stimulation scenarios include the man engaging in oral breast stimulation and manual clitoral and labial stimulation while the woman caresses his chest or penis; the woman manually stimulating his penis while she engages in a sexual fantasy and he's caressing her breasts; rubbing his penis against her breasts as she touches his testicles and inner thighs and they engage in romantic or erotic talk; engaging in mutual oral-genital stimulation.

MULTIPLE STIMULATION DURING INTERCOURSE

Multiple stimulation need not cease with the onset of inter-course. We strongly suggest integrating multiple stimulation into the intercourse scenario. The woman takes an active role in intercourse—the sexual activity during which women have traditionally been most passive. Whether orgasm occurs in the pleasuring period, or during intercourse, or in the afterplay period is not the chief factor in her enjoyment of intercourse. Women enjoy intercourse more when they are active participants. Multiple stimulation during intercourse can include kissing or caressing, fantasizing, manual testicle stimulation, having your breasts or buttocks caressed, changing intercourse positions and talking as you do so, trading who controls the type or rhythm of thrusting, stopping intercourse for five minutes and engaging in manual or oral stimulation, his providing manual clitoral stimulation during intercourse.

The couple can experiment with a number of intercouse positions, including woman on top, side by side, rear entry, standing, her sitting and his kneeling. There is nothing "natural" about the

The face to face intercourse position.

traditional man-on-top position. A major reason for its widespread use is it's the only position where the man can easily guide intromission. Also, in this position the penis is least likely to slip out of the vagina. Man on top is the best position to effect pregnancy. We are not against the man-on-top position—it can be pleasurable and satisfying. What we object to is the view that it is the ''right'' or ''natural'' position, and that intercourse is primarily for the man's satisfaction.

Intercourse can serve a number of functions—as a means of experiencing pleasure, as a sign of love and intimacy, and as a tension reducer (the latter is as legitimate for women as for men). Women need not apologize for their interest in and pleasure from sexual intercourse.

Olga

Olga was born in the United States, but was heavily influenced by her eastern European family and culture. Her father was a powerful, outspoken man who had very firm ideas about women and their role in life—as mothers and nurturers for men. He had even stronger feelings about sex—that it was primarily a physical need and that intercourse and orgasm was what it was really all about. For women, sexual satisfaction came primarily from knowing their husbands were satisfied. Perhaps the most preplexing thing for Olga was that her mother, for whom she had enormous respect and warmth, seemed quite happy in the marriage. It was not until Olga was in her mid-twenties that she had a personal talk with her mother about marriage and sex. Mother said she never took her husband's rantings very seriously. Under his blustery character, he genuinely cared about his marriage and was a considerate lover. Olga was shocked to hear that her parents engaged in cunnilingus and fellatio, and that her mother enjoyed sex.

When it came to Olga, her father's principle concern was to prevent young men from doing to his daughter what he bragged he had done to women premaritally. He was obsessed that she not become pregnant. As an adolescent, she had to introduce the boys she dated to her parents. Her dates were intimidated by her father. As do many teenagers, Olga used rebellion against parents as a way to establish her sense of self. Her father was not

The vaginal rear-entry coital position.

one to openly rebel against so she became good at telling lies and acting behind his back (a habit that continues to get her in trouble in adult relationships). At seventeen she began to secretly date men who were four or five years older. She insisted they use condoms during intercourse, but because many young men are not terribly skilled in condom use she had an unwanted pregnancy and abortion at age nineteen. She didn't tell either parent, a decision she did not regret.

Olga enjoyed being involved in a relationship, and she saw sex as a way of expressing loving feelings. She especially enjoyed kissing and caressing. She was aware that men got automatic erections and wanted to have intercourse every time. Her partner usually ejaculated early so that just as she started getting into the rhythm of intercourse it was over.

Olga wanted to marry early and have children early, and she was surprised when her life developed in a manner different from what she'd planned. Encouraged by her mother and friends, she went to college and came under the influence of an excellent female economics professor who encouraged her to go to law school and helped Olga obtain admission to a prestigious university. While her friends from home were having their second and third children, Olga was clerking for a judge and finding that her social and sexual life was taking second place to her career—a distant second place. Olga enjoyed men, affection, and sexuality and wanted it to play a more important role in her life. Rather than pursuing the career path of being an associate in a large law firm, she chose to combine her legal and economic skills and obtained a position as legal counsel on a legislative committee. This proved to be an interesting and demanding job, but it did leave time to have a life outside her career.

Olga wanted to date men who were not intimidated by her professional accomplishments. She became active in a professional organization, and through one of her male friends met Joe. Two things appealed to Olga—he was physically active and he was a "toucher," not a mauler. Joe could be competitive on the athletic field, but he was tender and nondemanding when touching. In fact, Joe was the most affectionate man Olga had ever been involved with. Joe was interested in her sexually, but by then Olga had established a clear guideline for herself—she was interested in an ongoing, intimate sexual relationship, not brief, intense affairs. Olga wanted to feel assured this was a developing commitment, not to use sex as a way of rescuing a relationship or becoming sexually involved because it was expected.

Olga had come to appreciate the pleasure of sensuality—she especially enjoyed taking a long hot bubble bath. After a particularly grueling day, she was luxuriating in the tub fantasizing about being sexual with Joe. Her roommate answered the door when Joe knocked, and she told him Olga was taking a bath. Joe asked if he could come in and talk while she was bathing. Olga remembered thinking this was too romantic, like out of a movie, but she couldn't resist inviting him in. Joe volunteered to wash her hair and as he did Olga felt herself letting go and deciding this was a man she could enjoy making love to. Olga invited him to join her in the bath and they spent a sensuous half hour talking, touching, and washing each other. Before leaving the bath, Olga said she wanted him to use a condom (romanticism does not mean leaving yourself vulnerable to an unplanned pregnancy). The actual intercourse was enjoyable, although a bit anticlimatic. Joe was not the perfect lover—as usual with young men, he ejaculated early. Olga felt he was interested in her and wanted her to enjoy intercourse, not do it primarily for him.

As the sexual relationship developed, Olga discovered two keys for her pleasure. She enjoyed Joe's stimulation, but didn't like the typical "foreplay scenario" to get her ready for intercourse. Olga was more easily aroused and orgasmic when she was actively giving as well as receiving stimulation. Hugging, caressing, and kissing were more arousing when they were mutual. She enjoyed lying back and having Joe caress her breasts and vulva while she stroked his back. As she became more aroused Olga was responsive to a multiple-stimulation pattern in which she would orally stimulate Joe while he was manually or orally stimulating her. Olga was usually orgasmic before starting intercourse or at least was highly aroused. At times she would manually or orally bring Joe to orgasm so he would know that intercourse was not the end all and be all of sexuality.

The second key for Olga's pleasure was to continue multiple

stimulation during intercourse. She became aroused by watching Joe's arousal build and realizing she had the power to turn him on. Olga found it much easier to be aroused during intercourse if Joe continued hugging her and touching her breasts while she stroked his buttocks and thighs. Olga was more likely to be orgasmic during intercourse if she had previously been orgasmic during the pleasuring period.

Afterplay was an important time for Olga. She was bitter about ex-lovers who would ignore her, roll over, and go to sleep after they had ejaculated. If Olga and Joe had sex at night or in the late afternoon (before a nap) she would use sex as a way of getting drowsy and going to sleep. She remembered a joke that sex was more effective than a sleeping pill. Olga enjoyed touching and talking for three to five minutes after the sexual experience and before drifting off to sleep. She liked to be held by Joe and talk with him. When being sexual in the morning, which was her favorite time, Olga enjoyed showering with Joe and being playful. It was a nice way to wrap up the sexual experience and start the day.

CLOSING THOUGHTS

The woman's concepts of affection, sensuality, and sexual expression are a healthy contribution to the sexual scenario. Pleasuring, intercourse, and afterplay is a broad-based, integrated approach to sexuality. It encourages touching inside and outside the bedroom, and reinforces that sexuality is more than genitals, intercourse, and orgasm. Nondemand pleasuring and multiple stimulation are key concepts underlying female sexual response. Women need to give themselves permission to make sexual requests and develop sexual scenarios that promote couple sexual satisfaction.

11
ENJOYING SEXUAL FANTASIES

When you hear the term "sexual fantasy," what is your first association? It's probably with pornography, which is identified as a male interest. In X-rated movies and novels, the woman is used and abused, sometimes violently, for the man's sexual pleasure. Women Against Pornography is an active, vocal group that holds that pornographic movies, videos, and sexually-explicit books promote the acceptance of women as sex objects and give cultural permission for rape and sexual abuse. If this is indeed the case then why would a book on female sexuality include a chapter on sexual fantasies?

In the past decade, there has been a host of research on the relationship between sexual fantasy and sexual arousal, for women as well as men. Although it's a complex phenomenon with many individual differences, the basic finding is that sexual fantasy functions in the same way for both women and men. Sexual fanatasy serves to elicit sexual interest, build sexual arousal, and help the woman reach orgasm. Sexual fantasies occur in daydreams and in sleep and can be used during intercourse as well as during masturbation. Sexual fantasy can have a positive, integral role in female sexuality.

FANTASY AND BEHAVIOR

The crucial concept to be aware of if you are to use sexual fantasies comfortably is that fantasy and sexual behavior are two very different realms. Because you are turned on by a particular sexual fantasy does *not* mean you want to experience it in real life. It's perfectly normal to have "unusual" or "non-

148

socially-acceptable'' sexual fantasies. That's the joy of the fantasy realm.

Our behavior is rational, constructive, under our conscious control, and socially appropriate. Fantasy allows an emotional, irrational, sometimes downright crazy component into our moderate, well-ordered lives. Your fantasy of going on television and telling your boss exactly how she has goofed up, and thereby starting a mass demonstration that results in a million-dollar bonus for you makes great fantasy, but it wouldn't be acceptable or constructive real-life behavior. In the same manner, you might enjoy fantasizing being in prerevolutionary China with male eunuch servants catering to your every whim and being part of a ménage à trois with two strong soldiers who ravage you. Is that a sexual experience you'd want in real life? No, but it can make for an arousing sexual fantasy.

The second most common sexual fantasy theme, for both women and men, centers on forced sex—forcing, being forced, or switching roles. Does this support the old adage that ''women really want to be raped''? No more than it would that men really want to be raped. What makes a fantasy erotic is that it turns you on to a part of life and sexuality that is outside the norms of behavior. It allows you to experience events that you cannot and do not want to experience in the real world. Fantasy is a mental realm in which you can give yourself permission to enjoy otherwise undesirable people and activities.

Very few people, if any, regularly fantasize sex with their regular partners, in their own bedroom, in the ''missionary'' position. You may fantasize about being sexual with Tom Cruise, or your next-door neighbor, or an evil drug king. Sex occurs on a beautiful island, in a torture chamber, or in an auditorium with all your friends looking on with admiration and/or disgust. The sexual behavior is not intercourse, it's cunnilingus, or group sex, or being attacked by a gang of half animals–half humans with extraordinary penises. Women do not fantasize about ''normal sex,'' there's nothing erotic about that. They fantasize about ''kinky,'' nonsocially desirable, and even scary themes outside the realm of their actual behavior and desires. The five most common sexual fantasy themes are: 1) sex with a different partner, 2) forced sex, 3) group sex, 4) sex with another woman, 5) watching or being watched while having sex. These themes make better fantasies than reality. If you can stop worrying that it means you want to or are in danger of acting these out, you can take advantage of sexual fantasies to enhance sexual desire and responsivity.

THE ADVANTAGES OF SEXUAL FANTASIES

The major plus with sexual fantasies is that you are in control of them and can have them any way you like. You are the person who designs, develops, and choreographs the fantasies. You don't need to be concerned with censorship or someone else's opinion. They are yours to play with and enjoy. In fantasy, society's rules about appropriate behavior can be and are discarded. You can enjoy activities which, if you acted them out in the real world, would cause you humiliation and disaster. You get all the benefits without paying any of the costs.

Most people associate sexual fantasies with masturbation. In fact, the majority of women do masturbate and utilize fantasy as an integral component during masturbation. The old adage "friction plus fantasy equals orgasm" is as true for females as well as males. Especially important is the role of sexual thoughts in initiating a state of readiness (or in the colloquial, "horniness"). This facilitates the woman's sexual desire and receptivity to self-stimulation. The second major role of fantasy is as an "orgasm trigger." As fantasy arousal builds, so does the physical sexual arousal. A certain thought, image, or verbal sequence serves as a "trigger" to allow sexual arousal to pass into orgasm.

Another outlet for sexual fantasy is through dreams. Sleep research indicates that deep levels of sleep are necessary for physical and psychological well-being. Sleep rejuvenates the woman, while sleep deprivation has a number of negative physical and psychological side effects including irritability, depression, difficulty concentrating, lack of sexual interest. One of the most efficacious sleep levels is REM (rapid eye movement) sleep, which is strongly correlated with dreaming. Sexual dreams are very common during REM sleep.

A common clinical intervention with clients who are having sleep difficulties is to coach them in developing dream themes that are pleasant, involving, and nonconflictual. This facilitates the sleep process as well as allowing the woman to look forward to and enjoy her dreams. For example, a client really enjoyed "Masterpiece Theater" presentations about life in nineteenth-century England. She used these as the theme of her dreams and would incorporate a number of sexually attractive characters and scenarios to make the dreams more interesting. When she awoke in the morning, she was interested in initiating sex with her partner. Dream content is usually not remembered, but some women do recall particularly vivid dream images, some of which seem sexually "far out." Remember, dreams play out in irrational and emotional ways—we don't have to defend our dreams. Like sexual fantasies, dreaming about something does not mean you want to experience it—dreams and real-life behavior are different realms.

Another form of sexual fantasy is daydreaming. It can serve a number of purposes, perhaps the most common being to relieve boredom. Sitting through an interminably dull meeting can be made more tolerable by imagining what the speaker would look like nude or fantasizing having oral sex under the table. Your sexual daydream could take you out of a stifling room and place you at a ski resort skiing down the slopes in mid-March with the sun out and people in swim suits.

An additional function of sexual fantasies and daydreams is as a rehearsal. This can be of particular value for younger, less sexually experienced women. They can use fantasy to practice how a lovemaking scenario will develop. As the scenario unfolds in a woman's mind, she can change and revise it as she wishes so that she becomes more comfortable and builds her anticipation and confidence. Once imagined, she can suggest trying the scenario with her partner.

Fantasy rehearsal can be used to deal with difficult aspects of sexuality such as talking about contraception or putting in a diaphragm. In classes for women on how to prevent AIDS, some instructors utilize imagery or role-play rehearsals where the woman discusses the man's risk level for being positive for HIV and insists on his using a condom.

Fantasy can and is used by women as an accompaniment during partner sex, especially during intercourse. Perhaps as many as 50 percent of women utilize fantasy during partner sex. Fantasies serve as a bridge to build greater sexual arousal.

The experience of imagining having sex with another man (a movie star, a sexy man you saw on the street, or an old lover) while being sexual with your partner is the most common sexual fantasy. Many women feel an acute sense of guilt indulging in this reverie. This guilt is totally unnecessary, however, since changing a partner's identity in your imagination is not a sign you want to switch real-life partners. In the same way, using sexual fantasies of multiple partners, forced sex, or lesbian sex does not mean you want to engage in those sexual behaviors. Sexual fantasies are an erotic component that can heighten stimulation and arousal.

MISUSE OF SEXUAL FANTASIES

Sexual fantasies have a number of positive functions. However, like all good things, they can be misused and cause psychological and/or sexual difficulties. For instance, when a thought or fantasy is associated with guilt or anxiety, it may take on a power it should not have. The woman may feel bad about herself and become obsessive. The fantasy may control her thoughts, almost compulsively. In such cases, the fantasy may produce intense arousal, but also intense guilt—a very unhealthy combination. Women seldom develop the obsessive, addictive behaviors associated with male fetishes. However, women do experience conflict, guilt, and lower sexual self-esteem because of sexual fantasies. This self-punishment is totally unwarranted. There is no such thing as an unhealthy sexual fantasy as long as it remains a fantasy and does not control your behavior. Fantasies are meant to enhance your sexuality, not be a source of guilt, anxiety, or conflict.

Another possible misuse of sexual fantasy is developing a pattern of self-negation. For example, a client used a fantasy theme of being dominated and forced to perform sex acts. Her fantasies included being tied up, having to fellate six men, men tearing off her clothes, being penetrated by a horse's superlarge penis. Rather than seeing these as harmless fantasies that could be interspersed with other sexual reverie's, she became frightened and guilty. She saw them as a symbol that her sexuality was "perverse" and became afraid she would act them out. The greater the guilt, the greater the fear, the more controlling the sexual fantasy. After a few months of this cycle, the client decided the only thing she could do was to avoid sex as a way of shutting out the thoughts. This caused difficulties in her marriage that eventually brought her into therapy.

There are two ways to break the self-negating cycle in regard to sexual fantasies. The first is to remember that fantasy and behavior are two different realms. The woman's fantasies can be enticing and arousing in imagery, but would be disastrous in reality. Sexual fantasies make much better fiction than reality. The second is that the key to sexual fantasies is to use a variety, not to obsess on one situation or theme. You have open to you the widest possible range of thoughts, images, and acts. It is guilt and fear that traps you into one fantasy theme. Give yourself permission to break the cycle and enjoy a range of sexual fantasy without guilt or fear. You can use domination, group sex, sex with an inappropriate partner, or other socially undesirable but erotic fantasy themes without being afraid.

There are large individual differences in sexual fantasies. It might be worthwhile to discuss a case study to demonstrate the uses of these and show how one woman overcame her inhibitions and increased her pleasure.

Julie

At twenty-five, and married less than a year, Julie was concerned about her desire and arousal. She loved Bob, found him attractive, and wanted their marriage to be successful. When they had met two years ago, Julie remembers being attracted to Bob and wanting to be sexual with him every day. Her mind was full of images of him and fantasies about how and when they would make love. These thoughts abruptly ceased four months before the wedding. Julie and Bob were still sexually functional, but it wasn't as much fun anticipating sex. When she's with Bob she is aroused and orgasmic, but she has noticed a continued decline in desire.

Occasionally, when she's at the movies or when jogging, she'll have a sexual feeling about a man she sees. At times she fantasizes about engaging in an erotic, seductive scenario outdoors. Julie's reaction to these fantasies had been intense embarrassment. She would try to immediately get them out of her mind. Before meeting Bob she'd enjoyed similar fantasies (feeling a bit wicked as she did so), but felt these were inappropriate for a married woman. As Julie purposely tried to stifle sexual reveries that did not involve Bob, she found there were fewer fantasies, and it was not particularly erotic to fantasize about making love to Bob.

Julie went to a family wedding and at the reception talked to her favorite aunt, who was an adult education instructor. As they were discussing her life, Julie mentioned jogging and the aunt jokingly asked if she used her time while jogging for serious thinking or something fun. Julie blushed and stammered, but her aunt reassured Julie she need not be embarrassed. A speaker at an adult education workshop on aerobic exercise had said engaging in fantasy was very common as an accompaniment to exercising. It was a perfectly normal and healthy activity.

Her aunt's openness enabled Julie to ask why fantasies were so strange and different from what you wanted them to be. Her aunt said that in normal waking life your behavior needed to be rational and appropriate within a set of approved social norms. However, fantasy was governed by a set of emotional, irrational, and idiosyncratic rules (or lack of rules). She reassured Julie it was perfectly okay to have strange fantasies. Julie had always admired her aunt's marriage. Her aunt confided that she could enjoy looking at other men and fantasizing about them with no feeling of disloyalty to her husband. She said her favorite fantasy was of Paul Newman and Robert Redford fighting to get her attention.

Julie could understand her aunt fantasizing after thirty years of marriage, but didn't it indicate something was wrong if Julie fantasized after only being married a year? The aunt was careful not to judge Julie, but made the point that both women and men used fantasies of other people and other sexual situations to fan the flames of marital sexual desire. Once those flames were lit they could be saved and expressed with your spouse. Like a good educator, the aunt suggested that Julie read *My Secret Garden*, Nancy Friday's book of female sexual fantasies, and use the images that were fun and arousing for her and discard the ones that seemed silly or turn-offs.

The next time Julie went jogging she was open to the fantasies she'd previously repressed. She jogged by two good-looking athletic men in their early thirties and imagined them turning around and jogging with her into a deserted area covered by trees with an open meadow in the middle. They were obedient and subservient to her desires. One man slowly and tenderly undressed her while the other lay down, unzipped his pants, and took out his erect penis which she rolled and kicked around with her bare feet. The other man remained clothed but was an exquisitely slow and tender lover who turned her on with his hands and tongue. When she felt highly aroused she roughly tossed him aside and took the other man's rock-hard penis into her, told him he was not allowed to come, and rode him as hard as she could for as long as she wanted.

As Julie jogged back to her house she savored the erotic feelings, took a shower, and talked Bob into making love. Julie wanted sex and wanted Bob. Julie now understood she could enjoy her sexual fantasies and they could serve to improve marital sexuality.

TWO EXERCISES FOR INCREASING FANTASY AWARENESS

These suggested exercises are to help you apply what you've read. If you don't feel comfortable with these exercises or don't believe they are in your best interest, feel free to skip them.

The first exercise involves using written and/or pictorial erotica. Give yourself permission to utilize whatever material might serve to intrigue and turn you on. Try magazines like *Penthouse Forum, Playgirl, Oui, Playboy*, and/or *Penthouse*. You might read books like *Story of O, Diaries of Anaïs Nin, Women in Love, Fanny Hill*, or fantasy books such as *Women Write Erotica*. Consider sexually oriented videos (X- or R-rated) such as *Misty Beethoven, The Big Easy, An Officer and a Gentleman*, etc. Some women prefer romantic/seductive images while others prefer more sexually explicit/passionate themes. There is no right or wrong erotica; don't censor yourself or allow others to censor you. Or what is sexually exciting for you.

Use the erotica you've chosen to build sexual interest and arousal. Focus on the pictures or written sections that are particularly exciting. Don't be embarrassed to go over the material two, three, or more times. You might mix reading and looking with self-stimulation or, if with a partner, engage in mutual stimulation. Let the written or pictorial material serve as a bridge to develop and nurture your arousal. Some women are more comfortable just focusing on the erotic material and not touching. They find interest and desire are easier to build if they focus on one thing at a time. The feelings can be saved and expressed later. Most women prefer to combine erotica and touching. Fantasy and stimulation enhances desire and arousal.

Find two or three materials you are receptive to. Males have cultural permission to enjoy erotica and the advantage of more practice using it. Take time and be open to erotica to determine if it will encourage sexual fantasies and allow your sexual expression to be broader and more flexible.

The second exercise asks you to utilize your own images. Some women have two or three specific fantasies or fantasy themes while other women prefer to use five or ten different ones. It's like going to Baskin-Robbins 33 Flavors ice-cream store. Some women have one or two favorite ice-cream flavors, others have four or five favorites and occasionally will try a new flavor, while other women will experiment with all thirty-three flavors and enjoying making up some of their own. You can utilize fantasies of past sexual experiences and embellish them, or you can develop totally outrageous but exciting new ones, or you can incorporate things you've read about or seen.

Some women are aroused by their own fantasies while others find erotica is better. Give yourself a chance to play with your images. As with the first exercise, you can fantasize only, or mix it with self-stimulation, or combine it with partner stimulation. Do what is comfortable and arousing for you. You can utilize fantasies in daydreams and/or as a cue to help you get to sleep and as part of your dreams.

CLOSING THOUGHTS

No one can tell you how to fantasize or whether sexual images, daydreams, and dreams will enhance your sexuality. Many women report a sense of freedom and liberation in utilizing sexual fantasies. Some find they are great for building interest and desire and then stop fantasizing as they get more involved with the physical stimulation. Other women discover that sexual fantasies are an integral part of multiple stimulation and help to facilitate sexual arousal. Sexual fantasy serves as the primary orgasm trigger for some women. Some prefer to use sexual fantasy only during masturbation, while others prefer fantasy only during partner sex, and still others utilize sexual fantasies in a wide variety of circumstances.

The keys in accepting and utilizing sexual fantasies are to realize you are in control and that fantasy and real-life behavior are totally different realms. You need not feel guilty or apologetic about your fantasies.

12
COMFORT AND PLEASURE WITH ORAL SEX

Traditionally oral sex was considered the male's domain. The old view was that males wanted oral-genital stimulation (fellatio, "blow jobs") from women who were reluctant to give it. Oral sex was exciting, but dirty, and male-focused.

So why is there a chapter on oral sex in the section on enhancement? Because oral sex is as much for the woman as for the man. Cunnilingus (oral stimulation of the vulva) can be just as enjoyable for the woman as fellatio is for the man. More women are multiorgasmic with cunnilingus than with any other type of partner stimulation. Cunnilingus does not interfere with intercourse and women report great receptivity to intercourse and more lubrication after cunnilingus. On the other hand, if a male has an ejaculation during fellatio, he's not able to continue to intercourse, at least at that time.

Oral sex is not dirty sex. No one considers mouth-to-mouth kissing as dirty. Yet the mouth contains more bacteria than does the vulva or penis. The mouth and the genitals are two of the most sexually receptive and responsive parts of the human body. They are filled with nerve endings that promote pleasure. It is totally natural and normal that these two parts of the body should come together in the pleasuring process.

How did oral sex get such a bad reputation among women? In part, it has to do with the slang phrases and their negative connotations. Phrases like "Go down on," "Eat her out," "Suck him off," have a decidedly aggressive and male connotation. In movies and novels oral sex has this same "exciting but dirty" character. In pornographic movies, it is not unusual to have shots of men ejaculating all over the woman's face. The infamous *Deep Throat* made deep-insertion fellatio a male obsession. "Eating pussy" to drive the woman to heights of passion so she'd do whatever her partner wanted reinforces the theme that even when the woman enjoys oral sex there's something nasty about it. There was no place for a positive female view of oral-genital sexuality. Like other male-based sexuality concepts used to define female sexuality, the traditional view of oral-genital sex does not promote healthy sexuality.

A BROAD-BASED CONCEPT OF ORAL SEXUALITY

Let's begin by thinking about oral stimulation broadly. Kissing someone, whether on the cheek or lips, is a sign of affection. Engaging in deep or tongue kissing (also called French kissing) is a sensual, pleasurable activity. Other examples of sensual oral stimulation include kissing on the thighs or legs, taking little "love bites" on the body, and running your tongue over your partner's back or chest. Comfort with giving and receiving kissing, biting, licking, and tongue gliding is the basis of enjoying oral-genital sex. Mixing, manual-genital stimulation with oral stimulation of nongenital body parts facilitates the process of comfort, receptivity, and responsivity. The underlying guideline is to view oral stimulation, the body, and the genitals as part of a process of giving and receiving pleasure with an intimate partner.

We can almost hear readers saying "Yes, but when do you get down to real oral-genital sex? If it's all so normal and natural, why does it need such a gradual buildup?" For women who do not want or need this broader-based experience of oral sexuality, they can initiate oral sex quickly and directly. Our view is that oral-genital sexuality, like other forms of sexual expression, is made easier by the woman being aware of her feelings and putting sexual expression into a broader, more sharing, and more pleasure-oriented context. Women need not feel constrained to "play the game" according to men's rules. The woman's approach of integrating feelings into sexual expression and emphasizing a comfortable, nondemand, pleasure-oriented approach to sexuality (including oral-genital sexuality) is a superior way to be sexual for both women and men.

CUNNILINGUS

Most women find it easier to receive oral-genital stimulation than to give it. This is not true of all women nor does it imply a tit-for-tat mentality, but it is the most common pattern. A key element is to signal when she is receptive to beginning cunnilingus rather than moving at the man's pace. The woman needs to be aware of and responsible for her arousal. She can communicate her needs and guide her partner. Males begin giving oral stimulation when they feel aroused; they are focused and demanding in their giving style. It's as if the woman would give penile stimulation in a fast, rough, demanding way regardless of whether he has an erection. Fast, focused cunnilingus can heighten passion if she is already aroused. However, this technique is counterproductive if she is not ready. Cunnilingus is an effective stimulation technique only when the woman is sufficiently aroused and receptive to it.

Most women prefer beginning genital stimulation manually and intermixing it with kissing, touching, and caressing. As interest and receptivity heightens, the bridge to cunnilingus is kissing, licking, or tongue gliding around the mons and labia while continuing with rubbing stimulation. As responsivity increases, the couple can proceed to faster, demanding cunnilingus. We are not saying this is the only pattern or the preferred pattern for all women or all circumstances. You need to be aware of your response and preferences and share these with your partner.

Do you prefer cunnilingus as a pleasuring technique or do you enjoy being orgasmic with cunnilingus? There is no "right" answer or "best" pattern. It is up to you and your partner to develop a sexual style that is comfortable. Many women find cunnilingus the easiest way to be orgasmic; empirically cunnilingus is the sexual technique most likely to result in multiorgasmic response. The tongue is more sensitive and flexible than the fingers or the penis. Being orgasmic with cunnilingus does not preclude intercourse. Some women find it easier to be responsive and orgasmic during intercourse after being aroused and/or orgasmic during cunnilingus. Other women do not want to be orgasmic during cunnilingus, but find it a highly arousing pleasuring technique. Still others find that although they enjoy cunnilingus, the man finds it even more arousing.

FELLATIO

There are innumerable jokes about "blow jobs" and how men beg or coerce women into giving them oral sex. Pornographic movies and erotic novels are filled with fellatio scenes. When males go to prostitutes, they are often charged more for fellatio than intercourse. The theme is clear—fellatio is for the man, exciting and dirty, and degrading for the woman. What a lot of nonsense!

Oral-genital sex is neither dirty, degrading, nor coercive. Fellatio and cunnilingus are about giving and receiving sexual pleasure. Pleasuring is a voluntary activity in which coercion has no place. If you feel pressured or coerced by your partner concerning fellatio ("blow jobs") you need to confront him—preferably outside the bedroom in a nonsexual context. It is easier to be rational and assertive with your clothes on, sitting up, than while nude, lying down, in bed. He needs to listen to your sexual feelings and requests, but you need to listen to his feelings and requests also. In a good sexual relationship, both people have a veto power that allows them to say no to anything that causes pain or discomfort.

It is easier to deal with sexual requests than sexual demands. A demand says you have to do it my way, right when I tell you, and if you don't there will be strong negative consequences. A request states your feelings and wants, indicates an openness to your partner's feelings and wants, and does not threaten negative consequences if you don't get your way. A demand says, "Give me a blow job and swallow my semen or I won't love you." A request says, "I really like the sensations of your sucking on my penis and occasionally I'd like to go to orgasm that way instead of switching to intercourse. I care about your feelings and comfort, and want this to be pleasurable for you. Are you willing to experiment with fellatio to orgasm?"

There is a major difference between mechanically "doing" a partner, and lovingly "giving" to a partner. There is greater pleasure and satisfaction if there is a genuine sense of "giving." You need to be comfortable with oral sex as a voluntary, giving experience that is pleasurable for you and arousing for your partner. Many women find that fellatio is very arousing, in part because of the man's arousal, but exciting in its own

It is often forgotten that oral-genital stimulation of the penis can be extremely arousing for the woman.

right for the woman. This is equally true for males giving cunnilingus. The best sexual aphrodisiac is an involved, aroused partner.

69: MUTUAL ORAL-GENITAL SEX

Pity the poor high school or college graduate in 1969. They really tired of "class of 69" jokes. The 69 position—which involves giving and receiving oral-genital sex at the same time— is one of the most maligned of sexual techniques. It has the positive connotation of wild, abandoned sex. Yet, it also has the "dirty" connotation that nice women wouldn't do this unless really out of control, that it's an "animalistic" act.

Sixty-nine is an excellent example of multiple stimulation. Many women find that as their arousal builds through cunnilingus, they become more involved in the process of giving fellatio. This makes sense in that oral sex is most exciting when there is already a moderate to high level of arousal.

There are women who very much enjoy oral sex, but do not enjoy the 69 position nor the experience of mutual oral sex. They find it distracting or off-putting to engage in both at the same time. Many women prefer sequential oral sex where one person is giver and the other receiver and will switch roles later or during the next sexual encounter. Some women complain that they can't enjoy the sensations of cunnilingus because they're distracted by having to give fellatio. Others note that when the woman becomes very aroused, her rhythm of fellatio is too hard or demanding for the male. Conversely, the woman might feel the man is not sensitive in giving cunnilingus because he's too caught up in his fellatio rhythm.

Julia

Julia is a thirty-six-year-old divorced attorney who has been in a living-together relationship for the past twenty-two months. Her first experience with oral sex was as a seventeen-year-old high-school senior. Julia had liberal parents who encouraged independence and setting her own path in life. They had been active sex educators for Julia and her older sister. However, when the older sister had an unwanted pregnancy and abortion

Mutual oral-genital stimulation is one of many ways to heighten arousal level.

at age sixteen, they urged Julia not to begin intercourse until she was at least eighteen and in college. This made good sense to Julia, who was career-oriented. She was aware how emotional the pregnancy and abortion had been for her sister and did not want that experience in her life.

Julia dated throughout high school, but she didn't have a serious, involving relationship until her senior year. She had engaged in petting to orgasm for eight months, and she found it enjoyable as long as her boyfriend was not rough or demanding. He was an athlete, but, unlike the cultural stereotype, was a sensitive, caring young man. He wanted to proceed to intercourse (he'd had intercourse with two previous partners), which Julia did not feel ready for.

In couples a generation ago intercourse generally preceded engaging in oral sex. A major sexual change in this generation is that couples will have oral sex before having intercourse. Julia found giving and receiving manual stimulation very arousing, so she felt she would enjoy oral sex. Julia was enthusiastic about giving it a try and was relieved to not have to deal with the threat of pregnancy. Unfortunately, her first experience was an extreme disappointment. The first time she fellated him, he thrust very hard in her mouth and ejaculated. She did not expect that and half gagged and spit out his ejaculate. Even more upsetting was that he did not ask how she felt or attend to her sexual needs. He was self-absorbed and distant after the experience. Julia did not know what to say or do, and she felt embarrassed about the whole situation. The next time they were together, he wanted to repeat the same scenario. Julia resented this because it was not pleasurable for her and she desired to return to the mutual pleasure of manual stimulation. What had been a satisfying sexual relationship degenerated into a sexual tug-of-war.

Julia asked her older sister for advice, but she got the standard "Men like blow jobs" line. She was too embarrassed to talk to her mother and felt inhibited about discussing sexual details with girlfriends. Her relationship continued until the summer after graduation but was much less satisfying. He kept pushing oral sex, and Julia gave in about once a month. After one other uncomfortable experience with his ejaculating in her mouth, she would excite him orally for a matter of seconds and go back to manual stimulation.

As a college freshman, Julia got a prescription for the birth control pill because she felt ready to have intercourse. During sophomore year, she had her first experience with cunnilingus. Julia liked the sensations, but she did not like her boyfriend's technique. He lay between her legs so she could not see or touch him. Julia found this position too isolating and felt like he was servicing her rather than making love to her. When she tried to communicate this, he was unreceptive, and the cunnilingus abruptly stopped. When it came to oral sex, Julia felt she had two strikes against her.

Sexuality was covered in Julia's elective course, "Women and Mental Health." She learned that over 75 percent of couples experimented with oral sex and women rated cunnilingus as their favorite pleasuring technique. Intellectually, Julia believed that oral sex could be pleasurable and she was missing out on something, but she hadn't a clue how to integrate it into her sexual life.

Julia was proud of her LSAT scores and acceptance into an excellent law school. She wanted the final months of college and the summer to be an enjoyable time for her—she felt she deserved a reward for hard work. She met a nice guy who was planning to study linguistics in Holland in the fall. They were interested in a sexual friendship that included both romantic walks and sexual experimentation.

High on Julia's list was oral sex. This time she found a man she could talk to about sex generally and oral sex specifically. Julia wanted to try cunnilingus first, but not start until she was already aroused by manual stimulation. She wanted to experiment with positions in which she felt more connected to him and could touch him. They settled on a position where he kneeled beside her and bent down over her. She preferred beginning by his kissing and/or licking her vulva and labia before focusing on and using sucking movements around her clitoris. Within three weeks, Julia began having orgasms during cunnilingus and found them highly satisfying. She was more responsive during intercourse that was preceded by cunnilingus.

Julia felt open to attempting fellatio, but she made it clear she wanted to do it as a pleasuring technique, not to orgasm. She enjoyed intercourse and the sensation of the man ejaculating inside her vagina. They experimented with a number of positions including his lying on his back and her kneeling in front of him, his kneeling and her lying by his side, and the 69 position. Julia's favorite was her kneeling while he stood. She would begin stimulating by kissing the shaft of the penis and licking the head and shaft. When he had a firm erection she would suck on his penis with slow, long movements and when he was aroused they would switch positions and do cunnilingus where she could continue to manually stimulate him. The scenario would culminate in intercourse. Julia was sad to see him leave for Holland, but she started law school with the sense of herself as a sexually experienced and sophisticated woman.

Julia met her husband in the second year of law school and from the beginning they had a sexually fulfilling relationship. She especially enjoyed sensuous baths with him followed by oral sex. He liked going to orgasm with fellatio and Julia found that she could enjoy it on occasion, especially when she was very aroused. She enjoyed the sensation of his becoming more erect as she sucked on his penis, and he signaled her right before he was about to ejaculate so she could move her mouth. Julia did not like the sensation of the man ejaculating in her mouth, although she did know women who found this sexually satisfying.

Julia's marriage did not break up because of sexual issues, but over a lack of commitment and inability to balance career and family. After the birth of her child, Julia stopped working at a law firm and became a supervisory attorney for the government, a job in which there were minimal travel demands. Her husband stayed on his seventy-hour work schedule, traveling for weeks at a time, as he strove to become a partner in a very competitive law firm. When he did not make partner, he tried to soothe his ego by a series of affairs. A good sexual relationship, including excellent oral sex, does not guarantee a spouse will remain faithful. Julia knew sex could not hold together a failing marriage.

As a single professional with a child, Julia had to reorganize her social and sexual life. With awareness of the AIDS virus, she was more conservative and discriminating in choosing men. Specifically, she had a clear and direct conversation with any potential sex partner about his past sexual experiences, and if she had any doubts about his risk for AIDS (homosexual contacts, IV drug use, going to prostitutes, or being promiscuous), she insisted he take an HIV screening test. Julia hoped to eventually remarry, but meanwhile she desired to have a high-quality sexual relationship that included the pleasures of cunnilingus and fellatio.

CHOOSING NOT TO ENGAGE IN ORAL SEX

We have emphasized the importance of viewing oral sex as a pleasurable, giving, and mutual sexual activity. What about those women who simply are not comfortable with oral sex or who have tried it and do not find it pleasurable? Sex should never be demanding or coercive. You have every right to veto engaging in oral sex. There is nothing magical about it. Some women have strong preferences for manual, intercourse, or rubbing stimulation, and find oral stimulation either does nothing for them or is uncomfortable. You needn't be apologetic or defensive about your preferences—you have a right to them.

Some women find there are elements of oral stimulation they enjoy, and other elements they don't. They mistakenly believe that if you can't be wholeheartedly involved in all aspects of oral sex, you should forgo the entire experience. Especially prevalent is the "tit for tat" philosophy of oral sex. Let us be straightforward, more women enjoy receiving cunnilingus than giving fellatio. They don't want to be called "selfish" or a "tease" so they stay away from any oral sex activity. It's in your best interest as a sexual woman as well as promoting satisfaction in the sexual relationship to be an involved and giving lover. There are ways of giving that do not involve fellatio. Other women enjoy giving fellatio and their partner's arousal, but do not feel arousal with cunnilingus.

Discuss your feelings and preferences with your partner and listen to his desires. Don't assume you know what he likes or wants. For example, some males really enjoy giving cunnilingus, but feel indifferent about fellatio. Each couple needs to establish a sexual style that is comfortable and pleasurable for both partners. It might include fellatio and cunnilingus as a regular part of their sexual relationship, or it might not involve oral sex at all. It is a matter of the woman's and couple's sexual comfort and style.

SPECIAL ORAL SEX TECHNIQUES

Ever since the porno movie *Deep Throat* there has been a heightened fascination with exotic oral sex techniques. Whether this involves taking the penis deeply into the mouth, using flavored whipped cream on the vulva, putting the testicle in your mouth and sucking on it, combining tongue licking of the clitoris with manual anal stimulation, combining fellatio with manual testicle stimulation, or focusing on sucking movements around the clitoral shaft combined with manual stimulation intravaginally, the notion is the more inventive the better. Sex magazines are always trumpeting a new "magical" technique of oral stimulation. Although we encourage experimentation with sexual techniques, we do not believe there is one magical technique that guarantees ecstasy. What is extremely arousing for some is displeasing to others. After having read numerous research and clinical reports and, more important, listening to a number of clients, here are some guidelines that can assist your experimentation.

Perhaps the most common mistake women make is to undertake oral sex according to the man's timetable. Most women do not respond to cunnilingus unless they are moderately aroused. Most women prefer to start with cunnilingus instead of fellatio, and want it to be slow, tender, and gentle. They prefer to begin with tongue licking or kissing rather than sucking or rapid tongue movements. As arousal increases, quicker, more direct, and more focused stimulation around the clitoral area is preferred. Although some women enjoy direct clitoral stimulation and some women prefer intravaginal stimulation, most women prefer stimulation around the clitoral area.

A common trap is the rhythm of stimulation follows the male's arousal pattern rather than the woman's. Cunnilingus is not a speed contest. Give yourself permission to proceed at your pace of arousal. Feel free to guide your partner and share with him where you are and what you want. You are responsible for your responses. And sex will be more arousing for him when it's more arousing for you.

Women have to realize that the way they want to be orally stimulated is probably not the way the man wants to be. His typical request is for a quicker, more intense rhythm and sucking movements rather than kissing or licking. He wants you to enjoy giving to him and become aroused with him. Males relish the experience of faster, more intense, and especially more passionate sex. Male socialization places higher value on physical expression of "raw sex" than is emphasized in female sexual socialization. For example, males are particularly aroused by the concept of the woman "making love to my penis." The fellatio position where the man is standing and the woman kneeling is exciting for the man not because it's "dirty" or "degrading," but because it gives him freedom to move and touch her as she's stimulating him. Don't do something you're uncomfortable with, but do realize that males prefer a more intense mode of fellatio than women typically give.

The issue of movement during oral stimulation is very important. Some people enjoy being passive, lying back and receiving oral stimulation. However, the majority of both women and men have a preference to be active during oral sex, especially in making thrusting movements. Some women do pelvic thrusts during cunnilingus and men enjoy thrusting the penis into the woman's mouth. Again, there is no right or wrong technique, it is a matter of stating your preferences and being aware of your partner's comfort.

Women fear gagging or losing control during fellatio. If you put any object directly and deeply into your mouth you will gag—whether a finger or a penis. Two techniques are helpful in preventing gagging. Guide the penis to the side of your mouth, toward your cheek. The second is to hold the shaft with your hand so that insertion is not too deep or too fast. Holding his penis gives you a sense of control during fellatio. Manual stimulation of the penis enhances the oral sensations. Most males are uncomfortable with teeth touching their penis, they prefer lips or tongue stimulation.

Most women enjoy cunnilingus more when it's not the only thing happening. Being totally focused on cunnilingus can raise performance anxiety with the woman taking a spectator role in her own arousal. Oral stimulation is not a spectator sport; it's an interactive, involving activity. Cunnilingus can be part of a multiple-stimulation scenario that involves giving and receiving touching and other forms of stimulation.

CLOSING THOUGHTS

Cunnilingus and fellatio are a particularly complex part of sexuality. Changing attitudes and experiences concerning oral sex are some of the most important sexual developments during the past decade. Oral sex can be one of the most intense and satisfying pleasure activities or it can degenerate into a useless power struggle. Our chief guideline regarding oral sexuality is to be open to the kind of stimulation that you are comfortable with, that enhances your pleasure, and that can be integrated into your relationship. Oral sexuality is a part of emotional and sexual expression, not a magical technique separate from it.

13
SEX IN MIDDLE-YEARS MARRIAGES

Why do the middle years connote menopause to so many people? Is menopause the most significant sexual event of the middle years? Your grandmother might have said so and maybe your mother, but for you and women of your generation it's not true. Menopause is part of what happens during the middle years, but certainly *not* the most important part.

Menopause is a gradual process, typically extending over a two-year period between the ages of forty-five and fifty-five. Physiologically your body is adapting to the cessation of the menstrual cycle. You will no longer have menstrual periods and cannot become pregnant. The underlying physiological process is change in hormonal levels, specifically a decrease in estrogen. This can cause a number of symptoms including "hot flashes" (a sudden outbreak of sweating and feeling hot), sleep disturbances (including night sweats), headaches, decreasing vaginal lubrication, increased anxiety and depressive feelings. For some women these symptoms are severe, while other women report them as minimal.

There are several things a woman can do to reduce the impact of menopause. The first is to alter her attitudes and expectations concerning menopause. The second is to consult a gynecologist with a subspeciality interest in menopuase and/or endocrinology—someone you respect and have rapport with so you can make optimal use of medical consultation. The third is to be knowledgeable about the menopause process and to actively cope and problem solve if there are disruptive symptoms. The fourth is to have a supportive relationship with a partner in which you can talk about and deal with the process of menopause.

Throughout this book we emphasize the role of attitudes and expectations in regard to female sexuality. Any sexual process is a complex interplay among biological, psychological, relational, cultural, and situational factors. Your psychological attitudes are only a part of the complex process, yet they are crucial. Too often women have been victimized by negative attitudes toward their body and sexuality that turn into self-fulfilling prophecies. We urge you to adopt more realistic and positive attitudes and expectations concerning menopause. Menopause is not the "curse" that ends female sexuality. Menopause is a normal, natural, gradual physiological process in which hormonal functioning is altered resulting in the cessation of the menstrual cycle. The net effect of menopause is to allow the woman to express her sexuality free from the burdens of menstrual periods and pregnancy fears. Menopause is better viewed as a transition and a challenging process than as a curse.

Most women think of their gynecologist as someone they go to for a yearly checkup and a Pap smear. We urge you to choose a gynecologist interested in menopause. A gynecologist who you see as competent and you trust is a valuable resource in dealing with concerns during menopause. A significant percentage of women can benefit from estrogen-replacement therapy. Estrogen deficiencies can require correction, but it needs to be prescribed with care so as not to heighten the risk of cancer. Estrogen-based vaginal cream can be of help when there is poor vaginal lubrication, vaginal itching, or painful intercourse.

If there is a specific problem, a gynecologist who knows your medical history and situation can provide an appropriate referral. There is an ongoing argument whether a female or male gynecologist is preferable. Our answer is the most important variable is that the gynecologist be competent and have a specific interest in working with middle-years women and menopause. She or he should be someone you trust and have rapport with. An uninterested or condescending gynecologist, whether male or female, is best avoided.

There have been a number of excellent books recently written on menopause including Cutler, Garcia, and Edward, *Menopause: A Guide for Women and Men Who Love Them* and Budoff, *No More Menstrual Cramps and Other Good News.* The more aware and knowledgeable you are, the better. The most important factor is taking care of your general health—maintaining a regular sleep pattern, healthy eating, regular exercise, not smoking, if you drink doing so moderately, and having a regular and satisfying sexual life. When symptoms do occur and are disruptive, for example, hot flashes, accept the symptom as a time-limited nuisance. You need not be stigmatized or feel embarrassed by the symptoms. They are best viewed as unpleasant, but temporary, phenomena that you can actively cope with rather than passively allowing them to control your life and activities.

Males are fond of blaming all difficulties on "female problems." Contrary to popular myth, there is not a "male menopause." Males are able to impregnate into their sixties and later. The hormonal changes occurring with males are more gradual and less pronounced than those of menopause. Males have wrongly used this as evidence that they are the stronger, more stable sex not susceptible to "raging hormones." In truth, males are less aware of their bodily functioning than females, and males are awash in myths about female sexuality. Don't feel victimized by your partner's jokes and misinformation. Make it clear that you want him to obtain correct information about menopause and be supportive of you in dealing with this life transition. You need not tolerate being the butt of his jokes. Being supportive means he must listen to your feelings, encourage you to pursue a health regimen, help you problem solve and cope when you do experience symptoms, and "be there" for you in an emotionally caring manner.

Menopause is a challenge and opens the door to a new chapter in sexual expression. Being unencumbered by a menstrual period and no longer fearing pregnancy creates a new freedom. Rather than menopause ending a woman's sexual life, it can serve as a good transition into the middle years and continuing sexual enjoyment.

THE REAL ISSUES IN MIDDLE-YEARS SEXUALITY

Now that we have tried to lay to rest the myths and misconceptions about menopause, let us examine some factors that enhance middle-years sexuality and identify some traps that can inhibit it. Researchers consider the middle years as those be-

It is important for a middle-age woman to overcome the fallacy of a youth-oriented sexual culture.

tween forty-five and sixty. As we were writing this book Barry turned forty-five, and even though Emily has two years to go, both of us are looking forward to experiencing what we are writing about.

The most important factor in middle-years sexuality is the woman's acceptance of her body and openness to sexual pleasure. When it comes to sexuality, we are a youth-oriented culture. The image of the beautiful, desirable woman is one with firm breasts, no wrinkles, and no body fat. The only forty-five-year-old women who qualify by those criteria are beauty- and body-obsessed—and frankly we don't find those attractive personal characteristics.

What makes someone sexual? It's the woman's openness to sensual touching and to giving and receiving sexual pleasure. A woman broadly defines sexuality by the way she talks, thinks, and feels about herself and her partner. Physical attractiveness is certainly a factor, but even more important is how a woman carries herself and how she feels about her body image.

A religious, conservative middle-years friend of ours commented that when she was growing up women were taught to downplay their bodies and sexuality. You were expected to dress in a matronly, nonattractive manner or you were accused of being vain. As an adult woman she was shocked and pleased by how much she enjoyed sex and how good she felt about her body. Her joyfulness with sex was good for her self-esteem and for her marital relationship. Her husband told stories of men who were dissatisfied with their lives and after drinking would admit they were having trouble with desire, erection, or orgasm. He was glad his wife saw herself as a sexual woman because that enhanced his sexual interest and functioning. One of our favorite one-liners is that as people age, "they are less good sexual athletes, but better lovers." Middle-years women have greater comfort and confidence in their sexuality than they did at twenty. They don't have to pretend to be virginal or naïve. Sexuality fully belongs to the woman.

Another potential advantage is a greater sense of security in the marital relationship. This gives women freedom to be more sexually experimental and expressive. One of the hoaxes perpetrated on women is the belief that men need sexual variety and women cling to the relationship and ignore sexuality. Middle-years women value sexual variety in the context of a stable and emotionally connected relationship. The middle-years married woman might not gloat, but she understands she was right all along—sexuality works best when it combines the sense of fun and experimentation with a stable, intimate marriage. If she could only convince her partner—but more on that subject later.

A related issue is the role of responsibilities. Middle-years women are often squeezed in terms of feeling responsible for their aging parents as well as their adolescent or young adult children. In addition, their own careers are blossoming. With conflicting roles and demands, it is easy to deemphasize sex. This would be a mistake and loss. Sexuality has three positive functions in the middle years—as a shared pleasure, a reinforcer of the intimate bond, and a tension reducer. The latter function has been attributed primarily to men, but now women feel free to see it as legitimate for themselves. Making time for a sexual date rather than being overwhelmed by varied responsibilities can help reenergize you and the marriage. The popularity of a weekend away without children actually increases as children become adolescents. Sexuality is a vehicle to say, "I'm a person with my own feelings and needs. I can be a responsible adult as well as a playful sexual woman." One of the best sex-education messages for adolescent children is knowing that their parents are an active sexual couple.

Another advantage of middle-years sex is that it's an interactive, cooperative process and less a sexual performance. Women used to envy and resent the man's ability to achieve spontaneous erection. His desire, arousal, and orgasm seemed independent of her, while hers required her partner's cooperation and stimulation. The female view of sexuality has proven to be the better one. As men and women enter the middle years, sex becomes a more cooperative, interactive experience. The woman welcomes this but for many men, especially those trapped by macho beliefs, it is a very difficult transition. Seeing your spouse as a better lover when he needs more from you and gives more to you sets the stage for satisfying sexual expression not just in the forties and fifties, but in the sixties, seventies, and eighties.

Taking time to be sexual is yet another advantage. Sex need not be a rushed, silent experience late at night after the children are asleep. You have the house to yourself. Rather than searching for a babysitter, your adolescents are babysitters. You might have an hour or two to make love in the middle of the day. The question is whether you can relax and give yourself permission to enjoy the sexual experience without feeling guilty about what you "should" be doing, i.e., chores like paying bills, putting up wallpaper, volunteering for a community project. You need to attend to what is in your best interest first (including your best sexual interest) rather than doing other things first. A crucial balance in adult life is between doing good for yourself and doing good for others. Traditionally, women have first done for others, and not taken good enough care of themselves. In the long run you will have more to contribute to others when you take good care of yourself.

Is the quality of sex really better in the middle years? Can the woman between the ages of forty-five and sixty feel good about her body and sexual expression or is that a new sexual myth? We do not want to set unrealistic sexual expectations, but there is little doubt that a woman can have a high-quality sexual relationship during the middle years. There are two key components to this process: the first is for the woman to value sexuality, to see her body as desirable and attractive, and to give herself permission to be freer in her sexual expression. The second is to have a secure bond with her partner where she feels both attractive and attracted. For most middle-years women sexuality exists in the context of a relationship. If the woman doesn't value the relationship, she is less likely to value the sexuality. Women see sexuality as more closely tied to what is going on in the relationship than do men. This is not true of all women and it might not be true of future generations of middle-years women, but it is true of this generation.

Many middle-years women comment that their sexual lives are of better quality than when they were young. They are surprised and pleased since it's so different from what they were led to believe by the culture and their mothers.

Carole

Carole's mother was thirty-eight when Carole was born so when her mother was forty-nine (Carole's present age), Carole was eleven. She can still remember thinking how very old forty-nine was and could never imagine a woman of that age being sexual.

Carole had her children at a younger age, so at forty-nine she has one daughter who is twenty-five and married and a twenty-two-year-old son who is a senior in college. She very much enjoyed the "empty nest" phase. She preferred visiting her children at their place rather than having them home for a visit. When they return home they bring friends and regress to the role of children wanting to be cared for. Carole enjoyed being a mother, especially when the children were in the "golden years" of childhood—seven to eleven. Carole is loving and caring toward her adult children, but she is eager to get on with her life, including her sexual life.

After the birth of her son, Carole had obtained a tubal ligation since she was sure she only wanted two children. When her menopause began she was prepared and did not feel she was losing anything. Carole had read an excellent article on menopause and viewed it as a natural process. She looked forward to not having to put up with monthly menstrual periods. Carole consulted the gynecologist who suggested six-month monitoring appointments. At this point there was no need for any medical intervention. If need be, she would utilize estrogen replacement therapy, but did not want to alter her hormonal system unnecessarily. When Carole was feeling tired or irritated by hot flashes, her most distressing symptom, she coped by a combination of relaxing or engaging in her two favorite activities (taking a long walk with her best friend or reading a novel). She told herself that although the symptoms were unpleasant, they would pass.

Carole had been disappointed in the sexual relationship early in her marriage. Roger was interested in sex and cared about her sexual needs, but he was not a particularly skilled or sensitive lover. Carole's friends talked about how fragile the male's ego was so she did not voice her sexual dissatisfaction. Last year, their twenty-fifth wedding anniversary, Carole and Roger reminisced about the first two years before their daughter was born. Roger regretted that the quality of their sex had not been better, not only for her sake, but for his.

Roger remembered the turning point in their sexual life as occurring on their tenth-wedding-anniversary trip to Europe. He attributed it to having two weeks without children and the romance of discovering Europe. Carole agreed the trip was great, but she knew that was not the curative sexual factor.

After six years of marriage, Carole had discovered Roger was having short-term affairs while on business trips. They had two verbal blowouts; she had raged and he had placated her by saying that the affairs were unimportant and didn't change his love for her.

Carole had been a full-time homemaker at the time. She felt taken for granted and that her trust had been abused. She, too, had looked at other men, at times engaged in flirting, and on at least two occasions had seriously considered sexual invitations from attractive men in the neighborhood. Carole had not rejected their advances on moral grounds, but because she did not want the marriage to be disrupted. Yet Roger had engaged in extramarital sex with no regard to her feelings or possible repercussions. Carole hated the feeling of being played with. Roger wanted the issue to go away and to return to normal life as if nothing had happened. That simply wasn't possible for Carole. Their attempts at lovemaking were sporadic and unsatisfactory—Carole was not ready to reenter the realm of marital sex.

They received brief counseling from their minister. The story of Roger's affairs was shared separately with their best couple friends who are still their best friends twenty years later. Roger reluctantly gave up the affairs, realizing they caused more aggravation in his life than they were worth. Over the years, Roger became the unofficial counselor in his organization for colleagues who were dealing with the repercussions of extramarital affairs.

Carole decided she would engage in part-time catering to supplement their income as well as raise her self-esteem. Her contacts provided ample opportunity to have an affair and for several months she flirted with the idea. At an event her firm catered, the opportunity and a special man came together. He was two years younger than she, from out of town, clearly attracted to her, and possessing the two characteristics she most missed in Roger—a sense of playfulness and a love of the outdoors.

The first time they made love, two months after they met, was at a wilderness camping site. Making love outdoors, with a sense of adventure, without risk of pregnancy (she had by then had her tubal ligation), and repeating it in the morning when the sun had barely risen fulfilled Carole's richest fantasy. To add to the intrigue, she got a secret post office box where they could exchange love letters. The affair extended over nine months with some powerful highs (meeting for a weekend in New York and having more fun making love than ever before). There were costly lows, including the stress from piling lie upon lie with Roger, the feeling of not being as involved with her children, and her lover's increasing pressure to alter her life and spend more time with him. After six months, much of the bloom had gone off the affair. The characteristics she valued in Roger—his interest in fathering, sense of priorities, orderliness, and intellectual acuity were missing in her lover. The lover's traits—his selfishness, racial prejudice, and especially his disregard of time and money matters—grated more and more.

Carole talked about the affair with a female friend who had no contact with Roger. Carole admitted the sexual quality was better, not just because of the newness and illictness, but that he took more time in lovemaking and used clitoral stimulation during intercourse. Roger would never think of engaging in manual stimulation during intercourse. Her friend asked the perceptive question—"Can't you guide Roger and make sexual requests of him?"

Carole decided to end the affair and recommit to her marriage. Carole believes Roger never even suspected that she'd had an affair. Roger did not develop verbal skills about sexuality, but much sexual communication is nonverbal. Carole became a more active sexual partner and guided Roger's hands. Setting a different sexual rhythm was subtle, but effective. The anniversary trip was a good symbol of their sexual revitalization, but the groundwork had been set months before. Carole had ambivalent feelings about the affair, but she was glad to be done with it and excited about renewing her commitment to Roger. She would not have felt good about herself if she had accepted his affairs and let her feelings fester or if she had dealt with his affairs by assuming a martyr role. Rightly or wrongly, Carole felt she had needed her affair to reestablish an equitable power balance in their marriage.

Carole was looking forward to the next chapter in her marital and sexual life. She didn't exercise as much as Jane Fonda, weighed fifteen pounds more than at marriage, had not gotten a facelift (nor did she have any intention of doing so), and had significantly more wrinkles than ten years ago. When looking in the mirror she felt good about her body image as a forty-nine-year-old woman. She was a co-owner of a catering company that had expanded into a successful restaurant. More than at any other period in her adult life, she had time to pursue her interests. She did have additional responsibilities for her aging mother and her in-laws, but she did not feel burdened by them. She enjoyed the role of consultant to her young adult children rather than feeling completely responsible for them. She had plans and dreams about her business, traveling with Roger and couple friends, and a desire to run for community office.

Carole realized sexual roles had changed with Roger. She was the more interested partner, more easily and regularly aroused, and she enjoyed being orgasmic as much, if not more, than Roger. Carole did not intimidate Roger; her sexual enthusiasm and skill was welcomed by him.

The quality of their sexual life was not only better than most of their friends', but better than it had been in their twenties. Roger enjoyed Carole taking the sexual initiative and being creative in their lovemaking scenarios (a role she would have been self-conscious about years ago but very much enjoyed now). She would initiate ''nooners'' or take advantage of a luxurious hotel room provided free as part of a catering contract. These experiences put spice into their sex life. Carole enjoyed special touches in their bedroom (a scented candle, an X-rated movie on the VCR, a special lotion to rub on his body).

Carole guided Roger in using clitoral stimulation during intercourse. They would vary intercourse positions occasionally to include the sitting/kneeling position, variations on rear-entry, and her special position of Roger lying on his back and Carole guiding his penis in while she was sitting with her back to him. This was a particularly physical and ''animalistic'' position that Carole found highly arousing. Carole valued emotional intimacy, but she also felt free to be physical and erotic. Carole looked forward to being sexual with Roger for the next twenty years.

DEALING WITH DIFFICULT ISSUES IN MIDDLE-YEARS MARRIAGE

In an ongoing marriage, the couple inevitably face frustrations and disappointments both in the sexual and nonsexual realms. Sex should not be used to get even with or back at your spouse. That's a self-defeating strategy that robs you of sexual pleasure and drains the relationship of healthy feelings.

One of our most helpful guidelines is to deal with nonsexual problems outside the bedroom with your clothes on. Issues concerning careers, children, money, in-laws, personal habits, time commitments, etc., are much better dealt with in this context. Sometimes all the discussion in the world will not resolve a problem. And it can have a direct effect on the sexual relationship. Dealing with chronic problems—health issues, a difficult adolescent child, financial stresses, arguments with couple friends, etc.—drains energy from a sexual relationship. We suggest sex not be used to exacerbate the problem or to solve it. It is better to acknowledge that this is a difficult, draining matter (accepting reality is better than pretending), but not to let it control your life. The problem will not last as long as your relationship, and it shouldn't be allowed to dominate your sexual life.

Chronic problems are even harder to cope with when they involve sexuality. The traditional view was that women had more sexual problems as they aged than did men, but that's not true. As males enter the middle years they are vulnerable to developing sexual difficulties. Males can experience a loss of desire, difficulty in achieving erection, and problems with ejaculation. This is primarily because the man has learned to be sexual in an automatic and autonomous manner, and that simply doesn't work for men over forty-five. In the short run the double standard inhibits sexual development and expression for the young woman, but in the long run the double standard causes more trouble for middle-years males.

Often the first reaction to a male sexual problem is for the man to blame the woman and for her to blame herself. That is both self-defeating and incorrect. Each person is responsible for her or his own sexuality. It is not the woman's fault that the dysfunction has developed nor is it her role to be a surrogate therapist and "cure" him. Another self-defeating reaction is to be overly sympathic and tell him that sex doesn't matter, you only want closeness. He does not need someone to "mother" him. Being overly sympathetic and avoiding sexual touching only serves to ensure that you will be a nonsexual couple. The best reaction is to continue to express sexual interest and enjoy the sexual interaction for yourself. Your sexual life need not be controlled by the sexual problem.

You need to be together as a team, and to refocus on sexual comfort and pleasure rather than sexual performance. If the problem isn't resolved in three to six months, we advise seeking professional sex therapy. Chronic sexual problems are harder to treat because over the years overlays of frustration, hurt, blaming, and avoidance have developed. The woman did not cause the sexual problem, but she can be an active, cooperative partner in helping him (and them as a couple) regain sexual comfort and confidence.

MIDDLE-YEARS SEXUALITY AS A BRIDGE TO AGING

If you can maintain these attitudes and skills in the middle years, you will build a solid bridge for the transition to sex after sixty. Guidelines concerning acceptance of your body, reinforcing the couple bond, setting aside time to be sexual, emphasizing a broader approach to sexuality, and being a communicative, giving, pleasure-oriented, intimate team provides a solid base for sexuality and aging.

14
SEX AND THE AGING WOMAN

Sex and youth—they sell everything from cars to cigarettes. The American model of physical beauty excludes women over thirty. Can you imagine a sixty-year-old *Playboy* centerfold? It's a shame that media sources like *Playboy* have such power over our definition of feminine beauty.

There is a significant gender bias in regard to aging. The older man is described as "distinguished." Older men are not considered candidates for facelifts—that is the domain of women. It's women who are encouraged to buy and utilize a variety of facial creams, have surgery on everything from breasts to buttocks, go to "fat farms" to starve off excess weight, and hide their age from everyone, even family members. Ours is an "ageist" culture, especially concerning the attractiveness and sexuality of older women. People assume a younger man dates an older woman only for money—"he must be a gigilo." The roles of older women are as caretakers for their husbands and grandmothers for young children. A widowed older woman is viewed with pity as a "dried-up prune." She is not thought of as having an independent life of her own, much less a sexual life. The assumption is that if an older woman does not have a husband, she has to be celibate. What an irony that the premarital double standard is also dominant for women over sixty!

How far is this cultural image from reality? Very far! You are a sexual person from the day you're born to the day you die. Women experience fewer sexual changes with aging than do men. Women can be and are sexual into their sixties, seventies, and eighties, whether married, divorced, widowed, or single. Not only can women function sexually, but sexuality can be a joyful, integral part of their lives. The major enemy of older women's sexuality are myths, cultural stereotypes, and being controlled by the prejudices of men.

SEXUAL CHANGES WITH AGING

Let us consider some physical changes that affect women sixty and older. The great majority of women have completed the menopause process by age fifty-five. Pregnancy fears and menstrual periods are a thing of the past. Although estrogen-replacement therapy continues to be a complex and controversial issue, you can establish a working relationship with a gynecologist or endocrinologist to evaluate your medical situation. By sixty hormonal function is usually successfully regulated. For women with concerns about vaginal lubrication, topical estrogen creams or water-soluble (nonallergenic) lotions can be utilized as a lubricant. Pubococcygeal muscle exercises can keep the vaginal walls better toned and more elastic and can reduce any problems of pain during intercourse.

For most women physical changes with aging have a minimal effect on sexual activity and orgasmic capacity. The major change is taking longer and requiring more varied genital stimulation to reach levels of sexual arousal. This change need not be viewed as a deficit; be aware there are positive benefits. One of the prime advantages of aging for women (as well as men) is that sexuality is less of a time-focused performance and more of a sensual, pleasure-oriented experience. A psychological advantage of the aging process is that you have more time and privacy, which can be converted into a major sexual advantage. It allows you to enjoy pleasure-giving and pleasure-receiving and gives your body time to develop arousal and lubrication. This is of great importance with your partner because the physiological changes experienced by males are greater than those for females. One major change involves erections. Erectile response is slower and requires more direct penile stimulation. Secondly, the man has a lessened need to ejaculate at each sexual opportunity. Understanding and accepting these changes will facilitate pleasure-oriented sexual experiences. Taking more time for sexual expression and focusing on sexual pleasure rather than sexual performance will make sexuality a more physically and emotionally satisfying experience for both partners.

Another important consideration is the side effects of diseases and medications. No disease causes sexual functioning to totally cease, but being ill will alter it. The major effect of illness and disease is on sexual desire. When a woman is feeling bad about her body or body image, sexual desire is affected. You may no longer think of your body as a source of pleasure. If you are ill, especially with a chronic disease, you may focus on discomfort and symptoms and lose your sense of bodily pleasure.

Side effects of medication can have even more negative effects on sex than the illness itself. For example, some medications used to treat high blood pressure occasionally decrease genital vascular functioning and therefore interfere with sexual arousal. Several other medications can interfere with sexual desire and vaginal lubrication. The effects of illness and medication have been more thoroughly studied in males than females. Males are more performance-oriented than women, and are particularly sensitized to erectile performance, the most common side effect of medication. A common female complaint is that when males develop erection problems (commonly termed "impotence") they become obsessed with a sense of failure and stop being sexual.

Aging itself does not cause the cessation of erections or sexual interest. When couples cease having sex in 96 percent of cases it is because the male decides to stop. He doesn't announce it as such, but rather stops initiating and avoids it if the woman initiates. The man has decided that since sex is no longer easy and automatic it is not worthwhile. Rather than talking to his partner and working with her, he unilaterally quits the sexual team. For some women this is acceptable and even a welcome relief from an unsatisfying sexual life. However, many women want to continue active sex. Even if there is to be no sexual intercourse, they still desire sensual and affectionate touching. Some women want to engage in manual or oral stimulation to orgasm, and they find it frustrating that their partner takes the stance of intercourse or nothing. The withdrawal from physical affection and emotional intimacy is particularly unfair and upsetting.

There is a new trend to medically assess and treat male sexual dysfunction, especially erectile dysfunction, with surgery or injections. This trend has not transferred to treating female dysfunction, and hopefully it will not. In order to function sexually, the hormonal, vascular, and neurological systems must be intact and capable of responding. Most older women and men are physiologically functional, although at a different level of efficacy and sensitivity than when they were twenty. You can swim in your sixties and enjoy it. However, you are not the athletic, competitive swimmer you were at twenty. You cannot swim as many laps or as quickly, but you enjoy the process of swimming as much, if not more so, at sixty. This analogy describes the differences between being sexual in your youth as compared to your sixties. One of our favorite sayings is, "You are a better lover as you age instead of being a sexual athlete." A very important guideline for sex and arguing is "use it or lose it," which emphasizes the value of regular sexual expression.

Ellen and Frank

Ellen is a sixty-eight-year-old woman in a twenty-four-year second marriage to Frank, who is seventy-two. When Ellen grew up she was taught that it was marriage that validated the woman and that sex was primarily for the man. Her life experience taught her that the assumptions she had naïvely believed in her youth were untrue.

Like many women of her generation, Ellen married before twenty-one and had three children in rapid succession. She'd expected to center her life around home and children, but her husband turned out to be irresponsible both in terms of money management and having affairs when he traveled on business. Tired of coping with an increasingly unhappy marriage, Ellen intiated divorce proceedings eight years into the marriage. Her husband did not pay child support so Ellen had to assume sole financial and emotional responsibility for her three young children. These were stressful years for Ellen, but she was proud of her ability to cope. At that time, divorce had a social stigma, especially for the "children from a broken home." Ellen was proud of her children and pleased that they were independent and self-sufficient.

Ellen was forty-two when Frank came into her life and forty-four when they married. In the years between marriage, Ellen had not been celibate, but she was very particular about the males she became involved with. She had had a one-night stand to see what it was like, and vowed that once was enough. She preferred having "lover" relationships that lasted for months or years to short affairs. Until Frank came into her life, she had never seriously considered remarrying. Frank was the responsible, nice guy that Ellen told female friends she was looking for. He had gone through a tumultuous divorce in which his wife left him to marry a friend. Frank had been prime custodial parent for his son, and Ellen was impressed with Frank's parenting skills. Ellen had clear boundaries between her lover and her children, and Frank did not breach those boundaries. Her young adult children commented favorably on what a good person Frank was. Their decision to marry was greeted with approval by their friends and children.

One of the things Ellen valued in marriage was an ongoing sexual relationship. She enjoyed the rhythm of being sexual two to three times a week. At first Frank seemed receptive to that sexual frequency. However, two years into the marriage his interest took a slight but perceptible decline. This trend continued and by the time Ellen was sixty, sexual intercourse occurred two or three times a month. Early in their relationship initiation was jointly shared. Now the only time sexual contact proceeded to intercourse was when Frank intiated it. Nothing was said, but Ellen came to understand that if Frank wasn't interested in intercourse, he would respond with a kiss and hug but then go back to watching television or would roll over and go to sleep.

Over the years, Frank on occasion would lose his erection as intercourse approached. He would be mildly irritated, make a joke about being too tired or having had one drink too many and Ellen would be understanding and not think much of it. During their forties this would occur three or four times a year. As Ellen thought about the past year she realized it was occurring with increasing frequency—now about every third time they attempted to make love. Frank no longer made jokes or said anything. He did begin making comments about getting older as well as increasingly noting women in their twenties and commenting on their clothing. Ellen was feeling less like an attractive, sexual woman and more like a matron.

Ellen traveled for her job, and she took advantage of the time away and privacy to engage in masturbation. Her body responded to her touches and rhythmic stimulation and she was readily orgasmic. Her arousal pattern was not very different from when she had met Frank eighteen years before. What had changed was Frank's interest and response. Ellen still felt love and attraction for Frank. She appreciated his companionship and that he was an affectionate person. However, she missed being sexual. If there was not to be intercourse, Frank was uninterested in other sensual or sexual touching.

After considering the state of sexuality in her marriage and discussing the issues with her two closest female friends—one married and one divorced—Ellen decided she needed to deal with Frank about it. She did not want to put Frank down or make him defensive, but she did want more sensuality in her marriage. Instead of focusing on the erection concern, she emphasized enhancing their sexual relationship.

Ellen had read that taking a shower together is a nonthreatening step in reintroducing sensuality in a marriage. One evening when Frank was about to get into the shower, Ellen surprised him by asking if she could join him. Frank was intrigued especially when Ellen suggested washing his back. They kept it light and fun, and afterward did some pleasurable kissing and teasing genital touching. The next day on a walk, Ellen said how much fun the shower had been and that it would be nice to have more sensuality in their lives. Ellen made it clear this was not pressure to have intercourse. Frank was relieved to hear that he could enjoy her initiations and touches just for themselves.

The following month was like a second honeymoon—there was an openness and easiness between them that had not been there for years. There was more playful and sensual touching both inside and outside the bedroom. Intercourse frequency went up, almost always at his initiation.

The first time that Frank again had an erection problem, it appeared they would regress. Frank did not say anything, he just rolled over. Ellen realized this was not a good time to discuss the issue, but it was important to do something. She rubbed and scratched his back for ten minutes until he rolled toward her and they cuddled and caressed. Ellen went to sleep feeling closer and better about Frank and the marriage. The next morning she invited him for a short walk before work. She said she genuinely enjoyed last night even though they didn't have intercourse. Ellen told him clearly and directly that they could have a pleasurable, intimate time even when there was no intercourse. They could enjoy sexual touching for itself; intercourse and orgasm did not have to occur to justify their time together. Ellen was direct in saying she enjoyed giving to him and found it pleasurable to help him get an erection with her hand, or mouth, or rubbing her body against his penis. Did he want sexuality to be an ongoing part of their life? Frank said he was glad he had married Ellen—that she added spice and joy to his life. He felt lucky to have such an honest wife and an involved sexual partner.

Ellen realized that if their sexual relationship was going to flourish it would require her active initiation and involvement. Erections were not her responsibility. Frank, like so many men, was too performance-oriented in his approach to sexuality. However, she didn't have to fall into that trap—she wanted to give herself and them the freedom to enjoy a range of sensual and sexual experiences.

SEXUAL ISSUES FOR WOMEN WITHOUT REGULAR PARTNERS

The reality for many and, as they age, most adult women is they will be widows. Women live an average of eight years longer than men. For single, divorced, or widowed women over age fifty-five, only about 5 percent will remarry. The realistic expectation is that the woman organizes her personal, sexual, and social life with the intention of remaining single. We do not suggest that she fall into the cultural stereotype of the asexual woman. You have choices available to you—both in terms of self-image and how to express your sexuality. You can attend to your weight, exercise, and clothing. You can be proud of your body image at sixty-five, seventy-five, or eighty-five—not by trying to look forty-five, but by accepting the reality of your age and dressing and carrying yourself in a comfortable and attractive way.

The key is feeling good about yourself and your body based on your own standards, not those of the youth-oriented media.

You need to compare yourself with yourself, not with an ideal image of the perfect, unwrinkled woman who is trying to look like her daughter rather than herself. Sexuality is not a function of the perfect body, but of a positive, comfortable self-image and an openness to giving and receiving sensual and sexual touch.

The topic of masturbation among older women is one of our culture's strongest taboos. Yet masturbation is the most frequent sexual outlet among single, divorced, and widowed older women. Masturbation is the most practiced and least acknowledged sexual behavior of women and men, married and single. Why the embarrassment? It goes back to adolescence when sex was giggled about. Masturbation was present then also, but was not acknowledged even to your best girlfriend. Once you become an adult the expectation is you will have intercourse and abandon masturbation. The reality is that in adulthood masturbation rates increase for both married and single women. It is both appropriate and healthy to engage in masturbation as an older woman. It keeps you in touch with your sexuality and your body's capacity for pleasure and orgasm. The new term for masturbation is "self-pleasuring," and it describes the experience well. It is a pleasurable way to experience your body and the easiest way for women to reach orgasm.

What about dating and sexual affairs? The typical complaint is that all the good men are taken. Although you might not feel your choices are ideal or conform to the norm of dating men who are potential marriage partners, you do have choices. Perhaps the most common choice is to have an active social life that does not involve dating. It might include engaging in activities with female friends, extended family, adult children and/or grandchildren, organized social groups, by yourself and/or a club or church group. Men can be viewed as friends, not as potential dates or lovers.

Other women enjoy traditional dating arrangements, either as a couple or with a group of couples. Some favor dates of convenience—accompanying a man you might enjoy socially or as a companion for a dance or dinner, but not someone you feel sexually interested in. The man might be a neighbor, someone from work, an organization you belong to, or a friend from your married days.

Many women prefer to date men they can develop a sexual relationship with. The cynical joke is that the only sixty-year-old single men are alcoholic, gay, or extremely dependent. The truth is that there are a variety of available men, including those recently divorced or widowers. There are men who have active professional lives and enjoy sexual friendships with women. There are men who are younger than yourself. Another option is to date men who are married. These choices depend on your values, interests, and the availability of appropriate dating partners. Although you need to consider advice from others, especially good friends, your judgment must ultimately determine your choice.

The concept of "sexual friendships" is helpful in thinking about dating patterns and sexual involvements. Ideally, most women would prefer a level A relationship—a monogamous, committed relationship that could result in marriage. Many women are willing to try a level B relationship, which is an ongoing, close, emotionally involving sexual relationship. In a level C friendship there is comfort and enjoyment, but with no pretensions of deep involvement or commitment. Some women are open to a level D relationship—being sexual with an acquaintaince or casual friend. A smaller number of women are interested in a level E relationship—a one-night-stand with a man you don't really know. Our suggestion is to focus on sexual relationships in levels C, B, and A. This means establishing a basic level of comfort with the man, where you are attracted to him and trust him to deal with you in a responsible and caring manner. It might not be a perfect relationship and it will not last forever, but it can meet some of your needs. The question to ask yourself is whether this friendship will enhance your social and sexual life. You need to have realistic expectations about its role in your life. You are better passing up the opportunity to be sexual if the cost is personal discomfort, feeling used by the man, or putting up with his drinking or poor manners.

A common trap for older women is to marry with the expectation of a vital or at least companionable marriage, and to discover their new spouse did not want a partner, but a "caretaker." These women find that being single and dealing with loneliness is much preferable to the severe loneliness and responsibility of being in a caretaker marriage.

Jeanette

Jeanette became a widow at age fifty-two when her husband of thirty years died of a heart attack. Although theirs had been far from a perfect marriage, Jeanette did very much miss him. His death coincided with their children leaving home, and it was a difficult two-year adjustment period. Jeanette had money from life insurance and the sale of her home, but she was not financially carefree. Her job as a salesperson in a craft shop was satisfying but not lucrative. Jeanette decided against pursuing a more challenging and financially rewarding career—a decision that was made with a good deal of ambivalence. If she had to plan her life over again or had been five years younger, she would have entered a medical technician training program.

Sexually, Jeanette felt nothing for over a year, which she correctly attributed to the grieving process. She was a healthy, alive person and was pleased, although a bit uneasy, with her renewed sexual thoughts and fantasies. She went to a movie with three female friends and felt turned-on by a sexy scene. She joked about how erotic the scene was and that night in bed she touched her breasts and vulva. Although she did not proceed to orgasm, it was satisfying. Two nights later she masturbated to orgasm, and she felt as if her body had awakened from a long sleep. Jeanette began a regular rhythm of masturbating one to three times a week using images of past lovemaking, fantasies about men (usually much younger) she had seen on the street, and reading and rereading erotic sections from novels.

As her body reawakened, so did her interest in dating. Her social life revolved around extended family get-togethers and gardening and historical-society activities. In these social activities females vastly outnumber males. In her third year of widowhood, one of her friends died of a stroke. She did not know the friend's husband well, but she offered him her help. She was not surprised when he called and asked for assistance in weeding and replanting his flower garden. Jeanette found him attractive and he was a witty fellow. After working in the garden, they had a beer and an enjoyable chat. A week later, he called to invite her to a dinner dance. Jeanette hadn't been to a social event like that for years and was very enthusiastic. He drank too much and was a poor dancer, but she was willing to ignore those factors because she enjoyed meeting his friends and being part of a couple again. She enjoyed his kisses and hugs that night. A major source of upset was that he would not let her drive home, insisting that he was not impaired.

Since he was the only man expressing interest in her, Jeanette fell into the pattern of going out with him two or three times a week. Jeanette felt ready to advance the sexual relationship, but since he didn't initiate she did not push it. She met his adult children and went to his high-school reunion. Jeanette found this a worthwhile friendship, but considered it in the C level. Four months into the relationship, after a party where he again had too much to drink, he surprised her by initiating intercourse. Jeanette was open to sex, but she found him a rushed and clumsy lover. He had trouble with an erection, tried to force intromission, and ejaculated in the process. She was not upset nor critical toward him or the sexual experience.

Jeanette was shocked the next day when he proposed marriage. Although flattered, she was wary. She'd seen one of her best friends enter into a marriage and become trapped in the caretaker role and had seen an acquaintance who had rushed into marriage only to find that after the ceremony the man changed dramatically. Jeanette suggested they spend more time together, including overnights, but he seemed reluctant. Whenever Jeanette raised issues about their life together, he said he loved her and it would be good, but ignored her request to discuss specifics. Sexually, nothing changed. There were no sensuality or pleasuring experiences. He'd initiate intercourse only when drinking, and it continued to be very performance-oriented. Her sexual feelings and needs were being ignored. Attempts to talk about the emotional and sexual relationship were sidetracked.

He began putting subtle and not so subtle pressure on Jeanette to marry. He brought up his proposal to her friends and family, who told Jeanette that such an offer didn't come along often and to take advantage of it. However, the more she got to know him and the more activities they shared the more concerned she became. She was wary of his drinking, disliked his avoidance of dealing with issues, and did not believe he cared about developing a good sexual relationship. Although she enjoyed dating and the social activities, she decided to end this affair. Jeanette was not surprised to learn that he married someone else less than a year later—he was more interested in getting remarried than caring who he was married to. At times Jeanette feels lonely and desires an ongoing sexual relationship, but she has no regrets about not marrying that man. She knows she can have a satisfactory life as a single woman and prefers that to being trapped in an unhappy marriage.

CLOSING THOUGHTS

The sexuality of older women is still one of the most taboo topics in our culture. Although the older woman has to overcome the barriers of myth and misinformation, she can express her sexuality in positive ways. Difficulties with males, both in terms of their availability and their self-defeating attitudes about erections and women, add to the obstacles. Remember, you are responsible for your own sexuality and need to choose how you can best integrate it into your life and the aging process.

III. PROBLEMS—
DEALING POSITIVELY WITH
SEXUAL ISSUES

15
SEXUALLY TRANSMITTED DISEASES—
INCLUDING AIDS

Our culture has always used the threat of contracting a sexually transmitted disease (STD) as a way to control female sexuality. In the last few years, this threat has swept the country and the world in the form of AIDS (acquired immune deficiency syndrome). It is truly a terrifying disease. It is very sobering to realize you can die as a result of making love.

In this chapter we will try to put the topic of STDs and AIDS into an objective, rational framework based on what we know in 1990. This will be changing as more research is conducted. We will try not to exaggerate nor minimize the importance of STDs in female sexuality. Our belief is the more aware the woman is about STDs and AIDS, the more she will be able to protect her health and be comfortable in her sexual expression. As in other areas of life, knowledge is power.

THE INCIDENCE OF SEXUALLY TRANSMITTED DISEASES

A generation ago when people talked about sexually transmitted diseases they used the term VD (veneral disease) rather than STD. Throughout this chapter we'll be using the term STD because it is more descriptive and covers a range of diseases that are transmitted sexually. When Barry first began teaching a college sexuality course in 1970, the main STDs were gonorrhea and syphilis. In the 1970s herpes (herpes simplex II) began to spread and became the most feared STD because, unlike gonorrhea and syphilis, it has no cure. Herpes was and is a serious STD that affects over twenty million Americans. Now the most frequently contracted STD is chlamydia. However, all the STDs have been forgotten with the furor over AIDS, the STD that developed in the 1980s, and threatens to dominate sexuality in the 1990s. To keep this in a realistic perspective, new STD cases, in frequency, are chlamydia, gonorrhea, herpes, syphilis, and AIDS.

Do STDs occur only among prostitutes, homosexuals, and promiscuous people? This is the common stereotype which, like most stereotypes, is false. The likelihood of a woman contracting one or more STDs in her lifetime is better than one in three. The most common age range to contract an STD is fifteen to nineteen, followed by twenty to twenty-three. However, women in their sixties can and do contract STDs.

Let us be clear about one thing—contracting a STD is not a punishment for having sex nor is it a moral judgment on your behavior. An STD is a health problem, not a moral problem. If we remember that basic fact, we can examine the complex issues involved in diagnosis, treatment, and prevention in a more objective and helpful manner. Let us first consider the traditional STDs—chlamydia, gonorrhea, herpes, and syphilis, and then we will examine the new, frightening one—AIDS. Much of what we'll say about other STDs is applicable to AIDS. The emotionalism and fears surrounding AIDS is such that it is difficult for women to objectively evaluate information.

DIAGNOSIS OF THE TRADITIONAL STDS

How does a woman contract an STD? There are specific differences for each one, but basically an STD is passed from one person to the other through physical contact, especially genital contact. Genital contact includes but it is not limited to intercourse. Thus, STDs can be transmitted via oral and anal sex, in some cases via kissing or touching, and can be passed by lesbian as well as heterosexual contact.

A particularly distressing fact about STDs is that they are "sexist" diseases. It is easier for the male to infect the female. Males are usually symptomatic so they are aware they are infected. Women are usually asymptomatic so they are dependent on their partner to inform them in order to be diagnosed and treated. In addition, the effects of STDs are more severe for women than men.

Chlamydia is an organism that affects the genitals of both females and males. Females are usually asymptomatic while males typically experience a thin, clear discharge from the penis and mild pain on urination. Although it is considered the most benign of the STDs, it is the most frequent and is problematic for the woman if not effectively treated. Both partners need to be treated. If only one partner is treated, they will continue to pass the organism between them and become reinfected.

Gonorrhea (also known as "clap," "dose," and "strain") is passed by oral, anal, or vaginal contact. Again, women are usually not symptomatic, although some do feel pain while urinating and/or have a vaginal discharge. The incubation period (the time between infection and appearance of symptoms) is from two to ten days. The person remains infectious until treated. Most males are aware they have gonorrhea because they have a burning sensation while urinating, as well as a heavy whitish or yellowish pus discharge from the penis. Gonorrhea is diagnosed by a test in which a smear is taken from the genitals and cultured. A smear and culture for gonorrhea needs to be specifically requested and can be done at a doctor's office or clinic. Many women mistakenly believe it is routinely done during a gynecological exam. If you are sexually active with more than one partner, you need to be assertive with your gynecologist and ask for a smear and culture test for gonorrhea as part of your regular exam. If you are having oral and/or anal sex you need to inform the doctor so she can take a smear from either region as well as from the vagina. Untreated gonorrhea can cause severe problems for women, especially chronic pelvic inflammatory disease. If untreated, this can cause sterility, uterine infections, bladder infections, and kidney problems.

Herpes is a viral infection that once contracted remains in the person's body, although usually in latent form. Herpes can only be transmitted through contact with the infected area when the woman or man is in the active herpes cycle, i.e., there is an outbreak of the herpes sores. If the man has a herpes sore on his penis and the woman has oral sex or intercourse, herpes can be transmitted to her mouth or vagina. It is possible to reinfect the partner so that even if both partners have herpes, they should avoid contact if one has a herpes outbreak. The bad news about herpes is that there is no cure. The good news is that over time the herpes outbreaks decrease in frequency and severity. There is medication that helps control herpes outbreaks. Herpes is a "sexist" disease in that the herpes sores are harder to identify in women (because they can be internal) and women have more active herpes cycles (probably related to their menstrual cycle). Over twenty million Americans have herpes. In dealing with herpes, it is crucial to develop an awareness of your herpes cycle and refrain from genital contact when active sores are present. There are married couples where one partner has had herpes for years, but the other partner never contracts it.

Syphilis (also known as "pox," "bad blood," and "syph") is one of the oldest known STDs. Many famous people, including Christopher Columbus and Al Capone, have died of syphilis. It can be transmitted through kissing as well as genital contact, i.e., if you kiss your partner and he has a chancre in his mouth you can develop syphilis. The organism that causes syphilis can only exist in a warm, moist environment (mouth, anus, vagina, penis) so it is not possible to catch it through contact with unsanitary toilet seats. The primary symptom is a chancre and the person can remain contagious for years. Even when you stop being contagious, the disease is still active inside your body (the latent stage). Late-stage syphilis can cause severe problems including blindness, heart problems, insanity, and even death. It is diagnosed by a special blood test, VDRL, and is successfully treated with massive doses of penicillin. Syphilis is one of the few STDs that is declining in frequency because more doctors and hospitals have instituted routine blood tests.

This brief overview should make you aware that STDs are a serious medical problem that is of concern to all women, not just "certain types." Sexuality is meant to enhance your life, not cause fear and illness. You need to be aware of STDs and protect your sexual health.

Angelica

Angelica is forty-four and committed to being a positive sex educator for her two daughters, age nineteen and sixteen. She wants them to grow up very differently than she did in terms of sexuality. Angelica is realistically concerned that they have all the facts about STDs, and she's especially concerned about AIDS.

Angelica was born in the 1940s, so her adolescence and young adulthood occurred in the turbulent 1960s. Her parents came from the generation in which you had sex but didn't talk about it. Angelica was pretty sure her mother was pregnant with her at the time of marriage. She received no formal sex education from her parents, nor from school, nor from Sunday school classes. The message was "Just say no" until you're married. The problem is that's not been the reality of adolescents in our culture since the 1950s.

Sexual myths were prevalent among her female friends. At parties, the lights would go down, Johnny Mathis slow-dance records would go on, and it was "grope" time. Angelica and her friends giggled about how guys would get hard and rub themselves against the girl they were dancing with. She learned the necking-and-petting game of enjoying touching for a while and then "putting on the brakes." Angelica was smart enough to realize this was not an ideal way to learn to be sexual, but she had no adult to talk to about sexuality concerns. She made do with the resources she had. The main sex material to read and pass around were old *Playboy* magazines—not the greatest source of sex education. There were rumors of who had gotten "knocked up." Pregnant girls were stigmatized and ostracized. Angelica didn't remember any serious talk of STDs, only jokes, rumors, and accusations.

The guy she was dating senior year pushed sex, but Angelica refused to give him a "hand job" feeling that was a "dirty" thing to do. One weekend he and four buddies disappeared for a "great adventure." The week they returned there was a lot of bragging and innuendoes about being "real men." Angelica remembered feeling a curious mix of envy and disgust. The week after it turned to fright because the guy said he'd gotten "clap" and it was her fault. The relationship rapidly deteriorated and rumors spread throughout the school. Angelica was having a hard time piecing things together, but she knew it wasn't fair and was very upset about the gossip and wrongful accusations.

She was glad to graduate from high school and looked forward to going away to college. There were still curfews and rules against having guys in your room, but in comparison to living at home she found the freedom intoxicating. Life dramatically changed her sophomore year when she became involved with a junior who had an apartment off campus. This was the beginning of the "free love, free sex" movement. The late 1960s generation promised to revolutionize the world; everyone would be liberated, enjoying peace and self-fulfillment. Very heady stuff for a young woman of twenty.

Angelica did not want to be repressed like her parents. The promise of the sexual revolution was spread out before her and she dove in full force. However, no one talked about the unfortunate consequences. That year she developed a case of "crabs" (pubic lice), a common but less severe STD, and was told by a guy she'd been sexually involved with that she needed to be tested for gonorrhea. Although embarrassed, she immediately went to the public health clinic (she didn't want to see her own doctor) for a smear and culture, which was positive, and she was treated with penicillin. Contracting gonorrhea had a sobering effect on Angelica. She did not laugh it off as did many of her friends. The idea of having a disease that could permanently sterilize her was frightening because her life plan included having children. She decided to moderate her sexual life and practice safer sex. Unfortunately, it's easier to protect yourself against pregnancy than STDs. Angelica went to a young gynecologist recommended by the campus "hotline" and started taking birth control pills. She was sexually active with a steady boyfriend and between relationships would have briefer affairs.

The summer after she graduated from college, she worked at a lodge in the West before starting a regular job in September. Midway through the summer, the guy she was going with noticed an itchy rash and bumps on the base of his penis. He didn't know what it was and figured it would go away by itself. Meanwhile they continued being sexual and his rash did go away in a few days, so he didn't worry. However, two weeks later Angelica noticed itching and some discomfort from bumps on her labia. The next day it was distinctly uncomfortable. She consulted a local gynecologist who was very judgmental. He told her she had herpes, that it was incurable, there was nothing he could do, and that because of herpes she would not be able to have children. Angelica was devastated and felt punished by God for her sexual activity. Her boyfriend minimized the problem and said since they both had it they would keep being sexual with each other. Angelica was turned off by his insensitivity and the harshness of the male gynecologist. She decided to take a break from men and sex for the rest of the summer and enjoy hiking in the mountains.

When Angelica returned to work in the city, she searched for a more knowledgeable and sensitive gynecologist. He confirmed the diagnosis of herpes when she saw him at the next outbreak. He told her the boyfriend had been wrong; even if both people have herpes they need to avoid sexual contact during an outbreak. The gynecologist counseled Angelica to treat this as a medical problem and not as a psychological or sexual stigma. She could be an educated, aware patient, and over time the herpes would have minimal impact on her life and relationships. He advised her that with time there would be less outbreaks and they'd be less severe, but that she would be contagious whenever there was an outbreak. He recommended that when she was ready to have children she take the conservative approach of having a cesarean section rather than a vaginal delivery, to prevent possible infection of her newborn.

Angelica met Bill three years later, and when she trusted him enough to begin a sexual relationship, she told him she had herpes. She said he need not worry because if she did suspect an outbreak she would tell him and they would avoid genital sex until all the sores were gone. Bill was reassured by her honesty and did not contract herpes.

Angelica wants to deal with sexual issues in a helpful manner with her daughters. She wants them to have good information and access to competent, caring doctors. Angelica hoped to establish a positive, comfortable attitude toward sexuality, and from that context talk about the difficult issues of STDs, AIDS, sexual abuse, rape, and unwanted pregnancy. She did not want to scare her daughters away from men and sexuality, but she did want them to engage in sex that protected their personal integrity and health. She emphasized having a verbally communicative, respectful relationship with a young man *before* sexual involvement. Her guideline was that if you are not committed to using effective contraception, you are not ready to have intercourse. She emphasized the importance of using a condom to protect against STDs and AIDS. She told them she would be an askable parent and always be there to help.

THE ISSUE OF AIDS

AIDS (acquired immune deficiency syndrome) has caused terror in women and men, not only in the Untied States, but throughout the world. A few years ago, some mental-health people labeled the problem as FAIDS (fear of AIDS). Yet the fear of AIDS is not an irrational one. The AIDS virus and spread of the disease to women is real and needs to be dealt with seriously.

AIDS is a new disease, not diagnosed until 1980. It is a major public health problem and needs to be addressed as such. The current atmosphere of fear, stigma, and moralistic pandering to people's misconceptions by calling it God's revenge on homosexuals, or nature's way of condemning sexuality, or punishment for sexual excess, is counterproductive as well as being untrue. It is wrong to consider it a male disease and to say that the only women at risk are I.V. drug users, prostitutes, or women who have sex with bisexual men or drug users. These are the high-risk groups, but it is important for all women to realize that they can be at risk and to properly inform themselves. It is not high-risk groups, but high-risk sexual behavior that spreads the virus. As with other STDs, AIDS is spread by sexual contact. If you think for a moment about the extent of the social networks formed in our society through sexual contact, it will become obvious that most women can be at risk for contracting an STD and/or AIDS.

Let us first examine the currently known scientific facts about AIDS from an objective perspective and then discuss how you can be responsible and practice safe sex. AIDS is a virus spread primarily through the mediums of blood and semen. Although it is present in other mediums—saliva, tears, and sweat—it is exceedingly rare, if not impossible, to transmit the disease through contact with these fluids. The virus is present in vaginal secretions, but it is not easily transmittable through that medium. AIDS has spread most rapidly in the gay male community, but it is not a disease of sexual orientation. Both women and men, heterosexuals and homosexuals are vulnerable to the AIDS virus. The fact that in the United States the majority of victims at present are gay males comes primarily from two factors—the practice of anal intercourse, which is the highest-risk sexual behavior for transmitting AIDS, and a history of multiple sex partners.

When it involves sexual contact (as opposed to blood transfusions or the use of contaminated needles), AIDS is a disease carried primarily by males. In other words, the transmission is most often from male to female or from male to male. Female-to-male transmission is rare. The exception to this is childbirth—females can transmit the virus to their babies.

The carriers of AIDS are healthy people who have no symptoms and usually are not aware that they are infected. The virus that causes AIDS is called HIV (human immunodeficiency virus) and when a person is infected he will remain infectious indefinitely. It appears that most people who contract HIV will eventually develop AIDS, but perhaps not for many years. People who have the HIV virus, but are healthy, are the major transmitters of the disease. Once people begin developing symptoms, they usually stop being sexually active or practice safe sex. Since at present there is no cure for AIDS the best course of action is education and prevention. The more aware, knowledgeable, and responsible you are in your sexual behavior, the more you protect your health against AIDS and other STDs.

A common question is whether it's worth being tested for the HIV virus. If you have reason to believe you've had sex with a man who could be carrying the HIV virus it is worthwhile. There are three reasons for this recommendation. If the woman tests negative for the HIV virus, which is the most likely outcome, it will serve to energize her to actively protect her sexual health. If she tests positive for HIV virus then she needs to tell her partner (so that he can be tested) and to change her sexual behavior so that she is not reinfected nor risks infecting someone else. Thirdly, she needs to develop a relationship with a physician knowledgeable about AIDS who can monitor her health and quickly treat her for any AIDS-related symptoms. Also, it will encourage her to live a healthy life-style to retard the development of the disease. Although AIDS is not curable at present, it is now a more manageable disease.

Discovering you have a positive HIV test is psychologically devastating. Yet, if that is the reality, you need to deal with it in a constructive manner. First, you need to do all you can to protect your immune system. Choose a physician who is up-to-date on new research in AIDS and with whom you have a good rapport. The physician might recommend taking vitamins, eating healthier, and maintaining a regular exercise regimen. You should change unhealthy behavior patterns: stop smoking, drinking, taking illicit drugs. Sexually, it means using a condom during intercourse, eliminating anal sex, and limiting sexual partners. Some women decide to stop being sexual, and other women engage only in sex acts where there is no exchange of bodily fluids, for example, manual stimulation with a partner and/or masturbation and/or hugging and caressing.

PREVENTION OF STDS AND AIDS

There are four primary methods of preventing STDs. The first is to develop a monogamous relationship with someone who does not have an STD. This is the ideal solution, but it is not always possible. For example, it makes no sense to stay in a destructive relationship just because it is sexually safe. A backup to the first method is to be very discriminating about who you are sexually active with. Before beginning the sexual relationship have a frank and assertive conversation about STDs and safe sex. This requires women to be more candid about their sexuality and more assertive than they have ever been. It is in their interest to do so not only in regard to STDs and AIDS, but also in terms of preventing pregnancy and stating the positive things they want and need in a sexual relationship.

The second method of prevention is the use of the condom, especially if you are having sex with someone for the first time or have reason to question his sexual health. Condoms provide significant, although not perfect, protection against STDs and AIDS. It is important that the man has the condom on well before any genital (oral sex or intercourse) activity. Another precaution that somewhat reduces the risks of contracting an

STD is to urinate and wash your genitals with soap before and after sexual contact.

A third method is to avoid specific sexual activities. For example, the highest-risk sexual activity in regard to AIDS is anal intercourse. Unless the woman is completely sure her partner is HIV negative she should avoid anal intercourse. Oral stimulation to orgasm (fellatio), especially if it involves swallowing semen, is a high-risk behavior. If unsure of the partner's health, avoid sexual activity that involves contact with semen, i.e., use of a condom for intercourse or oral sex.

Another method to guard your sexual health involves early detection and asking for screening tests. This entails knowing the symptoms of STDs and refraining from sexual activity if you or your partner show any symptoms. You need a good communicative relationship with your gynecologist, you must be able to freely state your concerns. If you are sexually active with more than one partner your gynecologist should routinely take smear and culture, VDRL, and HIV tests.

CLOSING THOUGHTS

Throughout this book it is assumed that the best and most realistic criterion for judging if a particular sexual practice is acceptable is whether it is harmful in some way to you or your partner. STDs enlarge the possibility of harming others through sex or of being harmed by them. We strongly urge you to be aware and protective of your sexual health.

The concern about STDs and AIDS is real and rational. Like other STDs, AIDS is a "sexist" disease, in that women are vulnerable to getting it from male partners. This is not to promote hysteria or paranoia, but to make you aware that now more than ever it is important to establish a respectful, trusting, and communicative relationship with a man. You cannot let your sexual life be controlled by fears of STDs or AIDS. The basic premise of sexual behavior—to be aware, knowledgeable, caring, and responsible—will serve you well in dealing with the issue of STDs and AIDS.

16
RECLAIMING SEXUAL DESIRE

Inhibited sexual desire became the "hot" sexual issue of the 1980s. This was no surprise to the approximately one-third of women who have difficulty positively anticipating being sexual. It validated what many women had been saying for the past twenty years—the major media focus was on orgasm, but women knew that the core of the problem was not feeling sexual and being disappointed with sexual experiences.

Sexual desire is a different and more basic issue than whether or not you have orgasms. The naïve assumption was that if you could teach a woman to have orgasms or if the man was such a good lover that he would give his partner an orgasm everything would be great sexually. We've created a new "sophisticated sex myth"—that the only thing women need to feel satisfied sexually is to have an orgasm. It is not orgasm that causes sexual desire, and orgasm is not the solution to the problem of inhibited sexual desire.

Occasional lack of sexual desire is an almost universal phenomenon for women (this is also true for men, although they seldom admit it). Low sexual desire is viewed as a problem only when it extends over a long period of time. Inhibited sexual desire is the most frequent female sexual complaint. About half of women with inhibited sexual desire report primary desire problems, which means they have never really thought of themselves as sexual women nor have they experienced the positive role sex can play in their lives. The other half report that at some time in their life (often premaritally or early in their marital life) they had a good and healthy sexual appetite, but it has disappeared or is infrequent. The problem of secondary inhibited sexual desire is as much a difficulty for males as females. Primary inhibited sexual desire is almost exclusively a female complaint, in large part because women in our culture are not taught to value sexuality.

THE BASIS OF SEXUAL DESIRE

The three components of sexual desire are feeling good about yourself as a sexual woman, believing you deserve to experience sexual pleasure, and anticipating a warm sexual encounter. The old view was that as long as the woman was in love and the man was a good and attentive lover everything would go well sexually. This places the responsibility for sexuality with the man and his sexual technique rather than where it belongs— with the woman. We are not denying the importance of having a good emotional relationship with the partner. Nor are we negating the important role played by the man's sexual technique. However, the prime factor in sexual desire lies with the woman's attitudes, values, and experiences.

The crucial element is your sexual self-esteem. Positive sexual self-esteem entails overcoming myths and misunderstandings about female sexuality. It includes an awareness of the happy role sexuality can play in your life. Sex can serve as a pleasurable experience to reinforce intimacy, and as a tension reducer. Rather than viewing sex as being only or primarily intercourse, sexual expression includes a range of activities from masturbation to affectionate touching to caressing to manual or oral stimulation to fantasies and daydreams, and includes intercourse as one of a number of ways to feel good sexually. Be open to experiencing a range of feelings and sensations both as giver and receiver. Sexual arousal and orgasm certainly enhance sexual desire, but they are not necessary for sexual desire. Openness to sexual thoughts and feelings and positively anticipating being sexual sets the stage for arousal and orgasm.

Feeling undeserving of sexual pleasure is the single most prevalent roadblock for sexual desire. By age twenty-five, 95 percent of women have had at least one sexual experience about which they felt guilty, confused, or traumatized. These include unwanted pregnancy, childhood sex abuse, contracting chlamydia or gonorrhea, being raped, poor body image, sexual rejection or humiliation, being peeped on or exhibited to, or guilty feelings about masturbation or sexual fantasy. Any of these can leave a woman without sexual self-esteem. The psychological/sexual scars related to the past can rob the woman of sexual desire. The woman fears that if her partner or her parents knew about these prior sexual incidents they would be harsh and judgmental. She feels bad about herself sexually, and her sexual desire is inhibited.

Males are encouraged to masturbate and to engage in sex to validate and reinforce their masculinity. Women in our culture are not given similar permission about masturbation or other sexual experiences. When men have negative sexual experiences (and 95 percent of men do) they are encouraged to shrug off the bad feelings. Women are not given similar advice. A bad sexual experience is viewed as the woman's fault, reflects on her "reputation," and serves to lower her self-esteem. She is encouraged to act like a victim rather than being taught to be a survivor.

Women have to learn to incorporate unfortunate experiences into their sexual self-esteem without being controlled by them. For example, a woman who contracts herpes has a sexually transmitted disease that will continue to be a part of her life, especially when she has a herpes outbreak. It can serve as a cue to remind her of a negative sexual incident and she can feel embarrassed or labeled sexually. Or if she takes the stance that she deserves to feel positive as a sexual woman, she can accept the herpes as an unfortunate, but not controlling, reality. She can be aware of her herpes cycle and realize that with time the herpes will be less active and there will be fewer outbreaks. If she does have a herpes outbreak, she will tell her partner, not be guilty, and choose either to abstain from contact or continue with sexual contact while carefully avoiding the infected area.

Seeing yourself as deserving sexual pleasure is an affirmation of you as a woman. Deserving means accepting negative experiences, but not giving them control over your sexuality. Deserving means empowering yourself to choose when and with whom to be sexual. A woman who feels deserving does not have to prove anything to herself or anyone else. If she does not feel comfortable or attracted in a relationship, or if she feels disappointed or angry at a partner, she has a right to say no to sex.

An illustration of a creative position for sexual exploration and
foreplay arousal.

She deserves a sexual relationship that protects her health (freedom from unwanted pregnancy and sexually transmitted diseases) and encourages emotional well-being (promotes her enjoyment of life and the pleasure of a respectful, intimate sexual relationship).

Positive anticipation is an integral part of sexual desire. There are three major functions of sexuality in a relationship—as a shared pleasure, to build and reinforce intimacy, and as a tension reliever. Whether she is motivated by these or something else—for example, feeling close, sex as an affirmation of love, to become pregnant, or a break in the routine—it is important there be positive sexual anticipation. Women who approach sex with a sense of dread, performance anxiety, being coerced by the partner, or a sense of resignation are burdening themselves and their sexual desire. Integral to positive anticipation is the attitude that being sexual is something that is in their best interest, and adds to a sense of personal satisfaction and enjoyment of the relationship. Sexuality is best when it is a voluntary, involved anticipation of giving and receiving pleasure. Positive anticipation of sexual arousal and orgasm facilitates sexual desire. The woman who has an orgasmic dysfunction can still anticipate the sexual experience and enjoy sexual desire. Sexuality is more than intercourse and orgasm, it is looking forward to expressing affection, sensuality, and genital stimulation in the context of a caring and emotionally expressive relationship.

INHIBITIONS THAT BLOCK SEXUAL DESIRE

There are many physical, psychological, relational, and situational factors that can and do inhibit sexual desire. The most common cause of primary inhibited sexual desire for women is not accepting herself as a sexual person. The most common causes of secondary inhibited sexual desire for women is stress in the relationship or a sexual dysfunction. Common physical causes include alcoholism or drug abuse, side effects of medication, hormonal difficulties, poor body image caused by obesity or poor health habits, and sleep deprivation (this is common in mothers of babies). Psychological causes are more common and include depression, anxiety, a history of sexual abuse or trauma, anger, stress, or a sense of dissatisfaction with one's life. Common relational problems are dissatisfactions or power struggles in a nonsexual area (money, careers, parenting, household chores), lack of trust caused by an extramarital affair, dissatisfaction with emotional expression or lack of intimacy, and disagreement about sexual frequency or initiation patterns. Situational causes include lack of privacy, being sexual late at night, fear of interruption or discovery, and an environment that is not conducive to comfort with sexuality (for example, an ugly or depressing bedroom).

Women are not given cultural permission to value sexual expression. The idea that "good girls" have to protect their sexual reputations is one of the most harmful of the double-standard legacies. In this view, sexuality needs the justification of love, or marriage, or trying to get pregnant. Sexuality as a means of experiencing pleasure, expressing intimacy, playful experimentation, or tension reduction is not "right" for women. This constricted view of sexuality makes women particularly vulnerable to inhibited sexual desire. Men are given cultural permission to be sexual without having to justify that need or those feelings. This is why primary inhibited sexual desire is so rare for men. Many men, especially as they enter the middle years or develop a sexual dysfunction, experience secondary inhibited sexual desire.

If a woman has a traumatic experience such as childhood sexual abuse, rape, unwanted pregnancy, contracting a sexually transmitted disease, sexual humiliation or rejection, a likely casualty is her sexual desire. She punishes herself for this transgression (even though it usually is not her fault) by giving up her sexual desire. This self-defeating response is based on irrational guilt. Women must permit themselves to value their natural, positive sexuality and to express it in a manner that enhances their self-esteem and relationship. When negative events do occur, they can be dealt with, incorporated into self-esteem, and not allowed to control sexual image or sexual desire.

Relational problems are a major cause of secondary inhibited desire. When the bond of respect, trust, and intimacy is breached, lessened sexual desire is a frequent response. Women learn sexual responsiveness in the context of a sharing, cooperative relationship. When that relationship is challenged, it is easy for sexual desire to decrease. The woman may no longer feel as loving or open and her inhibition is expressed sexually. What the woman does not confront is whether this reaction is in her best interest or serves her needs. In other words, even though she is experiencing stress would it be helpful to her to continue to feel sexual and be sexually active? Sexual expression can provide an energizing force that will motivate the couple to deal with relationship difficulties. Sexual desire is a way to affirm one's self-esteem while dealing with interpersonal stress. Relationship problems need not negate a woman's sexual self-esteem or her sexual desire.

A sexual dysfunction, whether experienced by the woman or her partner, can inhibit desire. Dysfunction sets the stage for a cycle of negative anticipation, aversive sexual experience, followed by increasingly long periods of sexual avoidance. As the sense of frustration and failure builds, sexual anticipation and desire decreases. This can be even more of a factor when dealing with a male sexual dysfunction. Women believe it is their responsibility to turn their partner on, and a man's sexual problem may be experienced as a personal rejection, which serves to compound the problem.

A man's dysfunction is usually not a symbol of sexual rejection of the woman. The most helpful stance she can take is that his sexual functioning and problems are his primary responsibility, and not see it as a personal rejection or her fault. She can be an active, involved partner in working with him sexually, but she has to realize it is counterproductive to give up her sexual desire and responsivity. Having a sexually desirous partner will be helpful to the man in overcoming his sexual difficulties. The couple needs to work together to revitalize their sexual relationship.

When the dysfunction is the woman's (whether nonorgasmic response, vaginismus, painful intercourse, or lack of arousal), it does not have to automatically lower her desire. Sexual desire can serve as an activating force to encourage the couple to work on improving their sexual relationship. Being sexual can reinforce the intimacy bond, while inhibited sexual desire drains and stresses that bond. In other words, reducing sexual desire serves to compound other sexual and intimacy problems. This is not to say that the woman consciously or purposefully tries to inhibit sexual desire. Most of the time, secondary inhibited sexual desire is a result of frustration, avoidance, or unmet expectations and represents giving up on the sexual relationship. Although understandable, it is self-defeating. The healthy focus needs to be on making the sexual experience more comfortable, functional, and satisfying, not giving in to inhibted desire.

Nancy

Women who grow up in loving families, have parents who are a good marital and sexual model, receive honest sex education and values, have a history of enjoyable dating relationships, avoid sexually traumatic experiences, are sexually comfortable, and have a satisfying marital and sexual relationship are very lucky indeed. Very few women have the benefit of all those conditions. A woman like Nancy is especially to be admired because she was able to deal with a number of personal and sexual difficulties, including inhibited sexual desire, and make sexuality an enjoyable part of her life. Nancy is twenty-nine, married, has a two-year-old daughter, and is four months pregnant.

Nancy's parents divorced when she was seven. Her mother was angry toward men. Mother was concerned and involved in Nancy's childhood and adolescence, but did little to no sex education beyond a talk about menstruation. Mother dated intermittently, and was more upset and angry when involved in a relationship than when interacting with female friends. Mother gave up dating when Nancy was twelve, saying men weren't worth the trouble. Nancy received birthday and Christmas gifts from her father, who had moved to another state and remarried. However, she saw him only four or five times, and didn't know what to say to him because she did not want to appear disloyal to her mother.

Nancy had many advantages in childhood, including contact with her mother's extended family. Nancy felt especially loved and cared for by her grandmother. School was positive both academically and socially, and although they did not have a lot of money Nancy didn't feel poor or deprived. She had her own room in a house they rented for years. Nancy went to a Lutheran church and enjoyed Bible study classes and the social aspects of the church. She was particularly impressed by the minister, who valued his wife and family and was very positive in talking about the role of marriage (although sex was not mentioned). Nancy particularly remembered his advice to only date boys who have the characteristics you would value in a mate (for example, those who are bright, ambitious, and outgoing).

There were no family discussions about men, sex, or relationships when Nancy was growing up. Nancy's early dating experiences were confusing, disappointing, and conflict-producing. Although she was gregarious and outspoken with girlfriends and adults, she felt shy and intimidated with boys. At fifteen she had engaged in kissing and petting with boys a year or two older. Although enjoying the touching and sense of adventure, Nancy did not like being pursued by boys who had a stronger sexual desire. Her girlfriends joked about guys and how they would push their erections toward girls, but Nancy found it a disconcerting experience.

Nancy read romantic novels and identified with the women in the stories. As she would daydream about the sexually oriented scenes from the novels, she'd touch herself genitally. Her involvement in the scenes and the sensations caused by the touching increased and one evening Nancy had her first orgasm. First orgasms are particularly important learning experiences that can enhance a woman's sexual self-esteem or inhibit her sense of sexuality. Unfortunately for Nancy, it was the latter. She had heard jokes and derogatory comments about masturbation, and she felt it was a strange and perverse behavior that was the sole domain of males. The fact that she masturbated to orgasm, and kept doing it weekly even though she vowed to stop, was a very upsetting experience. She had a great need to keep it secret because she felt she would be judged harshly by girlfriends, boys, and especially her mother. Masturbation became Nancy's major "secret." She saw it as a taint on her as a person and her sexuality.

In an effort to escape fears about sexuality, Nancy made a mistake that would haunt her for years. She became involved with a twenty-year-old man who seemed sure of himself and who Nancy hoped would guide her through troubled times. Instead, they developed a powerful dependency that nothing nor anyone could break for three and a half years. Rather than being a strong person, Nancy slowly became aware that Joe was pathologically jealous and dependent on her. Nancy's friends, mother, and teachers all disapproved of the relationship. Nancy and Joe became more and more an isolated couple. They would have endless arguments over who loved whom more, how they would prove it, and whether they would ever make love with someone else.

Nancy would have sex frequently to prove her love for Joe, yet sex was disappointing for her. Joe resisted using a condom, and he might not withdraw in time (coitus interruptus), even though he promised he would. Each month there would be an anxious week waiting for her menstrual period to begin. After seven months of worry but no contraceptive change, it finally happened—she became pregnant. Nancy felt there was no one she could tell—they would all say, "I told you so." Although Joe was very emotional, he gave neither practical nor financial help. Nancy had to arrange for an abortion on her own—a difficult experience. The net effect was a lowering of her self-esteem, feeling even more guilty about sexuality, and being more dependent on Joe.

After Nancy graduated from high school, Joe fought her mother's plans for her to go away to college. Luckily, a healthy component in Nancy's life was her interest in learning—meeting people at college broadened Nancy's perspective. She was a computer major and took an elective course in interpersonal communication for business. As she read the material about appropriate communication and heard the professor lecture and give examples of good and poor communication skills, Nancy had a growing awareness of the poor communication between her and Joe. When she tried to discuss anything with Joe he reacted with defensiveness and anger. Joe talked about himself and the relationship the same way he had three years ago. Nancy was growing as a person. She had outgrown this relationship, and it was not a healthy one for her either psychologically or sexually.

It took Nancy a full six months to separate from Joe, and even when she was out of state in college, she was harassed by Joe's phone calls and letters. Nancy was glad to be free of Joe, but she felt scarred psychologically and sexually. Worst of all she believed her sexual secrets (masturbation, abortion, and being used in a relationship) would label her as a "bad person." Nancy focused her energies on her studies, was active in the computer society—partaking in both professional and social activities—and gained a reputation as being a solid, down-to-earth person. Nancy avoided romantic attachments and built a wall of sexual inhibition around herself.

It was not until her senior year that Nancy ventured out from behind her sexual wall and began dating again. She purposefully chose a junior with whom she was comfortable, who was sexually passive, and was more involved with her than she with him. She was not sexually attracted to Bruce. Their relationship lasted over two years and they became engaged. Her friends and mother loved Bruce and commented on how much better he was for Nancy than Joe had been. However, Nancy knew something was very wrong. They only had intercourse twice a month. Nancy experienced minimal pleasure, little arousal, and no desire for sex with Bruce. She kept delaying marriage plans, although Bruce was pushing hard.

Nancy had always been a reader, and she picked up the book *Becoming Orgasmic* by Heiman and LoPiccolo. Although Nancy could have benefited from professional therapy, she felt she was young enough and bright enough to try to puzzle the sexual problem out herself. In reading the book and doing the exercises on her own, Nancy became aware of a number of facts about herself and the role of sexuality in her life. No one had ever told her that masturbation was normal and healthy. At twenty-three, for the first time in her life, Nancy could enjoy the pleasures of self-stimulation and orgasm. The book helped her confront the destructive stigma she had attached to her sexual secrets. She had the courage to discuss the secrets with her best girlfriend and a Lutheran minister, and she received understanding and support, not condemnation. The reality of most women's sexual lives is that there are incidents and experiences that are confusing, or guilt-producing. These need to be dealt with and accepted rather than allowing them to control your sexual self-esteem.

Between reading the book and talking, Nancy was feeling better about herself as a sexual woman, but this did not transfer to her feelings about Bruce or them as a sexual couple. Nancy had to face the reality that Bruce made a better friend than a lover.

At about this time, Nancy became increasingly aware of feelings toward Tim, an industrial engineer she had worked with for over a year. It was this realization and her ambivalence about romantic relationships that caused Nancy to begin psychotherapy. The therapist was helpful in clarifying Nancy's perceptions and feelings. Most important was a realization that she deserved sexual feelings and that sexuality could be a positive, integral element in a relationship. Nancy had to accept that she could not have a successful intimate relationship with Bruce. He was too passive and sexually inhibited himself, and there was simply no sexual attraction.

Nancy didn't want to just fall into a relationship with Tim. She talked more openly with Tim than with any other man about what was important to her and what she was looking for in a relationship. Touching and sexuality developed slowly between them. They slept together three times before having intercourse. Nancy was not expecting "magic" with Tim where the sex was immediately wonderful. She realized it took time and communication for a couple to develop a satisfying sexual style. Nancy was anticipating developing emotional and sexual intimacy with Tim. She enjoyed feeling sexual desire and looked forward to sex being one of the best things in her marriage.

KEYS TO MAINTAINING SEXUAL DESIRE

Sexuality cannot be taken for granted nor can you rest on your sexual laurels. Developing and maintaining sexual desire is a lifelong process for the woman and the couple.

For a woman with primary inhibited sexual desire, the focus should be on establishing a positive sense about sexuality, understanding that being a sexual woman is an integral part of life and that she deserves to and has the right to choose a relationship that will enhance her sexual expression and psychological well-being. It means confronting the inhibitions, secrets, misinformation, shame, guilt, and lack of appreciation for herself that blocks sexual desire. Some women can do this on their own or with the help of books, women's groups, or with their partner. Many women can benefit from professional therapy. Therapy for inhibited sexual desire might be individual psychotherapy, couples therapy, sex therapy, or a therapy group focusing on issues of female sexuality. You owe it to yourself to develop an image as a sexual woman and to anticipate sexual expression.

Secondary inhibited sexual desire is even more common for women. Whether caused by prior sexual trauma, the stigma of contracting a sexually transmitted disease, work stress, or turmoil over an affair or discovering your partner's affair, the conflict can be successfully dealt with and resolved. Many women view a negative sexual incident as just punishment for too much sexual pleasure, and the lack of desire as the logical consequence of sexual overindulgence (the "you play, you pay" philosophy). It's as if sexuality really didn't belong to her, and she didn't deserve sexuality as a part of her life. You need not be a passive victim and watch your sexual desire dissipate. You can actively deal with problems, and your sexual desire can survive the negative experiences.

A common pattern in secondary inhibited sexual desire is the slow loss of sexual anticipation and pleasure, giving way to apathy and eventually to sexual avoidance. This can be caused by sex becoming routine, relegating sex to the last activity late at night after all the important, worthwhile things are done (like walking the dog and doing the dishes), children, or a job taking all your energy with nothing left for sexual pleasure, you or your partner developing a sexual dysfunction so that sex has become more a chore than a pleasure, or a creeping sense of frustration with the compromises and hassles of marriage. These are understandable, but they are not natural or healthy. An important role of sexuality is to energize the intimate bond. When a couple surrenders sexual desire they not only cheat themselves, but they are less likely to devote the time and psychological energy to deal with other problems and keep the relationship on track. Sex cannot save a marriage, but it can reinforce the bond so the couple see themselves as a team and deal with the issues that confront them. When sex becomes a weapon in a couple's power struggle, everyone loses. Nonsexual issues need to be dealt with, preferably outside the bedroom. Sexual issues are better discussed sitting clothed at the kitchen table than when naked in bed.

Sexual desire needs to be nurtured by the woman and in the

relationship. She can be aware of and open to things that enhance her desire—fantasies, sexually oriented novels or movies, romantic interactions, reducing stress in her life, taking time to do things that reinvigorate her psychologically, and exercising and taking care of her body. Be aware that a couple feels emotionally closer and more strongly bonded before and after a sexual experience. Be open to touching both inside and outside the bedroom, and realize that not all touching should nor need it lead to intercourse. Rather than arguing about the frequency of intercourse, a couple can focus on the quality of their emotional and sexual relationship. They can talk and laugh, sometimes plan sex and other times be spontaneous. Especially important is establishing a rhythm of being sexual at least once a week and reestablishing the expectation that sex will be a pleasurable and energizing part of a woman's life and a couple's relationship. This combination of emotional intimacy and flexibility in sensual and sexual expression is an excellent basis for building and maintaining sexual desire.

17
DEALING WITH AROUSAL AND
INTERCOURSE PROBLEMS

The Masters and Johnson book *Human Sexual Inadequacy* was published in 1970. It set off a national debate about the role of female orgasm, which made it appear that orgasm was the only important element in female sexuality. In the 1980s the role of sexual desire and the problem of inhibited sexual desire were rediscovered. However, there is more to sexual function and dysfunction than desire and orgasm. This chapter will focus on arousal and intercourse.

The key elements in sexual arousal are receptivity and responsivity. Receptivity involves an openness to receiving and giving pleasurable stimulation. Responsivity means allowing yourself to enjoy the sexual stimulation and respond with subjective and objective (e.g., vaginal lubrication) arousal.

Central to sexual desire is feeling good about yourself as a sexual person and feeling positive anticipation for the sexual experience. Without sexual desire, it is harder to be receptive and responsive to sexual stimulation, although it happens. The ideal sexual scenario is that the woman desires to be sexual, is receptive to receiving and giving touching, responsive to sexual stimulation, involved in and enjoys the intercourse experience, is orgasmic, enjoys afterplay, and feels emotionally satisfied with the sexual experience. It is not realistic to expect that each sexual encounter will match this ideal scenario.

A number of women experience sexual desire and are receptive to stimulation, but report difficulty with sexual arousal. The traditional explanation was to label the woman "frigid." Happily, that term has fallen into disrepute in the professional community and is also decreasing in popularity among the lay public. The new "sophisticated" explanation is to say it's the man's fault—"He's a lousy lover." The old trap was to blame the woman; the new trap is to blame the man. Calling someone frigid or a lousy lover is a facile response, but blaming does not solve the problem.

AROUSAL AS A COUPLE ISSUE

As with other sexual problems, arousal is best considered as a couple issue. The woman can work with her partner to enhance comfort, receptivity, and responsivity. She needs to take an active, positive role in the pleasuring process. A key element is to communicate with and guide her partner (either by putting her hand over his or making verbal requests) to show what she wants and needs. He can be open to requests and guidance instead of playing the "macho" role of male expert.

Traditionally the woman was passive while the man "serviced" her during foreplay to get her ready for intercourse. Although some women prefer this scenario and have partners who are aware and sensitive lovers, the majority of women prefer the "pleasuring" concept. Pleasuring refers to giving and receiving sensual and sexual touching that is nondemanding and non-goal-oriented. Its purpose is not to get the woman ready for intercourse, but to enjoy a range of pleasurable stimulation that will probably include intercourse, but intercourse is not the sole goal. Involvement and comfort, help the process of sexual expression. The woman is actively involved rather than being passive. She can give stimulation as well as make requests for the type and rhythm of stimulation she most enjoys.

Arousal problems in males have received an inordinant amount of attention in the past few years. The rationale is that a woman doesn't need to be aroused to have intercourse, but a man does. The obsessive focus on male arousal and erection has not served males well, and will not serve women well. Unfortunately, our culture has labeled erection as the measure of male sexuality and orgasm as the measure of female sexuality. These performance criteria inhibit rather than facilitate sexual expression.

The best focus involves pleasuring, receptivity, and responsivity. Initially, pleasuring centers around nongenital stimulation. This can include sensual kissing, caressing, massaging, and hugging.

These set the stage for receptivity to genital pleasuring. Most couples proceed at the man's pace rather than the woman's. This is generally a mistake, but especially so for women with arousal problems. It is important to proceed at the woman's pace. Rather than the man trying to second-guess her signals, it would be preferable if, when she is receptive to genital touching, she moves his hand to her breasts or vulva or starts giving penile stimulation. She will be more responsive if initial genital touching is tender, playful, and nondemanding. As responsivity and arousal increase, she is open to more focused and rhythmic genital stimulation.

If sensual, nondemand pleasuring is the key to receptivity, then multiple stimulation is the key to responsivity and arousal. Common forms of multiple stimulation are 1) woman receiving oral breast stimulation and manual clitoral stimulation while rubbing the man's penis, 2) receiving cunnilingus while fantasizing and rubbing his penis against your thigh, 3) engaging in mutual oral-genital stimulation (69), 4) his rubbing his penis against your breast while manually stimulating your clitoral area, and 5) standing up kissing while engaged in mutual manual genital stimulation. Multiple stimulation facilitates erotic sensations and builds higher levels of arousal as you move toward orgasm.

One of the most common misconceptions is that multiple stimulation ends when intercourse begins. Intercourse can be more pleasurable for the woman when there is more than just thrusting. Multiple stimulation during intercourse can include kissing, breast stimulation, buttock stimulation, fantasizing, testicle stimulation, clitoral stimulation done by yourself or your partner, sexual talk, etc. Arousal builds when there is erotic involvement rather than simply passive acceptance of sexual performance.

PAINFUL INTERCOURSE

The most common intercourse complaint regards pain. Painful intercourse can refer to pain on intromission (entry) or during thrusting. If the pain is chronic, we strongly advise consulting your gynecologist. Be specific with her or him about the location, onset, type, and duration of the pain so the gynecologist can conduct a thorough examination. There are a number of potential medical causes of painful intercourse, including infection, tears in the vaginal wall, remnants of hymenal tissue, etc. The most common causes of painful intercourse involve problems with sexual technique. The most common cause of pain at intromission is the male misguiding the penis into the vagina. The most common cause of pain on thrusting is lack of adequate vaginal lubrication due to low levels of sexual arousal.

Why should the man guide intromission? It's your vagina and you know it better than he. We suggest the woman initiate intercourse when she feels ready and guide his penis into her vagina. One reason male on top is such a popular intercourse position is it's the only position in which the male can easily insert without help. We suggest couples experiment with the woman on top intercourse position with her guiding intromission. This allows her to move from pleasuring to intercourse when she wants and to guide his penis into her. Many women find it easier to insert at an angle (about 45 degrees) and do so in a slower, more gradual way than men do.

If there is a lack of vaginal lubrication (which is also the main cause of pain during thrusting), we suggest using an artificial lubricant. The most popular lubricant is K-Y jelly, which is used in hospitals and for vaginal exams. It is a sterile medium so using it will not cause vaginal irritation or infection. Some couples prefer to use saliva. Our suggestion is to choose a lubricant that smells good and has a comfortable feel to it. You might shop at a store like Crabtree and Evelyn and pick a lotion (labeled as a body lotion) making sure the ingredients are nonallergenic. Lotions are also available in drugstores—examples are Aloe-Vera lotion or Johnson's baby oil. Your partner can help choose a lotion that smells good and is appealing. If there is discomfort on intromission, put the lotion on the man's penis as well as around the vaginal opening. If the concern is lack of vaginal lubrication, you can place the lubricant around the vulva and in the vagina.

Using a lubricant can help vaginal lubrication during intercourse. The key element in reducing pain during thrusting is for the woman to be an active, involved intercourse partner and maintain arousal. Set a rhythm of intercourse thrusting that reflects your level of arousal. Many women prefer longer, slower thrusting—not just at the beginning, but throughout intercourse. Other women enjoy changing the rhythm of intercourse thrusting. Instead of just doing in-and-out thrusting, mix it with circular thrusting or up-and-down thrusting. Use of multiple stimulation during intercourse is perhaps the best way to facilitate arousal. Many women enjoy switching intercourse positions as a way of increasing arousal. Another technique is to engage in manual genital stimulation during the transition to a different intercourse position.

A source of pain during intercourse is tears in the vaginal wall. The vagina is a very adaptable and flexible organ. When there is vaginal pain, we suggest the woman practice vaginal exercises to increase awareness and flexibility of the vaginal wall. These exercises focus on the pubococcygeal (PG) muscle—an intimidating and unpronounceable term, but a relatively easy exercise. The way to identify the PG muscle is to urinate and stop the flow midstream; the muscle you use to stop the flow is the PG muscle. To strengthen the muscle (which improves vaginal tone and strengthens the walls), you can engage in two rather simple exercises. The first is to squeeze the PG muscle for two or three seconds and then relax it. Begin by doing ten or fifteen squeeze-relax sequences and over a period of weeks build up to twenty-five or thirty. This only takes three to five minutes; try to do it twice a day. You can exercise the PG muscle unobtrusively—only you are aware of what you're doing. Women do these exercises when they're driving, standing in a grocery line, watching their children, or when sitting at their desk. The second exercise involves "flicking" the PG muscle. This is a faster, more intense exercise in which you rapidly tense and relax the PG muscle fifty times a minute. Some women flick the PG muscle when engaged in intercourse to increase vaginal feeling and their partners report noticing the difference.

You can reduce or eliminate pain during intercourse. The entire sexual experience—pleasuring, intercourse, and afterplay—should be a comfortable one for you. There is no reason to endure pain during intercourse.

VAGINISMUS

Vaginismus is a sexual dysfunction that causes a great deal of physical and mental anguish for the woman and her partner.

Vaginismus is not a well-known problem, and women who suffer from it are often too embarrassed to seek treatment. This is a disservice because vaginismus can be successfully treated in 90 percent of women.

In vaginismus the vaginal introitus (opening) goes into involuntary spasms so that intromission is extremely difficult and painful. In severe cases, intercourse is impossible. Many women seek treatment because they want to become pregnant, but intercourse is too painful or impossible. A definitive diagnosis of vaginismus requires an examination by a gynecologist. Explain your concern to the doctor before the examination begins. He or she can observe the vaginal introitus spasms as the speculum is inserted.

Vaginismus can be caused by lack of information, sexual trauma in childhood, rape, fear of the penis, or fear of pregnancy. Treatment combines sexual counseling and physical exercise to decondition the spasming. It is crucial that the woman learn to feel comfortable and in control of her body and her vagina. Teaching breathing techniques, deep muscle relaxation, and PG muscle exercises can be of value. The essential step is gradually inserting objects into the vagina. Use of the fingers is the most common technique, but some women use dialators of increasing size that can be obtained from a gynecologist. Once a woman is comfortable with her own vaginal insertion, she transfers this process to partner sex. Her partner must follow her requests and guidance, and honor her veto power. Penile insertion is gradual, for increasing periods of time, and with slow, nondemand thrusting. Few women overcome vaginismus without professional assistance, but with therapy it is a very curable problem.

Diane

Thirty-four-year-old Diane was frustrated with the state of her sexual life. She had been divorced four years earlier. Diane's marriage had been emotionally tumultuous and destructive. However, throughout the relationship, in good times and bad, sexual desire and arousal had been high. They even had sex five days before the final divorce decree. She and her son have lived with a divorced man for the past two years.

Diane was convinced that the traditional view of love and sex being invariably intertwined for women was not true, at least for her. She had stayed in her marriage three years too long because she believed if the sex was good it must mean she still loved him. After the divorce, Diane learned things about her ex-husband that caused her to feel humiliated. He'd begun an affair shortly after Diane became pregnant and had sex with the other woman the day their son was born. Babysitters had refused to return, not because her son was hard to take care of, but because her husband sexually harrassed them. He'd had an affair with a girlfriend of hers and in one instance had intercourse with Diane's younger sister.

Diane did not relish being single again, but she was proud of her decision to divorce. She knew being in an unhappy marriage was one of life's worst fates. Her major sexual outlet was masturbation, where she had no problem with arousal or orgasm. Diane's occasional affairs had been disappointing and intercourse was painful. Two of the men were rough and inconsiderate lovers. One was a rapid ejaculator and the other had a hard time reaching orgasm. Diane did not enjoy prolonged intercourse thrusting, especially after she'd been orgasmic.

Diane enjoyed the stability of a living-together relationship with George, but she did not feel in love with the intensity needed for a marriage. He would travel for a consulting job and stay for three to six months. Diane accepted this arrangement, but it would not be acceptable in the long run. Their sexual relationship was becoming increasingly bothersome to Diane. On some occasions George had difficulty with erections and would force intercourse. Diane did not want to hurt his feelings, but she was finding the sexual experience aversive. She began looking forward to his trips. Diane found masturbation easier, more arousing, and pain free as compared to intercourse.

Diane's arousal was muted because she was not receptive or responsive to George's touch. Most of the stimulation came from her, and as soon as he got an erection he immediately moved toward intercourse. She did not feel ready for penetration. Intromission was rough and often painful. He moved very fast because he was worried about losing his erection and wanted to have an orgasm before that happened. Diane had been easily orgasmic during afterplay, but was reluctant to ask because his stimulation was unenthusiastic and mechanical. Things were on a downhill track, and frankly she did not care.

Diane was shocked when George told her he wanted to consult a sex therapist and asked if she would be willing to participate. Diane took a day to think about it and went for a picnic with George. He valued the relationship and her help with the sexual problem more than she thought. She did not enter sex therapy just for him or to be altruistic. She desired to regain her sexual arousal and eliminate pain with intercourse. George located a professional sex therapist who had a good reputation and was licensed as a marriage and family therapist. Diane was pleased the therapist was a female, although she would have been willing to see a male.

The therapist conceptualized the sex problem as a couple one, and emphasized there could be positive lessons for Diane as well as George. She made it clear that successful sex therapy did not entail a commitment to marriage. Although George and Diane wanted a better relationship and better sex, neither was interested in taking on the permanence of marriage.

Diane was responsive to the genital pleasuring exercises, especially the sexual massage, which integrated nongenital and genital caressing. With George open and expressive in giving to her, Diane was surprised how her arousal returned. The pressure for George to have an erection was removed and Diane found the sex to be more fun and exciting. She especially enjoyed the multiple-stimulation scenario that involved rubbing his penis against her breast while he did manual genital stimulation. While he was giving to her, she could touch his penis, rub his arm, caress his testicles, or rub his back with her foot. Diane enjoyed keeping contact with George, his arousal was higher when he was being touched, and he was a more stimulating lover when he was highly aroused.

The exercises that integrated intercourse as a pleasuring technique were better for Diane than George. Diane had come to dread intercourse because George had made such a big deal about his erection and intromission was hurried and uncomfortable. The therapist suggested it be Diane who initiate when to move toward intercourse and that she guide intromission. She suggested that on a routine basis Diane use the vaginal lubricant Vaginsil. The most helpful suggestion was to think of George's penis in a friendly way, as something for her to play with. The therapist emphasized penile stimulation could be fun whether he was erect, semierect, or flaccid.

A common mistake women who have partners with erection problems make is to allow his erection (or lack of it) to govern their sexual feelings. His erection is not a symbol of his attraction to you, or your desirability, or your sexual skill. He is responsible for his erection; you're not. You can enjoy the sexual experience, including intercourse, whether or not he has an erection. Contrary to popular myth, the man does not need a totally full, rigid erection for intercourse. Especially with the woman guiding intromission, and if there is a focus on pleasure rather than performance, it is possible to have enjoyable intercourse with a semierect penis. For too long, female arousal and pleasure in both nonintercourse and intercourse sexuality has been governed by the male obsession with erection. Diane could feel good about her arousal and the intercourse experience independent of the strength of George's erection.

At the conclusion of fourteen sessions of sex therapy, Diane realized two things. She had gained more than George both in terms of sexual arousal and increased sexual self-esteem. Second, although the relationship was much improved, she knew he was not the person she wanted to spend the rest of her life with. All in all, Diane was pleased with the therapy and her increased understanding.

INTERCOURSE AS THE WOMAN'S DOMAIN

In both the old double-standard model and the newer, more sophisticated sexual scenarios, intercourse is the prime domain of the man. He is supposed to get the woman ready for intercourse and receive his maximum satisfaction during intercourse. The woman's role is to be the recipient of intercourse and if she's more active, moves more, or has orgasm during intercourse, all the better (especially for the man).

In writing for males and talking to male clients, we emphasize that touching, affection, and verbal expression are part of the pleasuring process and are just as valuable for him as her. In the same manner, intercourse is as much for the woman as for the man. Whether or not the woman is orgasming during inter-

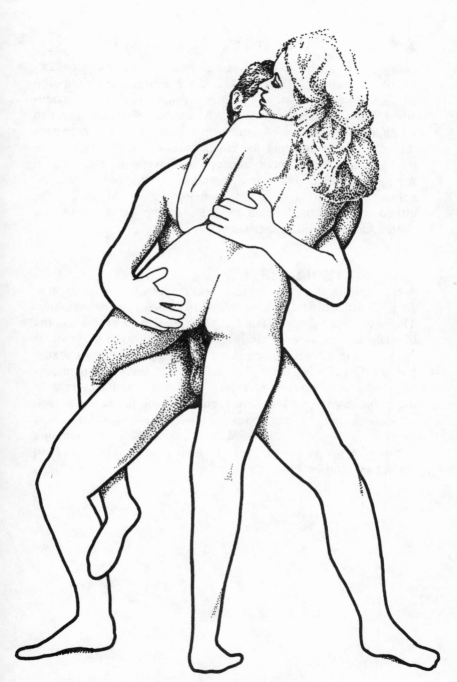

An example of a face to face intercourse position.

course, she can be an involved, pleasure-giving and pleasure-receiving partner. This goes beyond eliminating pain and emphasizes the woman enjoying intercourse as a natural extension of the pleasuring process. A number of techniques can facilitate the woman's pleasure and arousal during intercourse, including her controlling the coital thrusting, using intercourse positions that allow more freedom of movement, engaging in multiple stimulation during intercourse, and/or using simultaneous clitoral stimulation. More important than technique is the attitude between the woman and the man about intercourse as a shared, active, erotic experience.

CLOSING THOUGHTS

Our culture does not nurture healthy female sexual expression. The traditional double standard denied female sexuality. The new, sophisticated standard glorifies female orgasm as the ultimate performance demand. Healthy female sexuality involves sexual desire as well as receptivity and responsibility to sexual arousal. Orgasm is a natural culmination of involved, pleasure-oriented stimulation and emotional and sexual satisfaction with the intimate partner. We have focused on the problems of lack of arousal, painful intercourse, and vaginismus. Arousal and intercourse are best understood in the context of the woman's sense of herself as a sexual person and her active involvement in the sexual relationship.

18

YOU AS AN ORGASMIC WOMAN

Female orgasm was the hot sexual issue of the 1970s and 1980s. Two conflicting trends occurred in therapeutic and public discussion of orgasm. The helpful trend was to recognize that women had a right to expect orgasmic response as a natural part of their sexual expression. With increased awareness of female genitalia and sexual stimulation, more women experienced the pleasures of orgasm. The other trend was toward seeing orgasm as the "big O," making it into an unrealistic performance demand that inhibited sexual pleasure for women and men alike. What an unfortunate paradox that as we learn more about female sexuality, we negate that awareness by burdening it with the same performance obligation that has proven so harmful for male sexuality.

Let us state this clearly and unequivocally—orgasmic response is a natural, positive, integral part of being a woman. Female orgasm is a result of self-awareness, sexual self-acceptance, receptivity and responsiveness to effective stimulation, and the ability to let go and experience pleasure. It is *not* a measure of female sexuality, nor a performance goal, nor a means of proving something to yourself or your partner. The association is between "sexuality and pleasure," not "sexuality and performance." Orgasm is a natural result of high levels of pleasure and arousal. It is not a performance goal apart from the pleasure-giving and pleasure-sharing process.

Physiologically an orgasm is an orgasm, regardless of the means of stimulation. Whether it is achieved via masturbation, vibrator stimulation, intercourse, manual stimulation by partner, or by cunnilingus, the physiological processes are the same.

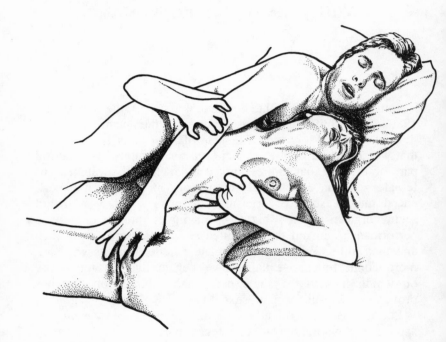

The principle of multiple stimulation heightens the woman's sexual responsiveness and enhances her ability to "let go."

There can be differences in the subjective sense of satisfaction, depending on your experiences, values, and feelings—this is as it should be. When "experts" dismiss a woman's orgasm as "immature," or not "real," or "inferior" they are stating their prejudice, not scientific fact. The plethora of books advocating multiple orgasms, G-spot orgasms, extended orgasms, six variations of orgasms, etc., are based on the wrong premise. The result of this performance-oriented, unscientific approach is to make the woman feel inferior and apologetic about her sexuality. Each woman develops her own pattern of orgasmic response that she can enjoy and celebrate rather than feeling intimidated by the "sexual experts" or the male who tells her she has to have a "more liberated orgasm." There is *not* "one right way to be orgasmic."

DATA CONCERNING FEMALE ORGASMIC RESPONSE

Sex researchers estimate that approximately 90 percent of women have experienced orgasm. Approximately 75 percent of women masturbate at some point in their life (this percentage has increased in the past decade as there has been more emphasis on female sexuality and the legitimacy of self-exploration). Female sexuality self-help groups, writing on female masturbation, and greater acceptance of vibrators have resulted in 95 percent of women being orgasmic during masturbation.

Over 80 percent of women have been orgasmic with a partner. This includes being orgasmic with partner manual stimulation, oral stimulation, vibrator stimulation, and intercourse stimulation. The most common couple sexual complaint is that the woman is not orgasmic during intercourse. Interestingly, men voice this complaint more than women. Although research studies differ greatly in their percentages—20 percent being orgasmic during intercourse to 80 percent—the best estimate is that approximately 65 percent of women have been orgasmic with intercourse stimulation. Does this mean that 35 percent of women are sexually dysfunctional? Absolutely not! Most of these women are regularly orgasmic during partner sex and thoroughly enjoy the intercourse experience. The cause of this myth is that both women and men are overly influenced by the male model of having one orgasm that occurs during inter-

The increasingly wider acceptance of vibrators has resulted in many more women being orgasmic during both masturbation and intercourse.

course. The key is to understand that female orgasm is more variable and complex than male orgasm. (This does not mean female orgasm is "better or worse.") Thus the woman might be nonorgasmic, have a single orgasm, or be multiply-orgasmic, and her orgasm could occur during the pleasuring/foreplay period, during intercourse, or during the afterplay phase.

Sex-therapy definitions of female orgasmic response accept the fact that the woman's subjective sense of satisfaction with the sexual experience is of prime importance. In these definitions, satisfactory orgasmic response in partner sex occurs when the woman is regularly (this does not mean 100 percent of the time) orgasmic in situations in which she is aroused and desirous of being orgasmic. The manner and timing of the orgasmic experience is dependent upon the woman's preferences and patterns. As long as intercourse is pleasurable, whether orgasm occurs or not is irrelevant.

Perhaps 50 percent of women who are orgasmic are usually orgasmic with intercourse (often with simultaneous clitoral stimulation) and prefer that pattern. The other 50 percent of women find it easier to be orgasmic with manual and/or oral stimulation and prefer this pattern. Of women who can be orgasmic with both nonintercourse and intercourse stimulation, their preferences are divided almost on a normal curve. In other words, some women have strong preferences for manual stimulation, others for oral stimulation, others for intercourse stimulation, and the majority report enjoying the variability of their arousal and orgasmic capability.

Approximately 20 percent of women experience multiple orgasms. This phenomenon is quite variable, with some women having two orgasms five minutes apart, other women having four to six orgasms bunched closely together, and other women reporting forty to sixty orgasms during a twenty-minute lovemaking session. Men might complain that the woman who has four orgasms is having four times the pleasure he does or four times the pleasure of a woman who is singly orgasmic. This is an incorrect and unscientific way to view multiorgasmic response. There is no evidence that multiorgasmic women experience more pleasure than women with a pattern of being singly orgasmic. The whole concept of measuring orgasms, setting performance goals, achieving the "perfect" orgasm, and comparing your orgasmic pattern with someone else's is self-defeating. Each woman (and couple) develop their own pattern(s) of sexual pleasure and orgasmic response. The idea is to develop an awareness and comfort with an orgasmic pattern(s) that is satisfying and enhances intimacy in your relationship.

Sylvia

Sylvia is forty-two years old and has been married to her second husband, Jack, for one and a half years. Sylvia is attractive, well-dressed, and quite extroverted. She is successful in her second career as an account executive for a large computer firm. Her self-image is as a verbal, empathic person who can interact with many different kinds of people. She reports a good relationship with her sixteen-year-old son and fourteen-year-old daughter, and a cordial relationship with Jack's twenty-two-year-old daughter from his first marriage. Sylvia is a religious person who is committed to the success of this marriage—she met Jack at a softball game for divorced and widowed people sponsored by her church group.

It was Sylvia who initiated couple's therapy, although Jack was a willing participant. Interestingly, men are more willing to join their wives in couple's therapy when the focus is on a sexual issue. Jack wanted sex to be a good, energizing element in this marriage because the poor sexual relationship in his first marriage was a major source of discontent. Sylvia's first marriage ended when her husband laid the blame on Sylvia for their sexual problems and left for another woman. Although sex problems are often blamed for a marital breakup, they are seldom the cause. A dysfunctional sexual relationship can drain a marriage of positive feelings and damage intimacy, but in Sylvia's case, as in many other divorces, there were more basic issues, such as communication, respect, and commitment, that doomed the marriage.

In reviewing Sylvia's sexual history, it was clear she had not been comfortable or aware of herself as a sexual woman. Sylvia's mother, who was alive and widowed, was a good and loving person but closed when it came to sexuality. She did instruct Sylvia on what to expect before her menstrual period began, which is more than many mothers do, but she was silent about sexual issues such as masturbation, petting, intercourse, contraception, and sexually transmitted diseases. Sylvia seldom saw her parents being affectionate, and she believed it was mother who carried the marriage. Father cared more about his children than his wife, but gave no direct sex education. He would tell sexual jokes to his sons, but he said nothing to his daughters other than, "Be a good girl and stay out of trouble." Most of Sylvia's sex education came from friends and stories she heard in school. The message was that boys were sex-crazed, and girls had to be sure not to get a "loose" reputation or become pregnant.

Sylvia never even heard about female orgasm until she was nineteen and a sophomore in college. By that time, she had experienced being gossiped about in high school, felt coerced to manually stimulate males to orgasm, and had an unwanted pregnancy and abortion. Sylvia did not enjoy her attractiveness and sexuality; instead she felt it caused problems and pain. She married at age twenty as much to escape the hassles of the dating scene as to express hope for a stable, successful relationship.

Sylvia did not find premarital or marital sex with her first husband satisfying, nor did it result in her being orgasmic. Yet this was the best sexual experience of her life because she enjoyed feeling attractive, in love, and the object of sexual attention. As with many young couples, premarital sex was more frequent and enjoyable, while marital sex was disappointing. Frequency declined, quality did not improve, and it quickly fell into a routine in which he perfunctorily tried to arouse her and when it didn't work he satisfied himself. Sylvia became increasingly turned off and was just as glad that the sex was short and over with. Sex was not "lovemaking," nor was it arousing or orgasmic, nor did it serve as an emotional bond. When her husband left, Sylvia was overwhelmed with conflicting feelings of anger and betrayal, as well as a sense of relief. She looked forward to the challenge of being on her own again.

Sylvia remained single for five years before marrying Jack. Although she did not enjoy the dating scene this time either, she was pleased with how she conducted herself. Sylvia was committed to not being used or abused in dating relationships. She could be on her own and take care of herself. Sylvia found it more enjoyable to go out with female friends or be by herself on Saturday night rather than be with a date who made her feel uncomfortable or defensive.

Sylvia joined a women's sexuality group led by a female psychologist who had specialized training in sexuality. The group met once a week for ten weeks and consisted of eight women who were single, divorced, living with someone, or married. About half of the women were like Sylvia in never having been orgasmic. The other half had been orgasmic on occasion, but were not regularly so. The first session was very emotionally draining, but at the same time personally validating. Each woman spoke of her sex education and sexual experiences in an honest manner. In listening to their sexual life stories, Sylvia realized that she was not alone—her sexual experiences were similar to other women's. She found it refreshing to hear women talk honestly and openly about sex.

The group leader strongly reinforced the concept that each woman is the expert on her own sexuality. A second theme was that a woman *deserves* to be sexually aware and to enjoy sexuality in her life. Throughout the group, books such as *For Yourself, Becoming Orgasmic, Shared Intimacies*, and *The New Our Bodies, Ourselves* were recommended to supplement and reinforce ideas presented in the group. Sylvia was encouraged to set aside time during the week to do the "sexual exercises." These tasks involved reading, talking, writing, and thinking about sexuality. Other exercises involved self-pleasuring, beginning with body self-exploration.

As the group progressed, Sylvia enjoyed hearing about the progress of other members. She received support from the members and group leader to continue her attempts to change. Sylvia found it ironic that as a child she was told that masturbation was the cause of sexual problems, and now as an adult, divorced woman she was learning that self-pleasuring and masturbation was a crucial step in developing her sexual awareness and responsiveness.

Sylvia found using sexually explicit fantasies increased her receptivity to manual stimulation. After three weeks the combination of feeling aware and deserving, utilizing manual clitoral stimulation along with breast stimulation, and focusing on erotic written material and fantasies resulted in her first orgasmic experience. Sylvia was excited and embarrassed at the same time. It seemed strange to acknowledge she could masturbate to orgasm. With continued practice, she identified the types of stimulation that were most arousing. In nine years of partner sex that had not occurred because she assumed that it was the man's responsibility to turn her on. Sylvia and the other group members came to understand that the woman is responsible for her own arousal and orgasm.

The final sessions involved talking about sexual relationships with a partner and what made them satisfying or disappointing. The group leader encouraged the single women to choose a partner actively rather than wait passively to be chosen. She encouraged choosing a man you feel comfortable with, attracted to, and most important, trust to be your sexual friend. The idea of thinking of a male as a "sexual friend" was novel and intriguing to Sylvia.

Sylvia's life was not a Cinderella story in which Jack appeared right after the group. Sylvia had three years of dating and being sexual. She found the concepts from the group valid and helpful, but they did not guarantee that a relationship would work the way she hoped. Sylvia had sexual affairs, some of which she enjoyed while others were hurtful and disappointing. Sylvia learned to feel comfortable and enjoy sexual experiences even when the relationship did not meet her expectations. She did not want to risk an unplanned pregnancy so continued using the birth control pill regardless of whether she was in a sexual relationship at that time. Sylvia would only be sexual if she desired to rather than feeling pressured or coerced by the man. If sex was to be good for her she had to feel comfortable with the man, the sexual milieu had to be playful with no time pressure, she needed to be aroused with manual stimulation before she could be responsive to cunnilingus (Sylvia was usually orgasmic with oral stimulation), and she preferred to guide penile insertion during intercourse.

Jack and Sylvia developed an emotionally open and intimate relationship. Sylvia had read that it took a couple about six months to develop a sexual style that was comfortable and satisfying to both partners. She realized it would take practice and experimentation, but Jack was more of an unrealistic romanticist. He wanted sex to be natural, spontaneous, and exciting (without having to communicate or work at it). Sylvia found Jack a comfortable and attractive person, and she knew he cared about her sexual satisfaction.

The fact that the sexual relationship was "stuck" caused her to seek couple's counseling. Sylvia and Jack were excellent therapy candidates. They were a committed couple and wanted sex to be a happy part of their marriage. Sylvia needed to be clear with Jack, especially requesting use of manual and oral stimulation to arouse her, and assertively tell him not to pressure her to be aroused on his time schedule. She preferred to be orgasmic before beginning intercourse, and she had to educate him that for her (as with many women), it was easier to have a subsequent orgasm during intercourse if she'd already been orgasmic during the pleasuring/foreplay time. Sylvia enjoyed the intimacy of being sexual and the variability of her arousal and orgasmic pattern. She did not feel a need to be orgasmic at each sexual opportunity—she could feel physically good and emotionally satisfied without an orgasm. She enjoyed Jack's reaction the times she would feel highly aroused and have multiple orgasms. At forty-two years old, Sylvia was pleased with herself as a sexual woman and with her marital and sexual relationship.

ORGASM AS A NATURAL PART OF FEMALE SEXUALITY

The concept that is hardest for women to accept is that orgasm is a positive, integral, natural part of her sexuality, not something you have to work at or that a man gives you. When young girls are learning about their bodies and sexuality, many receive confusing and contradictory messages about sexual interest and the importance of orgasm.

Women need to increase their awareness and understanding of sexuality. The bedrock of female sexual response is an acceptance of her body, including her genitalia. This involves both looking and touching while developing an intimate awareness of her labia, clitoris, and vagina. Masturbation is not a prerequisite for learning to be orgasmic, but it is the most direct pathway for a woman to learn about her sexual responsivity and potential. In partner sex, she has a right to be comfortable and not be pressured or coerced. A woman has a right to have her conditions for good sex met, and these include trust in the man and a sexual relationship that is based on genuine friendship. She needs to feel free from the stresses of unwanted pregnancy, sexually transmitted disease, and being manipulated or abused in a relationship.

Orgasm is a natural result of being receptive to touching, responsive to genital stimulation, and letting yourself enjoy sexual pleasure. The key concept for receptivity is nondemand pleasuring. The milieu that facilitates nondemand pleasuring is the giving and receiving of touching such as kissing, hugging, massaging, and caressing. The touching can be slow, rhythmic and tender, or it can be light, flirtatious, and playful. It can be done with clothes on or off.

Major factors in responding to sexual stimulation are feeling that the sexual scenario is moving at the woman's pace rather than the man's and that she can make requests and he will follow her guidance. Some women prefer beginning genital touching with breast stimulation, others with vulva stimulation. There is no right or wrong response—you need to identify your receptivity-responsivity pattern(s) and share it with your partner.

Most women prefer indirect rather than direct clitoral stimulation. A common female complaint is that the male gets tired of rhythmic stimulation and wants to vary it according to his desires. This breaks the woman's rhythm of arousal. A solution to this dilemma and miscommunication is to focus on multiple stimulation. The sequence of nondemand pleasuring and multiple stimulation is the preferred arousal pattern. Multiple stimulation is most welcome when a moderate level of arousal has already developed. Multiple stimulation can involve maintaining rhythmic stimulation around the clitoral area and adding other forms of stimulation such as manual or oral breast stimulation, stimulation of the mons and/or anal area, kissing and caressing, intravaginal finger stimulation, use of vibrator stimulation, and/or rubbing the penis against the woman's breasts or vulva. Some women enjoy being passive and accepting stimulation, but most women prefer to be active in giving and receiving multiple stimulation. Examples of being more active include touching and stimulating the partner, closing your eyes and engaging in a sexually arousing fantasy, moving your body in a rhythmic way to increase sensations, giving and receiving oral stimulation simultaneously and/or being in a standing or kneeling position which allows more touching and movement.

Letting go and being orgasmic includes psychological, sexual, and relational factors. Psychologically, the crucial issue is loss of control. The woman learns to trust herself and her partner and gives up self-consciousness about being highly sexually aroused and orgasmic in front of someone. Movie depictions of sexual scenes focus on the aesthetic qualities, but in reality orgasm is not an aesthetic experience. Orgasm is a personal, intense, erotic experience that lasts only a few seconds. Psychologically, the woman feels she deserves to enjoy being orgasmic and allows herself to experience the pleasures of orgasm.

In terms of sexual technique, it is important to be aware of and use "orgasm triggers." These are techniques that allow you to heighten arousal to the point of orgasm. Orgasm triggers vary from woman to woman and can include tightening leg and/or thigh muscles to build tension until it bursts forth in orgasm, giving yourself over to a sexual fantasy and letting it culminate in orgasm, asking your partner to stroke faster or harder as you advance toward orgasm, and/or verbalizing that you're "going to come." Sexual stimulation has to be focused and rhythmic to result in orgasm. Once you've identified orgasm triggers, give yourself permission to use them.

Relationally, there needs to be a trusting bond with the partner. She feels he cares about her and her sexual desire, that he willingly gives to her and is responsive to her guidance. Especially important is for the woman to realize it is not up to the man to work his magic and give her an orgasm, but that arousal and orgasm are her responsibility. His role is being an involved, giving, and caring partner. Her orgasm is not a measure of his masculinity. She doesn't have to prove anything to him nor does she have to prove anything to herself. The key to sexuality is giving and receiving pleasure, not performing by having an orgasm.

CLOSING THOUGHTS

One of the most harmful mistakes of the "sexual revolution" was taking female orgasm out of the context of sexual pleasure and into the realm of unrealistic expectations. The media emphasis on sophisticated orgasms have led women down a dead-end alley just as the traditional Victorian inhibitions did.

It is time for women to reassert their responsibility over their bodies. Increasing comfort and awareness is the first step. Understanding your conditions for an intimate sexual relationship, being receptive to nondemand pleasuring, responsivity to multiple stimulation, and letting go and feeling you deserve sexual pleasure sets the stage for orgasm as a joyful, integral component of the sexual experience. Orgasm belongs to you as a sexual woman and is a natural part of the sexual experience.

19

A COST-BENEFIT APPROACH TO
EXTRAMARITAL SEX

Over the past generation there has been a sizable increase in the number of women who have extramarital affairs. Reliable statistics are difficult to obtain, but our best estimate is that approximately two out of three marriages will experience at least one affair. Somewhere between 50–60 percent of men and between 25–40 percent of women will have an affair. These statistics are not presented to make women cynical or disillusioned about marriage and fidelity, but to make it clear that affairs are a major issue for contemporary women.

In our society the ideal is sexual fidelity. We are not arguing against that ideal, but it is important that women be aware of the realities and not naïvely believe that all marriages live up to the ideal. Women need not feel stigmatized if they or their marriage has not met the exclusivity ideal.

Increasing awareness and understanding puts you in a better position to make choices and decisions that can enhance your sexuality and relationship. The area of extramarital sexuality is so shrouded in assumptions and secrecy that it is hard to take the explicit cost-benefit approach we are suggesting. As an alternative to an extramarital affair surprising you or your spouse, we advocate thinking about and talking out the implications and meanings of an affair.

Individuals have implicit beliefs about affairs, but often the couple do not share the same ideas. This stems from our old nemesis, the male-female double standard. According to the double standard, males have a biological need for variety and illictness in sexual partners. This makes for provocative articles in magazines and talk-show confrontations, but there is no solid scientific evidence to support that assertion. According to that view, a "real man" will take any opportunity for a sexual affair with every available woman. Of course, the woman has to defend home, marriage, and children—so if she is a "good woman" she will never have an affair. Only "bad" women have affairs. The premarital double standard does not go away with marriage. This harsh, outdated approach to extramarital affairs might be entertaining and provocative, but it is hopelessly sexist and does little to help us rationally understand and examine extramarital behavior.

VALUES AND TERMINOLOGY

It is worthwhile to look at extramarital sex in a more discriminating manner, to distinguish among different levels of extramarital involvement, and to weigh the advantages and disadvantages of extramarital sex for you as a person and for your marriage. We suggest you not be controlled by easy, ready-made opinions and cultural stereotypes, whether liberal or conservative in orgin. Each can exert its own brand of tyranny over your thinking.

The traditional moral stance is to condemn all extramarital affairs. Especially in this era of AIDS, there is a fear that anyone having an affair puts physical health and the marriage in terminal jeopardy. From this viewpoint, the discovery of an extramarital affair is reason to call the divorce attorney and immediately end the marriage.

The open-marriage viewpoint holds the 65 percent figure concerning affairs is an underestimate because the other 35 percent lie. Marriage cannot meet all emotional and sexual needs. According to this view, it is not extramarital sex, but sexual exclusivity that is the enemy of the relationship. This approach advocates being adult and accepting that "everyone does it and what's the big deal."

Both extreme views impinge on our humanity, our right to choose, and our ability to take personal responsibility for our marriage and sexual life. If we look carefully at the traditional and open-marriage viewpoints, they are equally black-and-white approaches (although they contradict which is black and which is white). They make better theoretical arguments than behavioral guidelines. To see how emotional and value-laden both are, we need to carefully examine the terminology they employ. Those who are opposed to affairs use terms such as "adultery," "cheating on your husband," "cuckolding," "being unfaithful." Those who support extramarital sex use terms such as "personal and sexual sharing," "co-marital affairs," "not being hung up by jealousy and possessiveness," and "open marriage."

In examining the reality of affairs, for both women and men, we will try to be as clear and objective as possible. We will attempt to avoid easy answers, judgmental pronouncements, and value-laden terms. We want to take a rational, understanding, and constructive approach to the complex phenomena of extramarital affairs. Even in this era of AIDS, there is no blanket judgment—good or bad—that can apply to all extramarital affairs. Each affair must be considered in the context of the individuals and their marital situation. The woman's and couple's religious and personal values must be taken into account.

TYPES OF AFFAIRS

Although there are special qualities to each extramarital affair, for the purpose of discussion it is useful to divide extramarital affairs into three categories: the high-opportunity/low-involvement affair, the ongoing affair, and the comparison affair.

HIGH-OPPORTUNITY/LOW-INVOLVEMENT

The high-opportunity/low-involvement affair is the most common type for males and the least common for females. Given the derogatory label "one-night stand," this kind of affair requires a minimal amount of emotional intimacy. Examples include meeting a man at a convention, while out of town for business, at a bar, at a party, or having a passionate sexual first date without the expectation of seeing the man again. Another pattern involves paid sex, either with a prostitute or at a massage parlor. This is almost exclusively a male phenomenon, and its frequency is a prime reason that high-opportunity/low-involvement affairs are the most common male behavior.

The high-opportunity/low-involvement affair follows the traditional male-female double standard. The idea is that a "real man" never says no to sex—if he has an opportunity to be sexual he will take it. Women, on the other hand, are believed to care only about romance and commitment and to have no desire for sexuality itself, the excitement of a sexual encounter, or to be tempted by sexual opportunity. As is true for almost everything regarding the double standard, the woman is judged much more harshly than the man. In reality, women are also influenced by opportunity. It is exciting and ego-gratifying to be found sexually attractive and desirable by another man. This is especially true if the woman is in a new environment or situation where it is possible to let loose and experience something different and exciting. There is the intrigue, and yes, titillation, to see how this will play out sexually. Instead of watching a movie where beautiful people spontaneously and passionately come together, she has a chance to experience it herself.

Let us examine the advantages and disadvantages of high-opportunity/low-involvement affairs. Perhaps the major advantage is the sense of excitement that accompanies an affair. It can be a shot of psychological adrenaline for the woman's sense of attractiveness and desirability. This type of affair is the least threatening to a marriage. It is least likely to be discovered, and unlikely to precipitate a marital crisis. The affair does not compete on an emotional level with the marital relationship. The sense of heightened sexuality and desirability can reenergize sex in the marital relationship. If there is a sexual dysfunction in the marriage, and the affair is sexually functional, it's reassuring for the woman to know she can respond sexually.

The disadvantages of a high-opportunity/low-involvement sexual encounter include those that exist for unmarried women as well—the danger of sexually transmitted disease, especially AIDS, and/or unwanted pregnancy. A particular danger with the casual affair is that the sense of excitement and adventure sweeps over the woman so she is less discriminating. Some women feel as emotionally burned by this kind of affair as did the woman portrayed in the film *Fatal Attraction*—even though their response is not so extreme. A major disadvantage is that affairs are easier to get into than out of, and what starts out as an "innocent fling" can become a full-fledged affair with disastrous results for the woman and her marriage. Hooking up with a male who turns out to be very dependent or very angry is another danger. The most feared consequence is that the husband will find out and place the marriage in crisis. Some women (and men) accept that their partner can have a low-involvement affair, but others feel it breaks the trust bond as much as any other extramarital involvement. The sense of hurt, anger, and betrayal can be devastating for the marital relationship.

ONGOING AFFAIR

The ongoing affair refers to a relationship that might continue for weeks, months, or even years. In addition to meeting emotional and sexual needs, the affair provides a regular influx of excitement and adventure. This affair is kept separate from the marriage and is not viewed as a challenge to the marital relationship. It supplements the marriage and fulfills needs not met in the marriage. Examples of this type of affair are once-a-week dates for dinner and sex with someone a woman met at a community group, having sex with a man who comes to town four or five times a year, or going for a day hike in the mountains and having sex before returning home. An intriguing film about an ongoing affair was *Same Time Next Year*.

An advantage of an ongoing affair is that it provides a continuing and presumably safe sexual relationship. Half the fun is anticipating the next sexual date. There are more emotional ties than in a casual affair. Often the man becomes a "sexual friend" in the best sense. Realizing that a man values you and wants to maintain a sexual relationship can be flattering. Another advantage is that the places you go—restaurants, hotels, bars, shows—add a special flavor to your otherwise predictable life. You might experience something sexually that you don't have in your marriage, for instance, your lover may be aroused by giving you cunnilingus but your husband treats it like a chore. It's exciting to have a secret life—to be more than a suburban worker, wife, and mother. Fantasizing about the past meeting and looking forward to the next can add pleasure to your life.

The potential disadvantages of an ongoing affair are the same as for the high-opportunity/low-involvement one with some significant additions. Leading a double life and maintaining an ongoing secret can be very stressful. Ongoing affairs often take more time and energy than you planned. You have to arrange to cover yourself at work and home, get someone to pick up the car pool, make an excuse to go to a meeting, etc.

A more threatening possibility is that what was meant to have a specific place in your life expands and becomes more complex and demanding than what you bargained for. You were going to be "lovers," but not "fall in love." Emotional and sexual relationships are not necessarily rational or predictable. It becomes especially difficult where one partner wants more from the relationship and the other wants to keep it contained. Contrary to media notions, it is often the man (especially if he is unmarried) who pushes the woman to increase her time and/or sexual commitment. Barry had one case in which the lover demanded that the woman stop having sex with her husband. Perhaps the most explosive possibility is the husband finding out. The feelings of betrayal and anger are greater with this type of affair. The husband can be vindictive in threatening to withhold money, tell her family or friends, use the children to make her feel guilty, and, if the affair is work-related, to create a confrontation at her job. Males react with a greater sense of personal injury, jealousy, and anger at a wife's ongoing affair than wives do at a husband's ongoing affair. It is harder to rebuild the trust bond because once deceived the spouse is vigilant and wary.

COMPARISON AFFAIR

The affair that is most disruptive and threatening to a marriage is the comparison affair. Not coincidently, this is the most common female affair. In the comparison affair, more of the woman's emotional and/or sexual needs are met through the affair than from the marriage. You are comparing your spouse with your lover with the threat that the spouse will be the loser.

The major advantage of a comparison affair is the very special feelings of being in love. Many women object to calling this an affair, feeling that term denigrates a very special relationship. A woman who had several previous affairs did so primarily to meet her sexual needs. She felt that in the comparison affair she was loved and "making love" for the first time in years. It's a "romantic love" feeling many women have not experienced since they were young adults. In this kind of relationship people make major changes in their lives, including leaving their marriage. This type of affair can dramatically increase desire, arousal, and orgasm. This sexual reawakening rebuilds the woman's sexual self-esteem. Many experience greater sexual openness and experimentation than there ever was in the marriage. Other women report the man listens to them, respects them, and cares more for them than their husband ever has. Being valued as a person, not just taken for granted as a wife, can boost self-esteem. It is tantalizing to consider a different life with a different person. The comparison affair is an intensely passionate relationship in which factors like juggling household chores and children are not involved. The affair exists apart from your real life.

The same things that make the comparison affair so exciting and enticing can serve as the downfall of both the affair and the marriage. The reality is the magic cannot last. The comparison affair is an inherently explosive and unstable situation. In addition to all the disadvantages of the first two types of affairs, there is a sense of a ticking bomb. Ultimately, the woman is going to have to make a choice and it could cost her the lover, marriage, or both. This type of affair elicits the strongest reaction from the husband. He is most likely to fight to keep his wife, but it's not clear whether he values her and the marriage or he just doesn't want to lose to the competition. Hurt feelings and vindictiveness usually accompany this type of affair. Emotions run high and your life is in tumult. Life can feel like an out-of-control roller coaster.

The woman finds herself squeezed between two angry and demanding men. A particularly harsh outcome can result if she discovers that the other man makes a better lover in an affair than a partner in an ongoing relationship. As they deal with hard issues, she finds him less attractive and stable. For many women the ultimate cost of a comparison affair is extremely high.

Perhaps the major disadvantage of a comparison affair is the effect it has on your life with your husband and on the sense of trust and intimacy in the marriage. You put less time and energy into your marriage during the affair, and this gap in intimacy, affection, and sexuality is very difficult to bridge and rebuild even when both partners make a good-faith effort to do so.

Pam and Jeff

Pam was seen by others as an attractive woman, although she did not see herself that way. When she married Jeff at twenty-seven, Pam was relieved to be out of the dating scene. She felt awkward when men asked her out or "hit on her" sexually. Pam was sure that wearing a wedding band would protect her from those situations. She was shocked when this did not prove to be the case.

Fourteen months into the marriage, Pam had her first affair, a high-opportunity/low-involvement type. Pam was an inhalation therapist at a hospital and went to a three-day training workshop held at a hotel two hundred miles away. A man from a different city pursued her. Pam flashed her ring and said she was happily married, but it had little effect. She agreed to go for a drink with a group of people after the second day's presentation. He insisted she stay for a second round, and by the third drink he and Pam were alone. Pam went along because it was the path of least resistance. She was surprised how sexually responsive she felt. They had sex twice the next day and he promised to call or write her at work. Pam looked forward to hearing from him and was terribly disappointed when she didn't. The affair left a bad taste in Pam's mouth.

A year and a half later, Pam became involved in an affair with a physician at the hospital. He was married but constantly complained that his wife did not understand him or medicine. Pam admired his skill and dedication as a physician and imagined he would be an involved and good lover. Instead she found he was often distracted and was an early ejaculator. They got together for sex according to his schedule, although he would always pay for the hotel room. At first it was exciting and a break from her work routine, but taking compensatory time and getting someone to cover for her at work became an increasing hassle. He expected her to be available any time he was. Although he promised a weekend away at a medical convention, it never came about. Six months into the affair, Pam was becoming increasingly disillusioned.

In Pam's case two adages about affairs proved true: it was much easier to get into than out of and it took more time and energy than she expected. The physician simply would not take no for an answer. Tension built and he became more threatening and vindictive at work. The straw that broke the camel's back was when he filed a formal complaint with the head of the inhalation therapy department concerning Pam's handling of a case. There had been a problem with the case, but it was clear to Pam that this was a ploy to get back at her for refusing to meet him for sex. Pam considered filing a sexual harassment complaint, but after reviewing the facts with her supervisor and a competent and supportive woman in personnel, Pam decided it was not worth her time and emotional investment. The woman in personnel told Pam she had some leverage and options. When a work affair goes sour, it is usually the woman who is discriminated against because she is in a less powerful position and more vulnerable economically. Pam decided, with her supervisor's support and letter of recommendation, to switch jobs to a hospital where the physician did not practice. He dropped his complaint. At the exit interview Pam raised the issue of sexual harassment. The personnel department pursued the complaint against the doctor, and he received a formal reprimand. Although it wasn't the perfect solution, Pam felt better about herself and went into her new job with a sense of her personal integrity intact. She vowed to avoid any work affairs in the future.

Dealing with the effects of the affair on her relationship with Jeff was more complex. Affairs are very stressful on marriages. The time and emotional energy consumed by the affair has to come from somewhere, usually from the marital relationship, parenting, or the job. In Pam's case it came from her emotional relationship with Jeff. In the past year they had lived distant, parallel lives. Although they shared the same house and bed, they were like strangers passing in the night. Sex continued, but was perfunctory and decreased to two or three times a month. The sometimes difficult early years of marriage require the couple to focus on the relationship and forge bonds of respect, trust, and intimacy. Since most affairs occur in the first five years of marriage, one of the side effects is to sabotage the process of creating a viable marital bond.

Unbeknownst to Pam, Jeff had a series of low-involvement/high-opportunity affairs. Both Pam and Jeff felt they were getting away with something and wanted their secret kept from the other. However, both were aware something was wrong and felt guilty—this was truer for Pam than Jeff. Once Pam was in her new job and out of the affair, she wanted to turn her attention back to the marriage, but she found it a difficult task. Jeff continued to be distant, partly because his affairs were continuing.

Pam finally suggested they seek marital therapy. There was a tension-filled initial couple session where more was being guarded than said. In the individual meetings, the affairs were discussed. The therapist told Pam that even though her affairs were terminated they hung heavily over her marriage, and she told Jeff that marital therapy could not proceed as long as his affairs continued. Discussing affairs in detail and playing "tit for tat" feeds hostility, not openness. Not all affairs need to be nor should be revealed. In Pam's situation, if her marriage to Jeff were to have a chance of being revitalized, the secrets of the affairs had to be "put on the table." This was done in the couple feedback session and was very emotional yet at the same time relieving. At some level, both Pam and Jeff were aware of the other's affairs. One of the consequences was an agreement that neither Pam nor Jeff would have affairs of any type. This would help them begin rebuilding trust and intimacy.

Pam's struggle was to overcome her guilt and develop a sense that she deserved to achieve emotional and sexual satisfaction in her life. Marital therapy lasted eight months and was of great value to Pam and her marriage. It was not easy work, but it was worthwhile. Pam regretted the affairs, but learned important lessons about herself, sex, intimacy, and relationships and now felt more in control of her life. Pam and Jeff had an agreement that if an opportunity or a desire for an affair occurred in the future they would examine their motivations and discuss the situation with their spouse before acting on the impulse. Pam's expectation was that affairs were a thing of the past for her and her marriage.

TAKING RESPONSIBILITY FOR DECISIONS

Women have traditionally looked to books, self-help articles, ministers, Ann Landers, friends, to tell them what to do, especially in the area of sexuality. The traditional advice about extramarital affairs was that "good women" don't have them.

If your husband had an affair, one school of advice was to immediately kick him out. The other school said "boys will be boys" and as long as he was discreet and his affair didn't affect income, the house, or the children, it should be ignored. These simple pieces of advice do not account for the realities and complexities of extramarital affairs. Like most black-and-white judgments, they are of little help in dealing with the problems of women and relationships in the 1990s. It is patently unfair to label the 25–40 percent of women who have had an affair as "bad." Simplistic advice on how to deal with your husband's affair is just as absurd. Each marriage is different, and the type and meaning of an extramarital affair has to be understood in the context of the woman, her marriage, and that particular affair.

We can give information, psychological guidelines, and suggestions, but ultimately you need to take responsibility for your life and sexuality. Weigh these guidelines in the context of your attitudes, emotions, and behavior as a sexual woman, your marital relationship, and the choices that confront you. No matter how carefully we consider the pros and cons of different types of extramarital affairs, we can never balance one side against the other in an objective, dispassionate manner. The issues involved in marriage and extramarital sexuality are very personal, value-laden, emotional, and complex.

In an ideal scenario, early in the marriage (and even before marriage) the couple would have an open and frank discussion about the role of sexuality in their marriage as well as share their thoughts and feelings about extramarital affairs. This is seldom done and the consequence is that it's not unusual for a couple to be sitting in a therapist's office dealing with the crisis of a discovered extramarital affair. It's not surprising that each person had a different implicit assumption about affairs. Typically, the woman's assumption is that there will not be any affairs, and the man's assumption is that there can be brief or discreet affairs—that no harm is done if it "doesn't mean anything" and his wife doesn't find out. We have never met an individual or couple who've agreed to a comparison affair.

With the publication of *Open Marriage* in the 1970s, many couples discussed and some tried out the concept of mutual consensual extramarital affairs. Other couples took it one step further and experimented with "swinging," also called "mate swapping." In swinging, sexual partners are switched with the knowledge and permission of the spouse. Advocates claimed these "new age" relationships challenged hangups about jealousy and possessiveness that had thwarted personal growth. Some couples considered it to be harmless fun. As with other "pop psychology" theories, these extramarital relationships looked better on paper than in the reality of people's emotional and sexual lives. The evidence is clear that open marriage and swinging relationships do not work for most couples. The repercussions are harmful for the marital bond and are successful for very few women. If you choose to have an extramarital affair, the best guideline is to keep it apart from the marriage.

OUR PERSONAL MARITAL AGREEMENT

We were proud that we discussed a number of issues before marrying. We reached agreements about children and contraception, where we would live, careers, sexuality, money, dealing with in-laws, etc. However, a notable subject we did not discuss was extramarital affairs. In retrospect, we had the typical anxieties and inhibitions of other young couples. As our relationship progressed, we began having more open conversations about sexuality, making requests, and trying to improve the quality of our marital sex, although we still studiously avoided any discussion of extramarital affairs.

The topic came up in a serendipitous fashion. One of the male teaching assistants Barry knew had a female student who was flunking. She approached the teaching assistant and offered to do anything he wanted Saturday night if she could only pass the course. The teaching assistant was ethical and told her what she needed to do Saturday night was stay home and study. This story was greeted with great laughter, but afterward Emily asked Barry what he would do if a young woman came on to him. Barry tried his best to avoid dealing with the question, but Emily insisted she wanted to talk this out and understand his viewpoint and feelings. Barry assured her if he ever had an affair it would be totally separate from the marriage and would just be a fun fling for excitement and variety. This was Barry's implicit assumption about extramarital affairs, but it sounded strange being made explicit. Emily was adamant that if Barry had an option to have affairs then to maintain a sense of equity she would want the same option. She was not interested in a one-night stand or a quick fling, but would want a sense of involvement if she was going to have an extramarital affair. Barry was upset by this, saying that kind of affair would be a threat to their marriage. Emily replied that if they were going to make an agreement about affairs, it had to be an equitable one. Eventually it was agreed that neither would have an affair. One advantage of talking things out and making an explicit agreement is that things are clear. A potential disadvantage is that if one or both partners break the agreement they will need to confront feelings of disappointment and anger, and can't excuse themselves by saying it wasn't any big deal or they didn't know.

Our agreement has been helpful and worked well for us. We weren't suspicious when one or the other traveled or went to dinner or to a meeting with a friend of the opposite sex. This is how we've chosen to deal with the issue of extramarital affairs, but it does not mean it will be the right choice for you. Each woman needs to consider her situation, marriage, spouse, and values and choose what is best for her.

DEALING WITH THE MAN'S AFFAIR

We imagine several readers are saying to themselves, "This is very interesting, but when are they going to get down to the real issue—what to do about my spouse's affair?" It is true that more men than women have extramarital affairs and men often have more than one affair. The most common male affair is a high-opportunity/low-involvement affair; some involve paid sex (for example, at a massage parlor, with a prostitute at her apartment, or with an outcall prostitute who comes to the man's hotel room). Many men (and women) accept these affairs as "boys will be boys." The rationale is that it's totally apart from the marriage and not a threat to the spouse. It's the extramarital extension of the premarital double standard. Many women find this type of affair disgusting and are very angry when they discover their husband had a fling. However, they do not feel personally threatened.

If she discovers an ongoing affair or a comparison affair, it can be profoundly disturbing. A major element is wondering how he could have kept this secret from her. Feelings of jealousy and deception can be very powerful. She feels threatened by the other woman, her sense of trust has been shaken, and she's unsure whether she should believe what he tells her now. Men typically minimize the importance of the affair. Even more distressing, the man might continue some contact with the woman, even if intercourse has ceased. There's a fear he will resume the affair, especially if the marital relationship becomes strained.

Often the husband's affair is revealed in a way that embarrasses the woman. It might come from an anonymous phone call or a friend telling her. Or she calls his office and finds he's not in town. Or credit card charges come through that have no reasonable explanation. She is unsure whether to confront her husband. She might not share her suspicions with anyone, but will have innumerable conversations with herself about what to do. If she does share her concerns with others, their advice might be confusing and contradictory. It varies from letting the situation ride to calling a lawyer—from talking lovingly to him to getting a private detective.

We strongly suggest confiding in at least one good friend who can be supportive and not judgmental during this process. An important factor is the present state of your self-esteem and your satisfaction with the marriage. The better you feel about yourself, the easier it will be to deal with your spouse. The more you value the marriage, the more motivated you'll be to try to deal with him about the suspicious behavior. Rather than starting with accusations and confrontation, it would be better to state your feelings and fears and state clearly that you want him to deal with you directly and honestly. It's not likely things will be clear for one or two conversations—the process of clarifying the situation might take several days or weeks.

Getting out of an affair is more difficult than getting into it. Make it clear that you cannot maintain a sense of personal integrity and marital commitment if there is a continuing affair. It is the norm to have several emotionally draining scenes with tears, anger, accusations, promises. You will cope better if you take care of your needs and feelings, have a sense of your own integrity, know that you can have a life independent of your spouse, and are not afraid to be assertive and confront him. Conversely, if your self-esteem is low, you feel helpless and powerless in dealing with him, do not believe you can survive emotionally or financially without the marriage, you are in for a terrible time and are in need of professional therapy to help build your coping resources.

In dealing with an extramarital affair, the marital bond of respect, trust, and intimacy is strained. However, if this is a marriage worth saving, that bond must be preserved. You can be disappointed and angry at your spouse and express these feelings, but don't destroy the bond unless you're convinced you don't want to be married to this man.

DEALING WITH THE MAN LEAVING FOR ANOTHER WOMAN

There are no guarantees in life, and you need to be aware that a possible outcome in a comparison affair is for the man to choose the other woman and leave you. If this is likely, one of the best things you can do for yourself is to seek professional therapy.

You need to accept the reality of your loss without surrendering your self-esteem. He made a choice, and it is his loss. You know and like yourself, and you will survive the loss of his love. It opens the challenge of being single again and appreciating the new options in your life. In the short term it is harder to be the one who is left than to be the one who leaves. The worst thing you can do is to accept his judgment of you. In the long term, you have much to offer and can rebuild a satisfying life.

Where children are involved, it is preferable to deal respectfully and cooperatively about parenting issues. Make it clear to your children that the divorce was an adult decision and it was not their fault nor do they have the power to change it no matter how good or bad they are. You need to emphasize that the divorce will not change your desire to parent the children. You can cooperatively parent, but it is crucial to keep emotional distance from your ex-spouse, especially the romantic and sexual aspects of your lives.

GUIDELINES FOR DEALING WITH EXTRAMARITAL AFFAIRS

Many women deal with the issue of extramarital affairs in their lives. Instead of feeling guilty, stigmatized and/or judgmental, you have to clearly assess your feelings and the situation and act in your best interest. You need to deal with reality instead of being controlled by fears or fantasies. Why did the affair occur? What was happening in your life, his life, and in the marital relationship? What was the meaning and the message of the affair? Is the marital bond still viable or is the affair an indirect way of ending an unsatisfactory marriage? Trust is the element in the marital bond that is most disrupted by an extramarital affair. If this marriage is to be revitalized, you need to restore that trust by making a clear agreement concerning future affairs (most couples choose abstinence from affairs and rebuilding their sexual bond).

Some couples learn valuable lessons from affairs that can strengthen their marital relationship. Examples include the freedom to engage in more uninhibited sex play, to plan sexual dates, to utilize oral sex more comfortably, to feel more attractive and desirable, to be open to different intercourse positions, etc. These lessons can be integrated, but not in a comparison way, into your couple sexual style to make it more comfortable, flexible, expressive, and satisfying.

The extramarital affair need not become a supersensitive topic, but should be accepted as a reality that can be dealt with and talked about. Avoid the extremes of denial or obsessive focus. Life, sex, and relationships are meant to be lived in the present, not controlled by the past.

Let us end this chapter with a word about prevention. A good guideline is that the better the marriage and the marital sex, the more reason to decide against having an extramarital affair. It is simply too disruptive and draining, and not worth putting a satisfying relationship under stress. When an affair has occurred and the choice is to revitalize the marriage, you need to discuss the meaning of the affair and how to deal with it so it will not constantly burden the marital bond. Extramarital sexuality is a serious and complex issue. We urge the woman and the couple to think about and talk out its meanings. Prevention is the most cost-efficient strategy.

20
SINGLE AGAIN

In the traditional cultural fantasy, once a woman marries she is set for life. It's like a movie in which THE END flashes on the screen with the assumption that she will live happily ever after. Her marriage is the most important thing she will ever do and represents security and permanence in her life. In many cultures, the family arranges the marriage so the forces of the state, religion, and family are all aligned to build and support the marital structure. In these cultures, it is the woman's role to take care of the husband, children, and house. For this caretaking she is rewarded with a stable marriage and a clear role in society. These cultures treat women as second-class citizens, and marital stability and security is paid for by a lack of personal growth and marital dissatisfaction. The trade-off is permanence for satisfaction.

Marriage and divorce in the American culture represents the other extreme of the continuum. Arranged marriages are extremely rare; we adhere to the model of "romantic love" and free choice. Women "fall in love" on the basis of emotional and sexual attraction, but many find over time that their spouse is a poor match.

Our culture does not have the divorce stigma other cultures do and our legal system accepts and facilitates the divorce process, especially since the advent of "no fault" divorce. The religious, family, and social pressures that produce unsatisfying and often abusive marriages in other cultures are less powerful in the United States. We believe this is a good thing—marriages that require external, coercive forces to maintain them are not worth maintaining. This is not to say we are in favor of the high

264

divorce rate in the United States. Divorce is not to be taken lightly; it is a difficult and often traumatic life experience.

We believe women need to be aware and empower themselves to view marital choice, marriage, and divorce from a clearer, more realistic viewpont. We have a promarriage bias and believe that choosing better and seeing marriage as an ongoing process requiring psychological energy and commitment from both spouses is the way to decrease the divorce rate. Most marriages that end in divorce should end in divorce. Such marriages are not viable ones and not in the woman's best interest. This is reflected in the fact that over 70 percent of American marriages are ended at the woman's initiative. She finds the marriage is not good for her and does not meet her needs.

The biggest trap is viewing being single again as a sign of "failure." This is especially acute for women because they have been socialized to feel responsible for other people and most feel it is their role to ensure that marriage works. The choice to divorce does not signify failure as a person; it means that this marriage was not healthy. The divorce decision is a sign of strength; you think enough of yourself that you deserve better than this marriage. Many women stay in abusive marriages for years because they wrongly believe they "should" or "for the sake of the children." It is *not* in any child's best interest to see her father abusing her mother, or to be caught between parents who are angry and fighting, or to grow up with a loveless, sexless marital model.

In certain ways being single again because of the spouse's death is more difficult than divorce. You did not choose to be single again, it occurred because of a circumstance beyond your control. When the death of a spouse is totally unexpected, for example in a car accident, the trauma is even greater. When a spouse's dying process is gradual and expected at least there is an opportunity for anticipatory grieving. The reality is that loss and grieving is always difficult.

SEXUALITY AND LOSS

You are a sexual woman throughout your life, including periods in which you are dealing with losses, such as divorce or death. Some people find discussions of sexuality during these times particularly unnerving. It's as if they should deny sexual thoughts, feelings, and expression during the grieving period. Sexuality is an integral part of the life process, and there are sexual feelings and issues during the period of divorce or spouse's death.

As a marital relationship sours, it is common that one of the first casualties is the sexual relationship. Sex might be less frequent, less satisfying, or become dysfunctional. It is not unusual for the woman to develop inhibited sexual desire or secondary nonorgasmic dysfunction. Sometimes couples try to be sexual as a way of breathing life into a dying marriage, but sex cannot save a marriage.

The majority of happily married, sexually functional women occasionally masturbate. Masturbation is a normal, healthy behavior that can serve a number of positive functions. During a period of loss, masturbation can serve as a sexual outlet, a tension reducer, a way of reaffirming your capacity to be sexual, and as an acknowledgement of your ability to be independent.

Some women have affairs, especially before and during the divorce process. Affairs can serve to reinforce attractiveness and desirability. A good love affair can ease the transition into being single again. When there is sexual dysfunction in the marriage, it is invigorating to discover you can be sexually responsive and functional with another partner. The danger of an affair at such times is that the woman may expect it to be more than it is and may then become too dependent on the man. Most affairs are transitory; you need to be realistic about the role of the affair in your life. A woman is vulnerable at this time and might choose an inappropriate or abusive partner, in which case the affair adds to the sense of chaos and loss of control instead of providing a pleasant refuge.

SPECIAL ISSUES FOR THE DIVORCED WOMAN

Even when the marriage was an unhappy one, the transition to divorce is not easy. You get used to having a man in the house and of thinking of yourself as married. Many women realize they did not like their husband, but did like the married state. Let's be frank—one of the burdens of being a single,

The woman astride the man while both continue caressing each
other. This can be considered "pleasuring" as much as intercourse.

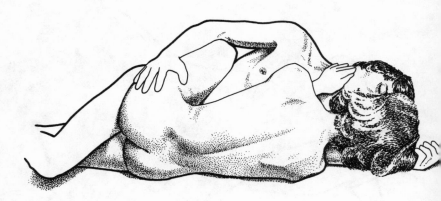

An example of the lateral (side) entry position.

divorced, or widowed woman is being approached by men in their endless search for sexual encounters. Even women who are comfortable with their sexuality and have strong prosexual attitudes are annoyed by men constantly coming on to them as if they were sex objects. Men assume you are sexual (which is true), but they mistakenly believe they are entitled to have sex with you just because they want to. Being a sexual woman means you have the right to choose who you want to be sexual with and who you don't.

The psychological process of a divorce and dealing with the stages of denial, anger, and depression is highly variable and individualistic. On the average, it extends over two years. It is not easy, but the great majority of women do successfully complete the transition from the married to the single-again state. Crucial to the process is finding friends and/or family members who respect and care about you and are supportive and constructive. It's important to stay away from people who are judgmental and blaming or who say they know what's best for you. Unfortunately, family members, especially parents, tend to take that role. They see divorce as a failure that reflects badly on them. Be clear that this perception is their problem, not yours. The other extreme is friends and family who try to protect you by putting down your ex-spouse and feeling sorry for you. You don't need their anger or their sympathy—you need their respect and support.

One of the chief decisions concerns dating. Rather than falling back into the dating cycle, we strongly advise that you carefully consider what kind of relationship would be in your best interest at this time. How much intimacy are you ready for? Do you want to maintain your sense of personal independence or are you open to an intimate relationship? Are you interested in greater security and stability or is this a time you'd be better off dating different men and keeping your options open?

There is a myth that all women desire and need marriage to feel complete. That's nonsense—you don't need a man to be a whole person or a sexual woman. You can take care of yourself, develop and maintain high self-esteem for who you are, develop friends and social activities, and create a diversified, satisfying, and secure life for yourself. The decision to become involved in an intimate relationship that could develop into a marriage is a positive decision. Starting a new relationship based on deficit needs such as dependency, loneliness, or desperateness is not in your best interest. Positive motivation promotes good decisions, negative motivation leaves you vulnerable to poor decisions and poor relationships.

Most women would agree that a stable and intimate marital relationship is ideal. However, so many marriages fall far short of that ideal. Because a couple stay together does not mean they have a satisfying marriage. In a good marriage, the woman has the freedom to develop herself as a person and have interests of her own as well as couple activities and shared interests. Each partner is an independent person, choosing to be in an interdependent give-and-take relationship. In many second marriages the woman takes care of the man and gives up her independence and personal interests. Is that trade-off in your best interest?

You needn't be married or in an intimate relationship to justify being sexual. Being sexual needs no justification. We do recommend against one-night stands and entering into unhappy or abusive relationships. Remember the basic guidelines about sexuality: 1) sex is a good thing in life, 2) sexuality is an integral part of you as a person, and 3) you can choose to express your sexuality so that it enhances your life and does not cause pain, trauma, or negative feelings. One-night stands and relationships with destructive men cause health and psychological problems.

In a new relationship it is crucial that you talk to your partner about sexual health—especially use of contraception and protection against sexually transmitted diseases. Many women prefer the birth control pill or IUD because it does not require any immediate action. If you are not using either of those forms of contraception you need to insist upon time to put in a diaphragm, sponge, or use foam.

If you do not know the man well, we strongly advise that you insist on use of the condom, both as birth control and to protect against sexually transmitted diseases. It is perfectly appropriate to visually examine the man's penis to see if there are any signs of infection or discharge. The risk of contracting gonorrhea, herpes, and chlamydia are much greater than that of contracting AIDS, but the consequences of AIDS are life-threatening. So in any new relationship, but especially a short-term one, be conservative and protect your health. Equally important is to use good psychological judgment in choosing a man. At a minimum, you need to trust he wouldn't hurt you and ideally he would be a friend with whom you shared a positive and exciting sexual relationship.

Our bias is toward an ongoing sexual relationship—the notion of having a lover rather than an affair. A sexual friendship might have the potential to develop into a permanent relationship, but most do not. They are like other friendships in that you are attracted to the man, trust him, and have a sense of caring for him. He might be in your life for six weeks or three years. You will share a variety of experiences, including sexual and emotional ones. Sometimes the sexual friendship will end amicably and other times disappointingly. The hope is that you will look back on the sexual friendship with good feelings and memories.

Linda

Linda was twenty-five when she married and thirty-three at her divorce. As she was growing up, Linda could not understand her parents' marriage. They seemed like such different people who bickered a great deal and had few good times together. Linda's mother stayed home until her last child was five and in school and then returned to work as a residential real-estate agent. Unlike other mothers who worked for extra family money, Linda's mother viewed real estate as her career and took great pride in her successes. At this point in her career, Linda's mother makes almost as large a salary as her father. Her father is a retired Navy officer who is the executive vice president of a professional association. His passion in life is golf. Linda thought her father was resentful of his wife and family because he had to financially support them, but seemed to get little enjoyment from them. Her parents had married before age twenty-one, and Linda was convinced that was the core of their problems.

Linda decided not to marry until twenty-three at the earliest and to marry a man very different than her father. Linda met Brad at twenty-four and from the first date was sure Brad was the husband for her. Brad enjoyed team sports like basketball, volleyball, and baseball. He was gregarious and always had people around him. Best of all, Brad was casual about his career and talked easily about feelings and relationships. There was no doubt in Linda's mind that she'd have a more exciting and fulfilling marriage than her parents.

Sometimes we are so committed to avoiding traps our mothers fell into that we inadvertently fall into a whole different set of snares. A positive characteristic of her parents' marriage that Linda took for granted was fidelity, but that was not in Brad's makeup or value system. Linda enjoyed couple time, but Brad preferred socializing with friends. When he went out he was totally unaccountable to Linda. She resented her father's planning and control, but was shaken by Brad's impulsiveness and irresponsibility.

One result of the impulsivity was a pregnancy six months into the marriage. Linda wanted to talk out feelings and options with Brad, but he said it was totally up to her. Linda wanted children, but not at that time and opted for a therapeutic abortion. Linda found the abortion experience more emotionally draining than she had anticipated and was very put off that Brad was not there for her.

Linda did have a planned, wanted pregnancy two years later, and she wanted Brad to go with her for prepared childbirth classes. He agreed to, but he missed over half the classes because of athletic or social conflicts. The childbirth went fine, but again Linda did not feel Brad had been there for her. She hoped for his emotional and practical support in taking care of the baby, but it was not forthcoming. Brad enjoyed playing with the baby and bragging about his son, but he refused to assume caretaking responsibilities. Brad maintained his athletic and social schedule, and unbeknownst to Linda, had an ongoing affair that had begun three months into her pregnancy. Linda could not understand Brad's unenthusiastic response to her desire to resume their sexual relationship.

A child causes a major transition in a marriage. When the couple adjust well to being a family it strengthens the marital bond. However, when they go their own way, it can poison the relationship. Linda had growing feelings of disappointment and resentment toward Brad.

Linda received more support and good advice from her friends and siblings than from her mother, who told Linda she'd have to hang on because she needed Brad. The final indignity was a call from a male friend of Brad's who revealed the affair. Although Linda felt betrayed and was very angry, in truth she was not shocked. Over the next four months, they had innumerable conversations about the marriage, changing patterns, Brad breaking off the affair, etc., but to no effect. Linda knew that Brad's feelings and level of commitment were shallow. She worried about being a single woman with a young child, but as long as Brad made child support payments (which he did) she could survive as a divorced person.

Linda was pleasantly surprised by the support she received from her father. He helped her negotiate a more flexible work schedule and a child-care contingency system. Father was more matter-of-fact than mother, who seesawed between blaming Brad and feeling sorry for Linda.

Linda did not find being single again the happiest time of her life, but it was better than the scare stories she had heard and read. She could not tolerate being married to a man she did not respect or trust. Linda missed having a regular sex partner—the sexual relationship had been satisfying. Linda mused how myths she learned as an adolescent were not true, including the falsehood that you really had to love a man to feel aroused and orgasmic.

Linda took pride in how well she managed with limited financial resources. She enjoyed parenting her son and had a circle of female friends with young children who shared babysitting. Linda was pleased with how her career was progressing. However, dating and sexuality were a major source of dissatisfaction.

Linda was in the singles group routine of parties, athletic events, and being fixed up by friends. She absolutely hated the pat "lines," and the "pop psychology" talks. She heard men describe themselves as "sensitive, sociable, and open to a meaningful relationship." As she got to know them over three dates she would describe them as "wimpy, inappropriate, horny," and pushing for sex no matter what. Linda had no use for one-night stands, but she did have several short, unsatisfying affairs. She would hold on to a mediocre relationship because she didn't want to go through the hassle of finding a new date.

After a particularly disappointing relationship that dragged on for six months followed by a three-week relationship with a dependent, needy man who had a hard time accepting "no," Linda decided to take a six-month sabbatical from the dating scene. This proved to be an excellent gift to herself.

Linda became involved in a number of activities she'd postponed so she could be available to date men. She signed up for a course in personal investing and joined a coed soccer team that practiced on Saturday and played on Sunday. She enjoyed both activities, and she felt relieved to not be battling the "Saturday night date" syndrome. On Saturday nights she'd plan special activities with her son or have dinner with friends and their children, or (after her son went to sleep) read a novel she was interested in. Linda was feeling more comfortable and at peace with her life.

When you are not desperately looking for a relationship and are feeling better about yourself, you can view men and relationships in a better perspective. Four months into this period, Linda became aware of what a nice guy Rick was. Two years before, Rick had injured his knee and no longer played team soccer. However, he would be at practices helping coach and at games cheering the team on. Rick still did light-impact aerobic exercise to keep active, but he did not want to risk reinjuring his knee. Rick was too years younger than Linda, but he seemed more steady and mature than the older men she'd dated. Linda was especially impressed by Rick's attention to her son—he had an easy way around children.

Unfortunately, Linda's team lost the big game and didn't make the playoffs. However, they did schedule an end-of-the-season picnic and Linda, her son, and Rick spent a lot of time together. Afterward, Linda invited him back to her house for a beer. When Rick asked about dating, Linda told him about the sabbatical and then impulsively said she'd break it for a special guy like him. Rick was flattered and invited her the next weekend to his favorite activity—a musical play. Linda knew little about musicals, and she was intrigued by his interest and delighted by his sharing information and stories with her. Linda decided it was time to open herself up to a new relationship. If this was a Hollywood romance, they would have fallen head-over-heels in love, married in six months, and lived happily ever after. This makes great fiction, but it doesn't fit the reality of most women's lives.

They dated for over a year and discussed the whole range of issues that can interfere with a stable and intimate marriage. They talked about easy subjects (preferences in music) and hard topics (Rick's career and personal preference meant he'd move to Maine within three years). They talked and worked together to improve their sexual relationship, which was hindered by Rick's problem of early ejaculation. Linda was impressed that Rick cared about her sexual needs and was not the kind of "macho" man who could do sex, but not talk about it or admit he needed help from the woman. When Linda decided to marry Rick and start a second family with him it was based on awareness and choice. Linda knew that successful marriages required continual communication, problem solving, and psychological time and energy. She trusted that they would continue to develop and maintain their marital bond.

GUIDELINES FOR DECISION MAKING AFTER A DIVORCE

Not everyone can find a man like Rick and have a successful second marriage, although women do report greater satisfaction with second marriages. There are always trade-offs in life and relationships. What was impressive about Linda's story and what should serve as the prime guidelines for single-again women is her ability to successfully organize her life as a single person. If you develop a single life you are comfortable with and respect, you will realize the choice to remain single is an acceptable one. Therefore, you can clearly assess and evaluate a man in your life rather than having a desperate need to remarry and romanticizing how perfect your new partner is. More women are choosing to remain single and enjoying a satisfying life, including a sexual one. They view women who settled for an unsatisfactory marriage partner with a sense of pity. Women who feel they are not worthwhile without marriage or at least a man in their life often wind up in abusive or depressing relationships. You might not have chosen to be single in some ideal world, but you can be a fully functioning single-again woman. Enjoy the challenge of developing your interests and talents and take advantage of the independence and control you have in your life. Remarriage is only worthwhile if it will enhance your life.

THE REALITIES OF BEING A WIDOW

Over 80 percent of married women will become widows. For some women this will occur in their twenties, but the majority become widows in their fifties, sixties, seventies, or eighties. There are many similarities between divorcees and widows in terms of feelings, the grieving process, and reorganizing life as a single-again woman. There are three major differences: 1) the death of a spouse is final, 2) it's not a matter of choice that the marriage ended, and 3) the woman is usually older, has had a longer relationship, and has often nursed her husband during the dying process. Widows, especially those over fifty, are less likely to remarry than divorced women.

The reality, which is usually not mentioned, is that a significant number of widowed women are satisfied to be independent and living on their own. This is not to imply that they wanted their husbands to die. Some marriages are difficult and it is especially draining to nurse a spouse through a chronic, debilitating illness. When he dies there is a sense of relief mixed with guilt about feeling that way. There is a cultural myth that women are meant to be long-suffering without complaining, but in truth it is very hard to take care of a dying person. This is especially true when the marriage had been stressful and disappointing.

When couples stop being sexual, it is the man's choice in over 90 percent of cases. One of the major causes of the cessation of marital sex is the husband's illness. Few women have the desire for or the opportunity to have an affair during the husband's illness. Thus, their major sexual outlet is masturbation. The majority of married women occasionally masturbate as do the majority of widows. Masturbation can and does serve a number of positive functions—as a pleasurable activity, a tension reducer, and a way of maintaining your sexual response pattern. The adage about sexual functioning with aging, "use it or lose it," is applicable to masturbatory sex.

Some widows become involved in sexual affairs, including those with younger men and married men. These can be quite rewarding and personally satisfying. Other times, they turn into disappointments or even disasters. Use good judgment and follow your intuition. Be sure it's a good sexual friendship and the man is trustworthy and has no hidden agendas (e.g., he's more interested in your money than you or he's looking for a caretaker, not a partner).

Irene

Irene became a widow at fifty-four. This was the second time she was single again, having divorced at twenty-eight and re-married at thirty-two. Irene had been very pleased with her second marriage. Herb was an electronics engineer who enjoyed entertaining and traveling. They had high-quality sex once a week, which Irene would miss. Herb died of colon cancer—the doctors believed they had gotten it all during surgery, and were saddened to learn the cancer had spread. Irene spent the last three months surrounding Herb with a sense of love and caring as did their two children and stepson (Irene's son from her first marriage, who was genuinely fond of Herb).

Friends and family were very attentive at the time and during the month afterward, but then Irene had to begin reorganizing her life. The grieving process began while Herb was still alive. Although they did not have intercourse those final months, they continued to be a warm, affectionate couple. Those moments of physical closeness meant a great deal to Herb and Irene. So often as death approaches, people stop touching and stop discussing their feelings, fearing it will be too difficult. In truth, they miss an important opportunity to share a painful but important life experience.

Irene had no expectation that she'd marry a third time. Friends who married older men often found they functioned more like a mother and caretaker than a spouse. Irene was a healthy, vital woman, and she had no desire to be a caretaker. She had the benefit of Herb's life insurance and retirement fund, which provided a solid financial base. She did her homework and established a professional relationship with a competent broker and accountant, and she was actively involved in managing her money. In addition, she worked thirty hours a week. This job allowed her the flexibility to take longer vacations and to plan long weekends. She visited her adult children and grandchildren and traveled with female friends.

Irene visited a male friend in San Diego three or four times a year, and they had a sexual affair that lasted almost ten years. Although it was far from ideal, it met her sexual needs to some extent and added a sense of adventure to her life. Irene's regular sexual outlet was masturbation one or two times a week. For fantasy material she used erotic fiction, and she would reread six or seven passages while stimulating herself. A few years earlier, she had overheard a friend talking about the pleasures of vibrators. Irene went to a local department store and bought herself one with three attachments (it was sold as a body or back massager).

Irene was proud of how she had dealt with Herb's death and how she had fashioned a vital life as a widow, personally, financially, socially, and sexually.

CLOSING THOUGHTS

Although women would prefer not to be single again, it is a distinct possibility for most women. Rather than reacting with depression and helplessness, you would be better to view it as a challenge. You need to deal with the sense of loss and the complex emotions of the grieving process. Rather than seeing yourself as half a person without a man in your life, you can see yourself as a competent woman who is responsible for herself. You can live a satisfying life without marriage or a man. You need to be aware of the common pitfalls women fall into and use good judgment and act in your best interest. Don't let yourself be used or abused just for the sake of being in a relationship.

Knowing you can take care of yourself—personally, practically, and sexually—forms a good base from which to consider the role of a new man in your life. When you make decisions based on strength and positive motivation you are more likely to be successful. When there is a new man or even a marriage, don't give up the friends activities, and competence you developed while single again. Marriage should add to your life rather than be your whole life. Your self-esteem need not center around marriage. You do not need to be married to justify feeling good about yourself as a sexual woman. Sexual expression, by yourself or with a sexual friend, can add to and energize your life as a single-again woman.

21

UNDERSTANDING LESBIANISM

Few topics cause as much emotional reaction as does homosexuality. When homosexuality is mentioned, the immediate association is to male homosexuality. Lesbianism, female homosexuality, is one of the least discussed and least understood sexual behaviors. Derogatory terms such as "fag," "queer," "fairy," are consistently used for gay males. The derogatory terms for gay women, "dyke" and "femme," are seldom used, and then mostly by men. Female homosexuality is an important phenomenon that needs to be understood and accepted by heterosexual women as well as lesbian women.

Let's begin by looking at estimates of the incidents of lesbianism in our culture. Sometime in their lives almost all women have a thought, image, or fantasy involving being sexual with another woman. At some point, usually in adolescence or young adulthood, approximately 15 percent of women engage in sexually arousing touching with another woman that might proceed to orgasm. Approximately 5 percent of women have more sexual contact with women than men for at least a year of their lives. About 1.5 to 2 percent of women are lesbian in their sexual orientation.

What does sexual orientation mean? In our view, sexual orientation involves a major life commitment. It is not like deciding whether you prefer strawberry or butter pecan ice cream. Having a lesbian orientation means she finds greater emotional and sexual satisfaction with a woman than a man. Having a heterosexual orientation means she receives more emotional and sexual satisfaction from a man. We emphasize the concept of *both* emotional and sexual commitment because

the common myth is that lesbianism is an impulsive or immature sexual decision. Far from it.

It is easier (in our culture and other cultures) to be straight
than gay. This is true for women as well as men. Sexual
orientation is not the major life decision a woman makes, but it
is a very important one and is crucial for her psychological and
sexual well-being. She has a right to unbiased and clear information in helping her make a commitment in regard to sexual
orientation. She deserves the support of everyone—family, friends,
and the culture—to make a decision that is truly in her best
interest. She would benefit from professional therapy in making
this decision and dealing with its implications. If you do seek
therapy be sure you choose a therapist who is open to both the
lesbian and heterosexual options. It will not help you to work
with a homophobic therapist nor with a strongly prolesbian
therapist during the decision-making phase. In most cases, a
female therapist is preferable to a male. Guidelines for choosing
a therapist are available in the Appendix.

MYTHS ABOUT LESBIANISM

In any area in which there is little research or writing, myths
abound. This is certainly true of lesbianism. Perhaps the most
common and the most harmful myth is that lesbians hate men
and therefore have sex with women because it's the only alternative. Lesbianism is a *positive* emotional and sexual commitment to women. The lesbian woman loves another woman, not
merely turns to her. The majority of lesbian women do not hate
men, and, in fact, usually have friendly relationships with them.
They simply are not sexually attracted to men. Another myth is
that lesbian women cannot have sexual intercourse. The majority of lesbian women have had intercourse, many married, and
many had children. Yet there was a basic lack of fulfillment in
the heterosexual relationship. Another myth is that lesbian women
have high rates of prior incest, child sexual abuse, rape, etc.,
and this is why they turned to women. This is another variation
on the theme of lesbianism being inferior or second class. It is true
that the rates of sexual trauma are higher for lesbian than
heterosexual women, but the majority of lesbian women do not
view themselves as passive victims. Nor were the negative

factors primary in committing to a lesbian orientation; comfort, attraction, trust, and arousal with women is and was the primary reason for lesbianism.

The myths surrounding lesbianism focus on the supposed deficits and negative motivations of lesbian women. An example is that lesbian women do not like children. A significant minority have children and empirical research indicates they are just as good parents as their heterosexual peers. Another myth is that lesbian women are likely to sexually abuse young girls or boys. The truth is that the great majority of child sexual abusers (pedophiles) are heterosexual males. Women (whether lesbian or heterosexual) have low rates of sexual offenses. This list of myths could go on endlessly, but let's wrap it up with one of the silliest—lesbian women don't have orgasms because they don't have penis-to-vagina intercourse. Lesbian women have high rates of orgasmic response to manual and/or oral stimulation and are more likely to be multiorgasmic than heterosexual women.

WHY WOMEN COMMIT TO LESBIANISM

The question of "why" usually means what went wrong to cause lesbianism. This is especially asked by parents or ex-spouses with a sense of guilt or blaming. The science of human sexuality has not advanced to the point where we know how and why people become heterosexual, much less lesbian. There are a number of unsubstantiated hypotheses based on working with gay males, but anyone (whether a minister, psychiatrist, or social scientist) who claims to know the cause of sexual orientation is not being truthful. Like other complex human behavior, it is likely to be multicausal, with many individual differences.

A favorite hypothesis is the biological-predisposition view. This theory holds that either genetically or hormonally the fetus has a predisposition to develop a lesbian orientation that is subsequently triggered by environmental events. A second hypothesis comes from psychoanalytic theory that emphasizes that the failure to resolve the "Electra complex" by age five guarantees the woman will develop a lesbian orientation. The social-learning hypothesis is that sexual events in adolescence and early adulthood, especially revolving around masturbation fantasies and first orgasmic experiences, heavily influence later

The lesbian experience often involves deep sexual and emotional commitment and few outside relationships.

sexual orientation. Orgasm is a powerful reinforcer so if orgasm is paired with female images and experiences it will facilitate lesbianism. A fourth hypothesis is that women who are hetero-sexually anxious (whether caused by trauma or social shyness) find experiences with women are comfortable and easier. Some or parts of each hypothesis might be true for a number of women, but are totally different or wrong for others. Some people believe you have no control over sexual orientation, others believe it is established at a very young age. If it was that simple then almost all would take the socially acceptable route and choose heterosexuality. Our belief is that it is a learned behavior and a major life commitment.

There are numerous examples of societal, vocational, family, and social discrimination against lesbian women. The decision to lead a lesbian life is a major commitment, not easily made or easily changed. A lesbian woman accepts that emotionally and sexually she feels more comfortable and sexually responsive with women than with men. For the woman who has made this commitment, it makes little sense to agonize over the question of "why."

In considering the commitment, the woman needs to look at all the data she has about herself—her thoughts, feelings, fanta-sies, sexual responses, and interpersonal behavior—and make the decision that is in her best interest. Family, friends, minis-ters, etc., suggest what they think is best for you. You can and should listen to their views, especially when those views are tied to their personal knowledge of you. However, almost al-ways, others suggest doing what is easy or socially desirable (i.e., embracing heterosexuality). Especially for married women with children there is intense pressure to give up or stay away from lesbian involvements. Only you can know your feelings, preferences, and commitments. That is why we recommend therapy with an objective professional who can help you sort things out and reach a decision that will be right for you.

LESBIAN SEXUAL BEHAVIOR

What is it that lesbian women do sexually? Are there special lesbian behaviors? If you are particularly aroused by cunnilingus does that mean you are a "latent lesbian?" The phrases "latent homosexual'' and ''latent lesbian'' are scientifically useless. Their only purpose is to make people anxious about sexuality. They have been used to control women's sexual expression. ''Experts'' have said that enjoying masturbation, or preferring woman-on-top intercourse, or being orgasmic with cunnilingus are signs of latent homosexuality—what nonsense!

There is *no* sexual behavior that is uniquely lesbian. Both lesbian and heterosexual women might or might not enjoy kissing, caressing, manual stimulation, vibrator stimulation, oral stimulation, etc. Some lesbian women enjoy intravaginal finger stimulation—others do not. The only behavior heterosexual women engage in that lesbian women don't is penile-vaginal intercourse. Some lesbian women do engage in dildo stimulation, but that is not a major lesbian activity. It is not the sexual behavior that makes an experience lesbian or heterosexual, but whether the partner is female or male.

DISCRIMINATION AGAINST LESBIANS

Discrimination against lesbians is not as great as against gay men, but it is a significant problem. Discrimination is especially severe in certain employment areas (for example, teaching), in determining child custody, among certain religious groups, and with family members. People think of lesbians as second-class citizens so they can justify their prejudice. Let us state it as clearly as we can. The lesbian woman is a normal, healthy person in every way. She is a first-class citizen in every respect. The problem of prejudice and discrimination is that of society, not that of lesbians. Whether the discrimination is against blacks, Jews, the physically handicapped, the divorced, etc., it is not the fault or responsibility of the group being discriminated against. Discrimination harms everyone in our society. As a people and a culture we would take a giant step forward by ridding ourselves of occupational, housing, and social discrimination against lesbians and other minority groups.

The rationale for discrimination against lesbian teachers is they will have a corrupting influence on children—it's as if being around a lesbian woman will contaminate you and lesbianism could be catching. There is a myth that lesbian women seduce impressionable youngsters. These fears have no rational justification. Lesbianism is a major emotional and sexual commitment. It's not culturally transmittable like a preference for yogurt rather than ice cream. Myths and fears die hard and are used to rationalize prejudice and discrimination. Evidence clearly shows that being raised by a lesbian mother neither increases nor decreases the likelihood of homosexuality in female or male children. A lesbian is first a person and a woman. In some parts of her life, her sexual orientation might play a major role (such as her friendship patterns), but in most areas such as vocational competence, parenting skills, housing, and managing finances it has no effect. It would be in the best interest of society and lesbian women to eliminate prejudice and discrimination.

DEVELOPING A LESBIAN RELATIONSHIP

Most lesbian adolescents and young adults struggle with their increasing awarness of dissatisfaction and ambivalence concerning romantic relationships with males. Although a small minority of female adolescents are aware and accepting of their emotional and sexual attraction toward women, they are the exception, not the rule. Sometime in early or middle adolescence, lesbians report feeling special interest in and attraction to other women—sometimes friends of the same age, other times women they particularly admire such as a Girl Scout leader, a friend's mother, or a teacher. The adolescent does not know what to make of these feelings and attempts to ignore or downplay them.

In junior high and high school, girls commonly talk about boys and how cute and sexy they are. Although they try to enter into these conversations, lesbian adolescents do not have the same feelings and interests. The majority of lesbian women do have sexual intercourse. Often there is sexual interest and response, but lesbian women report a missing ingredient of satisfaction. Some lesbians have close and romantic relationships with men, but note a lack of genuine connection and intimacy. It was best stated by a married client who said, "I felt cared about and loved, but realized he couldn't know and accept me for who I really am. I could only feel fully myself and satisfied in a relationship with my lover."

The first sexual relationship with a woman is an important

turning point. For most lesbian women it occurs between fifteen and twenty-five, but for some it does not happen until after forty. In our culture, women are more affectionate and emotionally expressive than men, especially with same-sex friends. Contrary to popular myth, having close friendships with other women or enjoying affectionate hugs with female friends does not promote lesbianism.

A lesbian encounter has both emotional and sexual components. A platonic back rub to reduce stress is a very different experience from a back caress that expresses attraction and arousal. Some women find such an initial encounter interesting, but not arousing. The woman with a lesbian orientation is aware of different and strong feelings. She feels in love or at least is experiencing a deeper level of emotional involvement than that experienced with males. Sexually she is aware of a different level of receptivity and responsivity to touch. Adult women who have not been particularly aroused after years of heterosexual stimulation might find themselves easily aroused and orgasmic in a lesbian relationship. Lesbian women value continuity and involvement rather than the anonymous sexual affairs that have stigmatized the gay male community. Relationships are likely to extend for months or years rather than days or weeks.

Most lesbian young women maintain heterosexual dating, and some continue to have heterosexual sex. With time and experience, the lesbian woman understands that she's more satisfied in a female relationship. The difference in sexual response becomes increasingly clear. It is not just the number of orgasms, but the sense of greater attraction to women and women's bodies. She finds herself enjoying the female partner's stimulation much more than a male's even when they do the exact same kind of stimulation. Most important is the sense of greater emotional integrity when involved in a sexual relationship with a woman.

Vicky

Twenty-seven-year-old Vicky is feeling very good about her life after three difficult years. She is at peace with her decision to commit to a lesbian life-style.

Vicky grew up the fourth child (second girl) in an Irish-Catholic family with seven children. Vicky enjoyed the comraderie and athletic activities of the family, but not its rigid Catholicism nor its pervasive religious, racial, and ethnic prejudices. Sexuality was not a topic of conversation in her home except to warn against the evils of unwanted pregnancies, homosexuality, and rape—all of which happened to "bad people"—people very unlike Irish Catholics.

Vicky knew her older brothers masturbated, and she thought of masturbation as an evil thing to do. She heard people talk about gays—who she thought of as desperate, lonely men who lived in a dangerous part of town. As a sophomore in high school, boys would push her to do more than kissing and hugging—they wanted to touch her breasts, rub against her, and move her hand toward their crotch. She saw sex as a male-oriented activity.

Vicky was sixteen when she met twenty-seven-year-old Andrea, who was a cousin of the girl her brother dated. Andrea lived in the neighborhood, was married, and had two young children. Vicky was impressed by what a warm and wonderful person Andrea was. Vicky babysat for her children, even accompanying them on weekend trips. Vicky found it exciting to sit up in nightclothes with Andrea after the children were asleep and talk. Vicky turned to Andrea with questions about school, boys, and family relationships. She continued babysitting until she went to college, well past when most girls stop. There was never any sensual or sexual touching with Andrea, and she was sure Andrea never suspected Vicky's special interest.

When Vicky returned home from Andrea's she would enter into the private world of her bed and fantasies. While fantasizing how it would feel to touch and be touched by Andrea, she would masturbate to orgasm. Orgasm is a powerful psychophysiological experience and the fantasies of lesbian activity accompanying it were positively reinforced. Vicky's body responded to her own touch and especially the thoughts and fantasies accompanying it much differently than it did when boys touched her or she fantasized about them. Questions about sexual orientation were in her mind, but she tried to push them aside and did not think of talking to anyone, friend or family, about it.

When Vicky left home for college, the person she missed most was Andrea, but she knew it would not be appropriate to keep in contact. Vicky threw her energy into the college scene—

going to sports events, loving the crowd scene at parties, drinking so she could force herself to go along with the touching her dates demanded, and trying to ignore feelings of sexual attraction toward women. Her sophomore year, Vicky took an elective course in women's studies—her academic adviser commented it was an unusual choice for a chemistry major. One of the topics covered was lesbianism, which was presented in a factual and accepting manner. This was the first time Vicky consciously thought she might be lesbian. The thought frightened her, and in a desperate overreaction she had three unsatisfying heterosexual affairs to ward off the feelings.

In her junior year, Vicky attended a not-for-credit six-week discussion group on sexual issues presented by the Newman Center, the Catholic group on campus. Male homosexuality was discussed and condemned at length, but lesbianism was never even mentioned. The emphasis for women was to not have intercourse and keep their bodies and minds focused on higher goals. As she listened, Vicky was shocked about how it was assumed that women were asexual but had to be strong enough to say no to the male's sexual advances. The double-standard view of females and males was alive and strong in Catholicism.

Vicky talked with three women after the fifth meeting, and they shared her dismay with the tone of the group. Vicky wanted to ask if any of them masturbated or had fantasies of women, but she was too inhibited. Almost all of Vicky's masturbatory fantasies involved women, especially those she saw on campus.

Toward the end of her junior year Vicky had her first sexual experience. Her partner was a Jewish activist woman who had "come out" when she was sixteen and was involved in the campus gay rights group. Although Vicky enjoyed being sexual with a woman, she was very conflicted about the relationship. She did not want to be as up-front about the relationship as her friend demanded. At this point in her life, she was not ready to "come out" to herself, much less to her friends, family, and the community. The conflict with her partner accelerated, and by the beginning of her senior year, the relationship was over.

Vicky had a stressful and ambivalent social and sexual life her last year of college. This badly affected her academic performance—she graduated, but just barely. In retrospect, Vicky considered this the worst year of her life. Vicky was at war with herself and her sexuality. She pushed herself to try to be heterosexual—she would go out with different types of males, trying to find the "magic man" who would turn her on to heterosexuality. She started with men who were friends and who she was reasonably comfortable with, but she felt little attraction or arousal. So Vicky went to the other end of the spectrum—trying "supermacho" men, first athletes and then truckdrivers. Vicky tried "rough sex" hoping it would bring out heterosexuality in her. Instead it caused her to feel badly treated by men and disrespectful toward herself. It also resulted in a case of herpes, which made her feel sexually "damaged." Luckily, after the first year she rarely had herpes outbreaks.

After seven heterosexual affairs that year, Vicky confronted the fact that although she enjoyed males as friends there was little emotional satisfaction with men and minimal sexual responsivity. Heterosexual sex was not for the real Vicky. She could get married and have a child, but it would be a sham life. Vicky wanted a congruent emotional and sexual life, not to live a double life or a sham heterosexual life. The best definition of lesbianism is having a strong sense of emotional and sexual satisfaction from being with a woman, and this was true for Vicky.

As Vicky entered the working world she also entered the lesbian world. This was different than two years before when she felt ambivalent about her sexuality. She wanted lesbianism to be a planned choice in her life. Vicky's first move was to join the local gay community organization. Although it was largely a male group, there was a core group of twenty lesbian women ranging in age from nineteen to seventy-three. Being part of a group that shared her sexual orientation, valued her as a person, and provided social support was a major step forward. It facilitated the process of "coming out" about her lesbianism to selected friends, professional associates, and hardest of all, family members.

The key element in coming out is the ability to come out to yourself, i.e., accept your lesbianism as a positive emotional and sexual commitment. Vicky had no need or desire to flaunt her lesbianism at work or in her neighborhood, but she was not willing to sit still and passively allow herself to be discriminated against. She considered herself a proud lesbian, not a radical lesbian. This meant having a positive self-view as a lesbian woman striving to have a personally, vocationally, socially and sexually successful life.

After she established a life in her new city and developed a solid core of lesbian and straight friends, she turned her energy toward finding an ongoing lesbian relationship. She thought of herself as a sexually oriented person and wanted a good sexual relationship. She was not turned on to women who wanted to role play "butch" and "femme" roles. She did not need a "forever" guarantee, but she did desire a partner with whom she could both give and receive sexual pleasure. She wanted a relationship in which there was a sense of equity and caring, and would not fall into the traditional problems of female-male relationships.

Relationships do not happen just because you're ready for one. Vicky had three affairs, which lasted for one month to seven months. She enjoyed the women and remained friends after the sexual affair ended. Carol was in a social science Ph.D. program. In entering into a relationship Vicky realized it would probably be limited by the fact that Carol would leave after completing her degree. Vicky was able to develop an intimate relationship without holding back. Intellectually and emotionally they were very compatible. As with heterosexual couples, it takes about six months to develop a couple sexual style. Vicky and Carol's sexual relationship continued to grow after the initial honeymoon romance had ended. Vicky really liked Carol being a touching person. They especially enjoyed sleeping close together.

In earlier relationships, there had been a good deal of oral stimulation (cunnilingus), but Vicky never felt comfortable with it and was more responsive to manual stimulation. Carol could talk about sexual feelings and suggested that the hangup might be less over stimulation techniques and more that Vicky didn't see cunnilingus as a loving act. Vicky agreed and added that she viewed it as tit for tat, and she did not feel comfortable or skilled in giving cunnilingus. Carol reassured her that although cunnilingus was arousing, it was not a demand. She enjoyed hugging, caressing, tongue licking, manual stimulation, and rubbing stimulation. Carol enjoyed giving oral stimulation, and until Vicky was ready to comfortably give cunnilingus it was not needed. Vicky found it difficult to settle back and receive, but once she felt permission to do so, she was surprised to find how responsive she was to cunnilingus. For the first time in her life, she was multiorgasmic, Lesbian women have higher rates of multiorgasmic response than straight women. Perhaps the major reason for that is the use of cunnilingus. Carol was a sensitive, skilled lover and Vicky was receptive, responsive, and orgasmic. Eventually Vicky became comfortable with giving Carol oral stimulation and found it exciting to see how aroused Carol became. The sexual relationship energized the emotional bond between them.

One of Vicky's hardest decisions was whether to share her lesbianism with her siblings and parents. She did introduce them to Carol, talking about her as a special friend. Her siblings seemed aware of and accepting of the relationship and genuinely liked Carol. They realized their sister was involved with a good person. Her parents liked Carol, but they did not want to discuss the relationship or sexuality and Vicky decided to let that ride. Vicky realized it required extra thought, planning, and commitment to maintain a successful lesbian life-style, but there was no doubt she'd made the right decision.

Nina

Nina is a twenty-four-year-old high-school physical-education teacher who confirmed her heterosexual commitment during the past year. The previous five years had been a source of ambivalence and turmoil for her. During high school Nina had been active socially and athletically but had few dates and no boyfriend. Nina was over six feet tall, the starting center on the woman's basketball team, and on the track team. She had a number of "buddy" relationships with guys, but no romantic ones. Nina was afraid this pattern would haunt her through the college years.

Nina established a special relationship with her sociology professor, and for a semester even thought of changing majors. When Nina became aware of the professor's lesbianism she was both intrigued and frightened. The professor had a lover, and

Nina envied the evident satisfaction and stability they possessed. A senior woman on the track team did have a romantic interest in Nina, and she decided to give it a try. Nina's first genital-stimulation experience (other than with high-school boys groping at her breasts and rubbing against her) was with this woman. When Nina had her first orgasm two months into the relationship, she was convinced she must be a lesbian.

Nina's attraction and masturbation fantasies involved both women and men. Nina was surprised and upset when her friend abruptly ended the relationship and started an affair with another woman. She was comforted by the professor who said that the stereotype of every lesbian woman preferring long-term, monogamous relationships was, like all stereotypes, untrue. Nina missed the attention and companionship, but not the sex. An older woman seemed interested in Nina, but she had to be truthful with herself and said she wasn't interested. Nina had a sexual relationship with two other women, but she had to face the fact they made better friends than lovers.

In her junior year Nina had a crush on one of the male basketball players, and she felt devastated when it was not reciprocated. Nina did not need another male "buddy." Finally, senior year Nina sought therapy with a feminist therapist. The therapist was not interested in trying to steer Nina toward either heterosexuality or lesbianism, but was confrontive about Nina's increasingly avoidant emotional behavior with both females and males. Although at the time Nina felt intimidated and a bit put off by the therapist, she appreciated being made to face the necessity of getting off the fence and taking some emotional and sexual risks.

When Nina started teaching, she took advantage of the excellent health insurance to begin therapy with a female therapist who utilized a cognitive-behavioral approach. The therapist helped Nina take a detailed inventory of her sexual experiences, fantasies, feelings, and values. Especially important was her encouragement to consider sexual orientation as a positive choice, not something you just fall into or go with what is easiest.

Nina realized that emotionally and sexually she felt closer to men and wanted a traditional life with marriage and children. The therapist helped Nina develop better social and assertive skills so she could tell friends she was interested in dating and pursuing a relationship with a man. The therapist helped Nina develop more understanding and comfort with heterosexual relationships. Nina found the books the therapist suggested to be particularly helpful. Perhaps the most helpful technique was to change her masturbatory fantasies and focus on men and the process of penile stimulation. Although Nina did not like female-male dating games, after her third heterosexual relationship she felt heterosexuality was the right commitment for her.

A RATIONAL APPROACH TO LESBIANISM

One of the most important commitments a woman makes is whether she will emotionally and sexually share her life with a woman or a man. Our culture, as almost all others, favors heterosexuality. However, society needs to accept that for some percentage of women, lesbianism is the commitment most in keeping with her emotional and sexual needs. Accepting lesbianism as a viable alternative without subjecting lesbian women to discrimination and prejudice would be a positive step for our society. Rather than family and friends asking what has gone wrong to cause lesbianism and seeing lesbians as second-class citizens, we would be better accepting that commitment and not questioning it. For the lesbian woman, it is her optimal decision and she doesn't have to justify it.

Although it would help to have a more tolerant society, ultimately, the woman must accept and feel good about her lesbian life. It is she who can celebrate her life and her sexuality, with or without the approval of others. Once accepting her lesbian orientation, it's crucial to be committed to leading a successful life as a lesbian woman—personally, socially, sexually, and vocationally. Many women succeed at this, and if we as a culture could take a more rational and accepting view of lesbianism, more lesbian women could lead fulfilling lives.

22

DEALING WITH SEXUAL TRAUMA

The specter of child sexual abuse, incest, and rape hangs heavy over America in the 1990s. Research by feminists and social scientists have discovered that these sexual incidents, once thought very rare, are perpetrated on a shockingly large number of women. One of the most upsetting, statistics is that by age fourteen approximately one in three female children will have had a significant sexual interaction with an adult. If you define sexual trauma broadly—to include unwanted pregnancies, contracting a sexually transmitted disease, experiencing sexual humiliation, guilt over masturbation, developing a sexual dysfunction, being exhibited to or peeped on, being sexually rejected, being sexually harassed (either verbally or physically), in addition to child sexual abuse, incest, and rape—you are confronted with a truly disturbing realization. Sexual trauma is an almost universal phenomenon for women. Over 95 percent of women can identify at least one sexual incident that caused them negative feelings, guilt, confusion, and/or trauma. These incidents can occur at any time from earliest youth to old age. The statistics are distressing and sad.

The resulting sense of stigma and victimization is often more psychologically traumatic than the sexual incident itself. For example, the nine-year-old girl who is sexually abused by a neighbor requires help, understanding, and most of all, acceptance. However, there is a tendency in our culture to "blame the victim," and when she tells her mother, teacher, or another authority figure, the reaction is often anger and blame, directed not only at the man but at the girl as well.

Traditionally, child sexual abuse (as well as incest and rape) has been ignored. The child kept the incident a secret, and this secret was devastating to her self-esteem. Revealing sex abuse is preferable to keeping it a secret. But often the child feels too confused, depressed, or guilty to confide in anyone so it becomes impossible to deal with the incident in a timely and helpful manner.

The central issue is whether the woman sees herself as a "victim" or a "survivor" of sexual trauma. Viewing herself as a "victim" and allowing this experience to control her life is a more severe form of "victimization" than the original sexual incident. It is vital to teach women to be sexual survivors, not sexual victims. The woman can accept the traumatic incident, acknowledge that she did survive, and commit herself to avoiding the victim role. She can decide not to allow the negative sexual experience to control her sexual and psychological self-esteem. A sexual survivor understands the trauma, learns from it, feels responsible for herself and her sexuality, and discovers how to express sexuality in a way that enhances her life rather than causes further problems. Her sexual self-esteem is that of a survivor and winner, not that of a victim and loser. There is a saying used by rape survivors: "Living well is the best revenge." The reality of sexual trauma cannot be denied or minimized. The woman needs support to cope with the trauma—to be an active survivor rather than a passive victim.

FACTS ABOUT SEXUAL TRAUMA

Who perpetrates sexual trauma? Men. In 95 percent of sexual crimes against women, the perpetrator is a man. In sexual crimes against boys and male adolescents, at least 85 percent of the time the prepetrator is a man. Although women do commit sexual crimes, including child sexual abuse, rape, and incest, they do so in considerably smaller numbers than men. In the majority of sex offenses, it is men acting out against women.

We could devote a whole book to why males commit sexual offenses, but succinctly there are two major factors. First is our old nemesis the double standard. Taken to its illogical extreme, it says a man can have sex with any woman, anytime, and in any situation. So, if there's not an available and willing female, he is justified in being sexual with children or committing rape.

The second factor is that somewhere between 2 percent to 5 percent of men have a variant arousal pattern and act on it. The technical term for this is "paraphilia," which can be defined as an inappropriate object of sexual arousal. Some paraphilias are benign, which means not illegal or causing harm to others. Examples are fetishes and cross-dressing. However, a woman in a relationship with a man who has a fetish arousal pattern knows it is problematic for her and her sexual relationship.

"Noxious" paraphilias result in harm to others and involve illegal activity. The most common noxious paraphilia is exhibitionism, which results in more arrests than any other sex offense. An astonishing 75 percent of women report having been exhibited to either as children, adolescents, or adults. About 50 percent of the cases of child sexual abuse involve "hands-off" abuse, most commonly exhibitionism. Other examples of hands-off sexual offenses include voyeurism ("peeping tom"), obscene phone calls, and verbal harassment. Hands-on paraphilias include frotteurism (for example, rubbing against a woman on a bus or subway). The most harmful paraphilia is pedophilia, which means sexual arousal with children.

Most child sexual abuse does not involve intercourse, and 85 percent of incidents are nonviolent. Child sexual abuse does harm principally by breaking the bond of trust between the child and the abusing adult. The activities, whether the adult fondling the child's breasts, buttocks, or vulva (clothes on or off), or watching the girl undress or taking pictures of her semiclothed, or the girl looking at or fondling the man's penis, are inappropriate sexual activities that cause guilt and confusion. Because force was not used and the abuse did not include intercourse does not make the sexual activity tolerable. Nor can it be justified by the man saying the girl was interested, or she enjoyed the touching and attention, or that it was she who initiated it. Sexual touching between children and adults is always inappropriate. Let us be especially clear that the ultimate responsibility for child sexual abuse lies with the perpetrator, not with the child. It is an adult responsibility to label a sexual interaction inappropriate and to confront it. It is a double victimization to put responsibility on the child for her abuse. The double standard that holds the woman responsible for saying no to sex (which is not reasonable anyway) has no bearing when children or adolescents are involved. It is the adult's responsibility to say no to sex with a child or adolescent. Child abuse is always the responsibility of the adult. Pedophiles act out against children to meet their own sexual needs, not because they have the interest of the child in mind.

THE WOMAN AS A SURVIVOR

Barry spent three years of his professional life giving workshops to help women become survivors rather than victims. Rather than letting the incident or series of sexual incidents control your sexual self-esteem, you need to deal with it effectively, acknowledge you survived, and retake control of your life. The key elements are to feel good about your body and to express sexuality so it enhances your life and does not serve as a source of further problems. A survivor is knowledgeable about herself and her sexuality, has learned from the past but is not controlled by the past, is active rather than passive, chooses a man and a relationship that will improve her life, and chooses when and how to be sexual. Sexual trauma is male-oriented, performance-oriented, and coercive. Healthy sexuality is mutual, pleasure-oriented, and open and voluntary.

Much therapeutic work has been done with adult survivors of incest or child sexual abuse. These incidents are best dealt with at the time rather than kept secret. If it can be dealt with effectively while the victim is still a child, she will not feel victimized as an adult. The child wants three things in regard to the abusive incident: 1) the abuse to stop, 2) to understand the incident in the least pejorative manner possible with an awareness that the responsibility was not the child's, and 3) if possible, to resume a nonabusive relationship with the man. The latter element is not applicable to stranger incidents, sexual assault, or rape. Most incidents of child sexual abuse involve a male the child knows and likes—say, a playground supervisor, neighbor, or someone from the church. Many incidents involve a family member—cousin, stepbrother, grandfather, in-law, or in the most difficult cases of incest, father or stepfather. These incidents can be dealt with so the girl has fewer psychological or sexual scars, and sees herself as okay. Much of the time, these incidents are mishandled by parents, counselors, mental health workers, or the court system, resulting in more severe victimization and trauma. Even in situations in which a woman has been revictimized, she can learn to be a survivor during her young adult or adult years. Women deserve to be happy; they should studiously avoid playing the victim role.

You can use available resources to reclaim your life. The support of others is vital in this process. The traditional trap of adults (especially males) is to blame the woman. A newer trap, especially among female friends and counseling personnel, is to be overly sympathetic and treat the child or woman as fragile, damaged goods. You need support and empathy, not sympathy. You need to be respected and have people there for you, listening to your wants and needs. This allows you to take back control of your life and act in your best interest.

DEALING WITH RAPE

The majority of rapes in the United States are committed by acquaintances not strangers. But the most traumatic is stranger rape using a weapon or inflicting physical violence. The victim feels out of control and fears for her life. It has been said that rape is more a crime of power and violence than sex. There is a certain validity to that view—rape is a crime and it is violent. But it is the combination of violence and sexuality that makes rape such a devastating experience. It is more traumatic being raped than mugged even when there is the same amount of physical injury. Sex plus violence does not just add to trauma, the combination multiplies the trauma.

One of the paradoxes for the woman who is raped is that she'll receive more support from the police and the man in her life if she is physical injured. When it is committed by an acquaintance (no weapon, and no physical injury) it's almost impossible to criminally prosecute. Even more psychologically damaging is that the woman is blamed for the rape. The twisted logic is that if she really wanted to stop it she could have. People question why she was with the man in the first place, or why she had a drink with him, or why she kissed him. The not-so-hidden innuendo is that it was her fault she was raped— she led him on by her actions, should not have worn a sexy outfit, should not have been drinking, should not have been in a bar or walking in a dangerous part of town. When a woman says no to sex, and the man forces, threatens, or coerces, then a rape has occurred. Sex against the woman's will is the meaningful definition of rape. Rape is not a "gray" area; if the woman says no and the man forces sex (whether physically or through intimidation) it is a rape—it's that black and white.

Although laws vary from state to state, the most common legal definition of rape is forced penile-vaginal contact. The major corroborating evidence involves semen in the vagina. The legal definition does not recognize the reality of the rape experience for women. Many rape incidents involve oral or anal penetration rather than vaginal. Many rapists are sexually dysfunctional and they do not ejaculate intravaginally. Many rapes involve coercion or threat rather than a weapon or physical force. It is very difficult to prosecute for rape unless the rapist is a stranger, there is a weapon or evidence of force, and the woman immediately contacts the police or goes to a hospital for a postrape examination.

The fastest growing type of rape in our culture is "date rape" on college campuses or among working young adults. The same theme repeats itself—the man says the woman really doesn't mean "no" and since she's not a virgin it's his right to carry through and have sex with her. Some men so badly misperceive the situation that afterward they ask whether she enjoyed it and had an orgasm. Some men even call and ask for another date!

Over two-thirds of rape survivors report psychological symptoms three months after a rape experience. The most common symptoms are fear of being alone, depression, nightmares or flashbacks, inhibited sexual desire or sexual aversion, general anxiety, obsessive thoughts. The rape is not only an attack on the woman, but has a negative effect on neighbors, other family members, and the community (who are co-victims). It has a powerful impact on the woman's relationship with her husband or intimate partner. Many of these relationships are unable to cope with the trauma and dissolve. The woman looks to her partner for support and understanding, and instead finds him questioning or blaming her, especially in the case of acquaintance rape.

A woman who has been raped needs two kinds of help. The first involves crisis intervention and support, whether from a trained paraprofessional companion, or nurses and doctors, or from friends and family. She has to accept the reality of the rape experience and to deal with injuries and fears of sexually transmitted disease or pregnancy. She has to decide whether to report the rape to the police, and if so, what to expect. She has to decide who to tell about the rape, and what type of help and support she needs from friends and family. She will need to deal with fear, depression, and anger and begin to take back control of her life. This acute phase lasts from a week to a month. About 20 percent of women deal well with the rape during this period and see themselves as survivors; 80 percent need further help and support in dealing with the rape trauma.

The second phase is conceptualized as a posttraumatic stress disorder. This means that the woman has to learn to deal with the physiological, cognitive, emotional, relational, and sexual effects of the rape. This might involve professional therapy; for example, many clinics have therapy groups for rape survivors. Individual therapy and couples counseling is offered as well as sex therapy. The six months following rape is the crucial time to see yourself as a survivor. Here the phrase "Living well is the best revenge" takes on a very personal meaning.

SURVIVING INCEST

Incest is the "shameful family secret." Most incest therapy is done with adults who had previously denied or repressed the experience. They enter treatment for another mental-health problem—alcoholism, eating disorder, phobia, depression, sexual dysfunction, etc., and in discussing that problem the past incidents of incest are uncovered.

Contrary to popular belief, most incest does not involve intercourse, force, or the father. The most common incestuous acts are fondling, voyeurism, and exhibitionism. Most incestuous activity is not violent. The more common incest perpetrators are cousins, brothers, uncles, in-laws, grandfathers, or step relatives. Incestuous activity involving more invasive or penetrative sex (oral, anal, or vaginal), involving force, and with a father or stepfather is more damaging.

Research studies find incest survivors more angry at mother than father. The women feel it was mother's role to protect her and she failed. Most women assume that mother consciously knew of the incest. Although it varies greatly with individual families, usually mother knew there was something wrong but not that it was incestuous sexual activity. Many of the mothers themselves had been victims of abuse. Often the mother was dysfunctional in some way—alcoholic or abusing drugs, depressed, suffering from a chronic physical illness, phobic, etc. Fathers are likely to have mental-health problems, especially alcoholism. It is estimated that the rates of incest are two and a half to three times higher in alcoholic families. Incest fathers tend to be rigid, defensive, and authoritarian. Incest families tend to be isolated and practice total secrecy about incestuous activity.

In the successful treatment of incest families the crucial element is communication about appropriate and inappropriate sexuality. This means the daughter(s) are able to say to the father that the touching is unacceptable, that the daughter will tell mother, and that mother will confront unacceptable sexual behavior. The rate of recidivism in treated incest families is less than 5 percent because the therapeutic approach emphasizes keeping channels of communication about sexuality open, confronting abusive sexual behavior, and helping the family function in a healthy manner.

If one daughter has been sexually abused, it is likely that other daughters also will have been, and sometimes sons as well. Incest truly affects the whole family, but it cannot be dealt with by the family alone. There is a need for professional therapy whether incest recently occurred or it happened during the childhood of adult survivors. There are books for adult survivors of incest and support groups that can help remove the stigma and serve as a positive resource. Women can be survivors of incest. If you experienced incest, you owe it to yourself as well as other family members including your children to confront the incest and see yourself as a whole person.

CHILD SEXUAL ABUSE

The majority of child sexual abuse is perpetrated by an adult the child knows rather than by a stranger. Most of the incidents are nonviolent and nonintercourse. The current conception of sex abuse is so focused on strangers and intercourse that the child abused in other ways often wonders whether what she experienced is really abuse and whether it's her fault. Much of the prevention literature focuses on very young children, but the facts are the average age range for child sexual abuse is between eight and twelve. By age fourteen, one in three female children have had a sexual interaction with an adult. Half of those children experience "hands-off" abuse—exhibitionism, voyeurism, sexual harassment, etc. "Hands-on" abuse is more traumatic and typically involves the male touching or fondling the girl's breasts, buttocks, or vulva, or the girl touching the male's penis or scrotum, being kissed or engaging in manual or oral stimulation of the penis. Less frequent, but causing more trauma, is oral, anal, or vaginal penetration. Continuous incidents of child sexual abuse are more harmful than a single incident. The use of physical force or the infliction of pain on the child multiplies the trauma.

Sexual trauma is a very individualistic and subjective experience. Often the child will blame herself and view the incident(s) as a shameful secret, which increases the sense of stigma and fear. The growing public awareness of sexual trauma, prevention programs, self-help groups, the books written by survivors who were abused as children all emphasize the importance of talking to someone rather than keeping abuse a secret. Women who deny or dissociate the trauma put themselves at risk of depression, low self-esteem and other mental-health problems. Sexual trauma is a sad but real phenomenon that needs to be dealt with directly rather than obscured by silence and blaming the victim.

Jena

Jena was a twenty-two-year-old senior in Barry's Human Sexual Behavior class. She was a communications major taking the class as an elective because she thought it would be a "gut" (easy) course. As the course progressed, Jena found herself becoming more emotionally uncomfortable. She was learning a good deal from the textbooks and lectures, but she was disconcerted by the suggestions to apply the knowledge to her own sexual development and decision making.

Jena could not get a handle on the source of her discomfort

until the class on sexual trauma and rape. As Barry explained what constituted childhood sexual abuse and incest, Jean flashed back to incidents that she'd never talked to anyone about or labled abusive, but now realized were. She recalled a male exhibiting himself to her and another third-grade girl while they were walking home. This occurred three or four times, but neither girl said anything to an adult. Even more upsetting was her remembrance of an uncle whom she liked touching her breasts, vulva, and kissing her on the lips when he was drinking. The family never confronted the fact that this uncle was alcoholic and sexually abused his nieces. Jena recalled an incident at the beach when she was fifteen in which a group of older guys pushed her into an alley and for about ten minutes harassed her and one of the men rubbed against her until he ejaculated. She blamed herself for these incidents and had tried to put them out of her mind. Jena was particularly upset about the uncle because she suspected he had abused her younger sisters and might be acting out against his grandnieces.

Jena's head was spinning during the break, but she was really shaken by the second part of the class, which was conducted by a counselor from the rape crisis center. Jena was surprised to learn that acquaintance rape was more common than stranger rape, and that date rape was almost epidemic on college campuses.

Jena had her first intercourse as an eighteen-year-old high-school senior. She saw herself as a sexually healthy and liberated woman who enjoyed having intercourse with young men she was emotionally involved with. She recalled two incidents over her college career in which she had felt forced, or at least coerced, to have intercourse with guys she knew only casually and had felt used. She was very angry when the one man called back and asked for a date. Jena felt upset, but she did not tell anyone because she worried people would gossip. She had not labeled these two incidents as date rapes, but that's what they were.

In talking with the counselor after class, she received a referral for a ten-session group for women who had been sexually victimized. Attending this group was a turning point for Jena. She felt understood, validated, and relieved to be able to talk about those sexual incidents. Psychologically and sexually Jena was committed to being a survivor. She had no intention of being "stuck" in the past or controlled by her anger. With her consciousness raised, she did her senior communications project on date rape. She talked to her younger sisters as well as her parents about the sexual incidents. They confronted the uncle who agreed to seek treatment for his alcoholism. Jena was feeling more competent as a woman and in control of her life.

SURVIVING SEXUAL TRAUMA

Ultimately the best way to deal with sexual trauma is through education and prevention. However, the sad reality in our culture is that the great majority of women have sexual experiences that cause confusion, guilt, and shameful feelings.

The first and most important step is to accept the reality of what happened rather than to deny and pretend it didn't occur. Be aware of the complexity of the incident(s)—the feelings, behavior, and your thoughts. A crucial element is not to blame yourself. The responsibility for a sexual incident lies with the perpetrator, not the victim/survivor. Acknowledge that you coped with the incident as best you could and did in fact survive it. Rather than feeling guilty, or resentful about the past, be committed to the present and the future. Learn from the incident and utilize your understanding and available resources.

A major element of becoming a survivor is feeling in control of your body and responsible for yourself and your sexuality. It includes having affirmative personal and sexual self-esteem. A survivor sees sexuality as a positive, integral part of her personality. She is aware and responsible and can choose to express her sexuality in a manner that enhances her life.

EPILOGUE

We have enjoyed writing a book that provides accurate information and helpful guidelines for women in the 1990s. The double standard that governed sexual behavior for generations is crumbling and will eventually disappear. The question is whether it will be replaced by a healthy model of female-male relationships and sexual behavior or whether it will be replaced by a different, but equally destructive, set of attitudes and problems or will degenerate into confusion and chaos. Our goal in this book was to outline a way of viewing sexual attitudes, behavior, and emotions that facilitates healthy sexuality and promotes respectful, trusting, and caring relationships between women and men.

What is the essence of sexuality? It is an acceptance of your body, including your genitalia. It is an acceptance of sex as a good aspect of life. Sexuality is a positive, integral part of you as a person. The crucial sexual choice is to express sexuality so that it enhances your life, self-esteem, and an intimate relationship rather than causing guilt, confusion, shameful feelings, or trauma. You deserve to feel good about yourself as a sexual woman and for sexuality to enhance your psychological well-being and an intimate relationship.

The female view of sexuality is a broad-based one. Sex is more than genitals, intercourse, and the few seconds of orgasm. Sexuality is the openness to giving and receiving touching and pleasure. Pleasuring is a way of expressing affectionate, sensual, and sexual feelings in a comfortable, nondemanding context. Sexual expression is an active, involved, pleasure-oriented process; you should not be a passive spectator controlled by male performance demands.

The sexually aware woman makes choices and plans about her own sexuality. She is knowledgeable about contraception, sexually transmitted diseases, and sexual trauma. She is not swept away by myths about romantic love, but chooses a man who she respects, trusts, is attracted to, cares about, and who cares about her. Her relationships with men are based on respect and equity—in every sense of the word she is a first-class sexual citizen.

You are a sexual woman from the day you're born to the day you die. Be aware of and celebrate your sexuality; let it enhance your self-esteem and add to the satisfaction in your life.

APPENDIX I
CHOOSING A THERAPIST

As we stated at the onset, this was not meant to be a do-it-yourself therapy book. Many women are reluctant to consult a professional therapist, feeling that to do so is a sign of "craziness," inadequacy, or weakness. We believe it is a sign of psychological strength. Seeking therapy means you realize there is a problem and make a commitment to problem solving, positive change, and psychological and sexual growth.

The mental-health field is a confusing one. You will need to find a therapist competent in dealing with your specific type of problem. Psychotherapy encompasses various techniques, and is offered by several different groups of professionals, including psychologists, psychiatrists, sex therapists, social workers, marriage therapists, and pastoral counselors. The background of the practitioner is of less importance than her or his competency in your special area of need.

One of the best resources for obtaining a referral to a therapist is to call a local professional organization (psychological association, mental-health association, or mental-health clinic). Another is to ask for a referral from a family physician, minister, or friend who might have information on the therapist's areas of competence.

Many people have health insurance that provides coverage for mental-health costs and thus can afford their services of a private practitioner. Those who do not have either the financial resources or insurance could consider a city or county mental-health clinic or a university or medical-school mental-health outpatient clinic. Clinics usually have a sliding-fee scale (that is, the fee is based on your ability to pay).

In choosing a specific therapist, be assertive in asking about her or his credentials and areas of expertise as well as fees. A competent therapist will be open to discussing this with you. Be especially diligent in discussing credentials (university degrees, licensing) with people who call themselves personal counselors, marriage counselors, or sex counselors since there are some poorly qualified persons (and some out-and-out quacks) working in any field.

If your problem principally concerns marriage or family issues, you can write the American Association for Marriage and Family Therapy, 1717 K Street N.W., Room 407, Washington, D.C. 20006, for a list of certified marriage and family therapists in your area. If you have a specific behavioral problem, such as phobia, lack of assertion, overeating, alcoholism, or sexual anxiety, you can write the Behavior Therapy and Research Society, c/o Eastern Pennsylvania Psychiatric Institute, Henry Avenue, Philadelphia, Pennsylvania 19129, for a list of certified behavior therapists in your area. If you are specifically interested in sex therapy, you can write the American Association of Sex Educators, Counselors, and Therapists, Suite 1717, 435 N. Michigan Avenue, Chicago, Ill. 60611 for a list of certified sex therapists in your area.

Do not hesitate to talk with two or three therapists before deciding on one with whom to work. Be aware of how comfortable you feel with the therapist, whether you can relate to her or him, and whether the therapist's assessment of the problem and approach to treatment make sense to you. Once you begin therapy, give it a chance to be helpful. There are few "miracle cures." Change requires your commitment and is a gradual and often difficult process. Therapy is not like going to a medical doctor who prescribes pills and tells you exactly what to do. The role of the therapist is that of an adviser or consultant rather than the one who decides upon a change for you. Psychotherapy requires effort, and it is well worth it in helping you change attitudes, feelings, and behavior, and making your life more functional and satisfying.

APPENDIX II
BOOKS FOR FURTHER READING

Andry, Andrew, and Steve Schepp. *How Babies Are Made*. Boston: Little, Brown, 1984.

Barbach, Lonnie. *For Yourself*. New York: Bantam Books, 1976.

————. *Pleasures: Women Write Erotica*. New York: Doubleday, 1984.

Barbach, Lonnie, and Linda Levine. *Shared Intimacies*. New York: Bantam Books, 1980.

Bing, Elizabeth, and Libby Coleman. *Making Love During Pregnancy*. New York: Bantam Books, 1983.

Blumstein, Philip, and Pepper Schwartz. *American Couples*. New York: William Morrow, 1983.

Boston Women's Health Book Collective. *The New Our Bodies, Ourselves*. New York: Simon and Schuster, 1984.

Budoff, Penny. *No More Menstrual Cramps and Other Good News*. New York: Penguin Books, 1981.

Butler, Robert, and Myrna Lewis. *Love and Sex After Sixty*. New York: Harper and Row, 1977.

————. *Love and Sex After Forty*. New York: Harper and Row, 1986.

Calderone, Mary, and Eric Johnson. *The Family Book About Sexuality*. New York: Bantam Books, 1983.

Carerra, Michael. *Sex: The Facts, the Acts, and Your Feelings*. New York: Crown Publishers, 1981.

Cutler, Winifred, Ramon Garcia, and David Edwards. *Menopause*. New York: W. W. Norton, 1983.

Downing, George, *The Massage Book*. New York: Random House, 1972.

Friday, Nancy. *My Secret Garden*. New York: Pocket Books, 1974.

Gordon, Sol, and Judith Gordon. *Raising a Child Conservatively in a Sexually Permissive World*. New York: Simon and Schuster, 1983.

Heiman, Julia, and Joseph LoPiccolo. *Becoming Orgasmic*. New Jersey: Prentice Hall, 1988.

Maltz, Wendy, and Barbara Holman. *Incest and Sexuality*. New York: D.C. Heath, 1987.

Masters, William, Virginia Johnson, and Robert Kolodny. *Masters and Johnson on Sex and Human Loving*. Boston: Little, Brown, 1986.

McCarthy, Barry. *Male Sexual Awareness*. New York, Carroll and Graf, 1988.

McCarthy, Barry, and Emily McCarthy. *Sexual Awareness*. New York: Carroll and Graf, 1984.

Sarrel, Lorna, and Philip Sarrel. *Sexual Turning Points*. New York: MacMillan, 1984.

Tavris, Carol, and Susan Sadd. *The Redbook Report on Female Sexuality*. New York: Dell, 1977.

FINE WORKS OF NON-FICTION
AVAILABLE IN QUALITY
PAPERBACK EDITIONS FROM
CARROLL & GRAF

- [ ] Anderson, Nancy/WORK WITH PASSION $8.95
- [ ] Arlett, Robert/THE PIZZA GOURMET $10.95
- [ ] Asprey, Robert/THE PANTHER'S FEAST $9.95
- [ ] Bedford, Sybille/ALDOUS HUXLEY $14.95
- [ ] Berton, Pierre/KLONDIKE FEVER $10.95
- [ ] Blake, Robert/DISRAELI $14.50
- [ ] Blanch, Lesley/PIERRE LOTI $10.95
- [ ] Blanch, Lesley/THE WILDER SHORES OF LOVE $8.95
- [ ] Buchan, John/PILGRIM'S WAY $10.95
- [ ] Carr, John Dickson/THE LIFE OF SIR ARTHUR CONAN DOYLE $8.95
- [ ] Carr, Virginia Spencer/THE LONELY HUNTER: A BIOGRAPHY OF CARSON McCULLERS $12.95
- [ ] Conot, Robert/JUSTICE AT NUREMBURG $11.95
- [ ] Cooper, Duff/OLD MEN FORGET $10.95
- [ ] Cooper, Lady Diana/AUTOBIOGRAPHY $12.95
- [ ] Edwards, Anne/SONYA: THE LIFE OF COUNTESS TOLSTOY $8.95
- [ ] Elkington, John/THE GENE FACTORY $8.95
- [ ] Farson, Negley/THE WAY OF A TRANSGRESSOR $9.95
- [ ] Gill, Brendan/HERE AT THE NEW YORKER $12.95
- [ ] Goldin, Stephen & Sky, Kathleen/THE BUSINESS OF BEING A WRITER $8.95
- [ ] Haycraft, Howard (ed.)/THE ART OF THE MYSTERY STORY $9.95
- [ ] Harris, A./SEXUAL EXERCISES FOR WOMEN $8.95
- [ ] Hook, Sidney/OUT OF STEP $14.95
- [ ] Keating, H. R. F./CRIME & MYSTERY: THE 100 BEST BOOKS $7.95
- [ ] Lansing, Alfred/ENDURANCE: SHACKLETON'S INCREDIBLE VOYAGE $8.95
- [ ] Leech, Margaret/REVEILLE IN WASHINGTON $11.95

☐ Lifton, David S./BEST EVIDENCE $10.95
☐ McCarthy, Barry/MALE SEXUAL AWARENESS $9.95
☐ McCarthy, Barry & Emily/SEXUAL AWARENESS $9.95
☐ Mizener, Arthur/THE SADDEST STORY: A
BIOGRAPHY OF FORD MADOX FORD $12.95
☐ Moorehead, Alan/THE RUSSIAN REVOLUTION $10.95
☐ Mullins, Edwin/THE PAINTED WITCH Cloth $25.00
☐ Munthe, Axel/THE STORY OF SAN MICHELE $8.95
☐ O'Casey, Sean/AUTOBIOGRAPHIES I $10.95
☐ O'Casey, Sean/AUTOBIOGRAPHIES II $10.95
☐ Poncins, Gontran de/KABLOONA $9.95
☐ Pringle, David/SCIENCE FICTION: THE 100 BEST
NOVELS $7.95
☐ Proust, Marcel/ON ART AND LITERATURE $8.95
☐ Richelson, Hildy & Stan/INCOME WITHOUT
TAXES $9.95
☐ Roy, Jules/THE BATTLE OF DIENBIENPHU $8.95
☐ Russel, Robert A./WINNING THE FUTURE Cloth $16.95
☐ Salisbury, Harrison/A JOURNEY OF OUR TIMES $10.95
☐ Scott, Evelyn/ESCAPADE $9.95
☐ Sloan, Allan/THREE PLUS ONE EQUALS
BILLIONS $8.95
☐ Taylor, Telford/MUNICH $17.95
☐ Werth, Alexander/RUSSIA AT WAR: 1941–1945 $15.95
☐ Wilmot, Chester/STRUGGLE FOR EUROPE $12.95
☐ Wilson, Colin/THE MAMMOTH BOOK OF TRUE
CRIME $8.95
☐ Zuckmayer, Carl/A PART OF MYSELF $9.95

Available from fine bookstores everywhere or use this coupon for ordering:

Caroll & Graf Publishers, Inc., 260 Fifth Avenue, N.Y., N.Y. 10001

Please send me the books I have checked above. I am enclosing
$_____ (please add $1.75 per title to cover postage and
handling.) Send check or money order—no cash or C.O.D.'s please.
N.Y. residents please add 8¼% sales tax.

Mr/Mrs/Miss _____

Address _____

City _____ State/Zip _____
Please allow four to six weeks for delivery.

WAIT—

Fuck. She's writing about me, now?

Not Smokey. *Me.*

She can *do* that?

I hate everything about this. I hate what I think she might say, I hate that she's thinking about me like that at all, but most of all, I hate that somehow she's dragged Jasper Graves into it. This is way, *way* over the line.

But I have to read it to know just how over the line it is. So I set my jaw and start reading.

38

FOREST WALKED THE SHORT DISTANCE BACK TO his trailer, dreaming of the moment he'd get to kick off Smokey's ridiculous boots and tight-ass jeans and slide into a pair of sweats and sleep all day until tomorrow's late afternoon call.

As his trailer came into view, he yawned, but he wasn't too exhausted to gaze at the pink blot of sky on the horizon. Sure, North Carolina was remote and full of rednecks, but it also had some of the most marvelous sunrises Forest had ever seen.

"Mr. Reed!" It always bothered Forest that the PAs here called him that, but North Carolina was in the South and no matter how many times he told them to call him Forest, their upbringing just wouldn't allow it.

Forest looked over to see his favorite PA running (they were always running) toward him. Lynn was endlessly friendly, whether it was midday or four a.m., and never batted an eye,